Music in American Life

A list of books in the series appears at the end of this volume.

Never without a Song

NEVER WITHOUT A SONG

The Years and Songs of Jennie Devlin,
1865–1952

Katharine D. Newman

Foreword by Alan Lomax

University of Illinois Press
Urbana and Chicago

Publication was supported in part by a grant from the John and Clara Higgins Foundation.

This book is printed on acid-free paper.

Library of Congress Cataloging-in-Publication Data
Newman, Katharine D., 1911–
    Never without a song : the years and songs of Jennie
Devlin, 1865–1952 / Katharine D. Newman ; foreword by Alan
Lomax.
      p. cm. — (Music in American life)
    Includes bibliographical references and index.
    ISBN 0-252-02081-2 (cloth : alk. paper). — ISBN 0-252-06371-6
(paper : alk. paper)
    1. Devlin, Jennie, 1865–1952. 2. Folk singers — United
States — Biography.   I. Title.   II. Series.
ML420.D534N5   1995
782.42162'13'0092 — dc20
    [B]   93-6387
                                        CIP
                                       MN

About the cover: Framed sketch of Jennie Devlin drawn from wedding photo; tag, "Philadelphia Folk Festival," 1938; Jew's harp and harmonica, instruments Jennie played in her early years, displayed on a "pretty hanky"; bust, "The Reading Girl," given to Jennie by her husband as a surprise gift in sympathy for her lifelong yearning for an education, c. 1915; quilt pieced by great-grandmother of Katharine D. Newman, Philadelphia, c. 1860.

Cover design by Robert Perine

To Ellen Eaves Henneke,

my lifelong friend who

so generously shared her

grandmother with me.

Please accept this book

with my love.

CONTENTS

Illustrations follow p. 58.

FOREWORD

Alan Lomax

In our day at last, we are hearing the woman's side of the human story told, not as in *Pamela* and *Moll Flanders* by men, but by women. The heroine of this singing biography—and she is heroic—takes us into the little-known world of the serving maids and working-class women of middle America early in this century. Jennie Devlin was everybody's slavey, and many were the slings and arrows of outrageous fortune that fell upon her. Her staying power reminds one of the indomitable protagonists of *Great Expectations* and of *Moll Flanders*. Indeed, the account of how this unwanted waif became a serving maid, survived her bitter destiny, found a mate, and managed to raise a family has a true Dickensian flavor.

Jennie differed from Pip and Molly in being a lover of ballads. Singing, she makes clear, kept her heart alive through all her troubles. For her the beloved old songs summed up the truth of existence. They broadened her view of human destiny, particularly that of other women, so that she felt less alone in her own sorrows. By immediately learning and keeping in memory every song that appealed to her, little Jennie Hess [Devlin] became a cultivated woman. Indeed, she was a folklorist, a historian of her period, storing up a treasure that all may now enjoy, thanks to the sensitive and devoted labors of Kay Newman, the author of this volume.

Samuel Pepys, the seventeenth-century diarist, early noted the importance of women in transmitting native musical traditions. In one entry Pepys unfavorably compares the performance of a fashionable opera singer to that of the English actress Mrs. Knipps. "She sings mighty well . . . just after the Italian manner, but yet do not please me like one of Mrs. Knipp's songs to a good English tune . . . [I] was in perfect pleasure to hear her little Scotch song, *Barbara Allen.* . . ." This middle-class Londoner extolled the musical talents of the serving maids of his household. "After dinner, talking with my wife and making Mrs. Gosnell (the maid) sing . . . I am mightily pleased with her humor and her singing." And of another maid, Mary Mercer, he wrote, "It being a very fine moonshine, my wife and Mercer came into the garden and my business being done, we sang till about twelve at night, with mighty pleasure to ourselves and neighbors."

These merry, musical maidservants of the seventeenth century were the cultural forebears of Jennie Devlin, who sang all day long at her work and was "as good a whistler as ever puckered a lip." She and they belong to a feminine mainstream that has kept the oral traditions alive across the centuries. Indeed in my lifelong experience in recording folksongs, it is the women who most stand out as the great song rememberers.

In the Haitian *vaudou* temples, the female servitors, the *hounsi*, lead the songs that bring the gods to the dancing floor. I have spent days recording these exquisite tunesmiths, as I did later on taping the great Bessie Jones of the Georgia Sea Islands, who required two months to tape the hundreds of folksongs that she knew. In the far Hebrides I found that the ancient Gallic worksong traditions belonged to the women — the songs for quieting and milking the cows on the shieling, and the rowdy songs for working up the tweed, essential to the safety of their fishermen husbands on the freezing waters of the western isles.

Two women of the Stewart clan of northern Scotland — Belle Stewart and the formidable Jeanie Robertson with her orientally ornamented style — stand out as the stars of contemporary British ballad singing. Majestic Texas Gladden, of the musical Smiths of the Blue Ridge, knew a fine version of every ballad I could think to ask her for and performed each one with the elegance of a ballet dancer. Way over in Arkansas, I met shy Mrs. Ollie Gilbert, and induced her to sing one ballad for me. Later collectors overcame her shyness and eventually Ollie poured out a river of more than one thousand folksongs. Jennie Devlin, as this collection illustrates, belongs in this select company, but there is more in her book than the songs.

It was a Kentucky woman, a true sister to Jennie, who taught us that traditional songs were not mere relics but had powerful emotional and social significance for the singers. Aunt Molly Jackson was possessed of great talent for song and a fearless intellect. Not only did she compose radical songs to help bring the union into the poverty-ridden coal camps of eastern Kentucky, but she remembered how many of her traditional songs had also functioned as means of feminine protest. According to Aunt Molly, there was a song sung by poor young girls like herself to protest against their forced marriage to some rich but unattractive old man:

> Old man come courtin' me one day,
> But I wouldn't have him,
> He come down the lane, walkin' on his cane,
> With his durned old beard a-flabbin' . . .

Aunt Molly's comments on women's problems in the southern backwoods provided a far more meaningful setting for the songs than the usual scholarly notes, and I threaded them through *Our Singing Country* (1937) and subsequent Lomax publications. These oral headnotes provided so much insight on the folk process that, in spite of the limitations of disc recording, I began to use the extra space on the ends of discs to elicit salient comments from the singers. With great talkers like Aunt Molly, Woody Guthrie, Jelly Roll Morton—these interviews grew into singing biographies. Indeed, the publication of the recorded saga of Jelly Roll, the flamboyant New Orleans jazzman, established the fascination of the genre that came much later to be called "oral history."

It was at this point in the growth of field recording method that Katharine Newman wrote me at the Library of Congress about the extraordinary singer she had found in New Jersey. This was welcome news because we lacked material from the Middle Atlantic area for our survey of American folksong. When we met, Jennie Devlin and I took to each other at once, as the chapter "Somebody," in this volume, makes clear. She had a fine quiet way with ballads, a trait she shared with the singers I had recently been recording in New England. She sang solo and unaccompanied in the impersonal style of the balladeer, so focused on the importance of the text that she was surprised when I expressed interest in the tunes.

Because of her northeastern style I felt quite confident that she would give me the risqué songs that she knew. I had discovered that in working-class New England, women were not excluded from the circle when bawdy ballads were sung. So while the other ladies whispered together in an upstairs bedroom, Jennie unblushingly confided in me a few salty rhymes, such as

> Some for the girl that dresses neat,
> Some for the girl that kisses sweet,
> But I'm for the girl with the lily white thighs,
> With a hole in her belly like a dead hog's eye.

Jennie was, in most respects, a reticent northeasterner, and it took years of painstaking interview and careful digging before the present singer biography was achieved. It is a deeply moving story, with sensitive insights into the heart of a folksinger. This unwanted child whose mother had literally tried to throw her away loved to sing the ballad of the lady who was haunted by the ghosts of her neglected babies. Small wonder that James Bird, who was hung for a crime he did not commit, was her favorite ballad hero, raised as she was by a series of demanding foster parents.

Not only did those foster parents work her like an animal, but, because they did not want to lose this perfect servant to marriage, they warned her against men and refused to allow her to go out. The night she was married, she was forced to stay in her room and her new husband was shown the door. Most males in her folksongs were threatening figures, like the murderous Henry Green and the Cruel House Carpenter. In this respect life fulfilled her fantasied expectations; she was abandoned, sometimes for years at a time, by her charming but wayward husband, and left to bring up three children with only the skills of a perfect housewife to fall back on. Nonetheless indomitable Jennie brought her family through and even cared for her husband in his declining years.

We must be grateful to Katharine Newman for weaving this poignant life history together, and to Jennie Devlin for teaching us how important song is in the lives of the women who do the work of the world.

ACKNOWLEDGMENTS

Four people contributed substantially to move this book from wish to reality: Ellen Eaves Henneke, Alan Lomax, Robert Perine, and Blaze Newman.

In 1936, Ellen encouraged me to ask her grandmother, Jennie Hess Devlin, to sing some of her old songs to me. When I realized that "Grandma Deb" (as Ellen called her) had a remarkable collection of songs — though I was too uninformed to evaluate it — I asked Alan Lomax to come from the Archive of American Folk Song in the Library of Congress to record them. He came in 1938, but he gave me advice I did not want to hear: "It's Gran's story more than her songs. Write a book about her." I did try. But I could not do it.

In 1985, my son-in-law Bob Perine suggested, "Why not just make a songbook? I'll design it for you." That sounded easy enough. But soon I was entranced again by the story of Jennie Devlin. Blaze Newman, beloved daughter but formidable editor, urged: "Write the whole book. You too can learn to use a computer. I'll teach you." But then she would be saying: "Are you sure that's what you want to say? Did you store? Both disks? Dinner's ready. Stay here tonight. You can boot it up and try it again tomorrow." To her belongs the credit for teaching an ex-teacher to become a better writer.

So now the book is finished, and my relief turns to joy since I can share it with all four of you. Without you, I'd still have just a collection of warped records and crumbling notebooks.

My love and my thanks go also to my backup team: Deborah Newman Silverstein and Diane F. Halpern. They read and reacted to version after version. My son-in-law Stanley J. Silverstein, reading this draft, gave a final word of approval. Grandma Deb would have loved all of you.

I regret that Janet Grimler died several years ago; I never thanked her adequately for her careful work in notating almost all of the songs. A few additional ones on the Lomax/Dealy recording have been transcribed by Alan DeVries. Pamela Richman, a folksinger herself, added guitar chords. Lawrence Czoka put the music on the computer, ready for the printer. I thank my stars that I found all these musicians.

Besides learning a great deal of American folklore, I have learned the true meaning of the word "scholar" from the generous assistance given me by Kenneth S. Goldstein, Ellen Stekert, and the late D. K. Wilgus. As an independent scholar, I have profited greatly by the suggestions of my editor at the University of Illinois Press, Judith McCulloh.

Throughout many wearisome revisions, from 1985 to now, one constant encouragement has been Robert Perine's promise to design my book. Now, at last, I have the pleasure to say thank you, Bob.

INTRODUCTION

Three Voices

This book is written in three voices in two different time frames. Jennie Devlin and I, as Kay Dealy, working together in 1936–38, were the first two; and now I add my voice as Dr. Katharine Dealy Newman, in the last decade of this century, remembering the singer and her songs.

Old age has advantages of its own. No longer must we prove ourselves or strive to fulfill our destinies. We are bound into failing bodies, but now we have the time to muse and meditate and tell ourselves the stories of our lives. We also have time — and willingness — to listen to other people tell their life stories. There is no more time for criticism of them or ourselves. Life has been amazing; all our stories hold great fascination. Of course we know how they will all end, but meanwhile, let us enjoy our memories and our matured understandings.

Recently, I discovered a quilt that had been pieced by my great-grandmother, circa 1860. It is a nine-and-bar pattern, with many tiny squares of more colors than I can count, made from all the scraps of material available to her. All was carefully hand-stitched: hundreds of identically spaced stitches taken by a patient old woman. Finding this treasure gave me the same feeling of excitement about reentering the past that I had when, a few years ago, I finally sorted out all that I had taken down, word for word, song for song, as given to me by Jennie Devlin when she was in her seventies and I in my twenties. Here I "own" the record of another humble woman; Jennie Devlin had stitched her life together with songs. What an inexpressible thrill to hold a bit of the past in one's hands.

When I realized the treasure I had — a life-documentary and a song collection — I wondered about its worth as a book. I took the songs (words, tunes, tapes, and my old research) to two folksong authorities: the late D. K. Wilgus, who was at that time professor of English and Anglo-American folksong at the University of California, Los Angeles, and Kenneth S. Goldstein, then chairperson of the Department of Folklore and Folklife at the University of Pennsylvania. They both thought I had a collection large enough to sustain publication. But when I showed them my bibliography of more than three hundred entries from so long ago, each said the same thing: there was no way that I could catch up on the research of the past fifty years. Each gave me a basic list of major collections and theories with which I should become acquainted. Each pledged to help me, and each did, as my notes show.

I found Alan Lomax again. In 1938, he had spent a day recording Jennie Devlin's singing and storytelling. Now he heads the Association for Cultural Equity at Hunter College. Here are stored the many hundreds of tapes he has made over all the world, music that, linked with stories and dances, demonstrates the connection between popular arts and the disparate cultural patterns of different peoples. That he has written the foreword for my book is a great boon. It links together the beginning and the ending of this story.

Being an independent scholar once more has been much easier for me than it was in the 1930s. When I entered a library back then, I carried pads of lined paper and several pencils; getting caught with ink in a library meant expulsion from the premises. How did I ever wheedle so many people into hand copying songs for me? I shake my head in gratitude over the many selections from songsters—those cheap little paperbound books in which song lyrics were printed—in my mother's exquisite handwriting. Some sets of words that I apparently thought might be of value were copied by one of my high-school students, and some are even in the handwriting of my obnoxious sister-in-law. I am impressed by the great talent I must have had in persuading people to sit with me in uncomfortable old libraries, plying their pencils.

Today there are too many resources. As I returned to my research, I tried to limit myself to studying only the material that could help me understand what I have in my old notebooks. My "social life" has included trips to my neighborhood library to pick up rare books located for me through interlibrary loan, and late-night visits to the duplicating center near the local college campus, where—a dozen years into retirement—I felt like a professor again. Now my new files, crammed with photocopies, bulk as large as the old folders with the handwritten copies. I have been excited to find important connections between my original work and that of the major folk-song collectors since the thirties. In those days I had contact only with John and Alan Lomax, H. M. Belden (in Missouri), and Colonel Henry Shoemaker, the Pennsylvania state archivist.

How ironic that when I returned to the University of Pennsylvania for my Ph.D. in Victorian studies (1961), I never learned that it had become a major center of folk-song scholarship. I even had a proseminar in research with G. Malcolm Laws, Jr., without knowing his "real" work. I winced when I learned, in my second immersion in the Devlin material, that Laws had cited some of her song titles merely as "sung in New Jersey," and, to deepen the irony, that he was the only scholar I ever found to have used the Lomax/Dealy material. It was a regrettable loss for me.

I did catch up with a bit of my past work in 1987 when Joseph Hickerson, archivist at the Library of Congress, sent me a copy of the *Check-List of Recorded Songs . . . in the Archive of American Folk Song to July, 1940* (where "Kay Dealy" was listed "among interested folklorists . . . with independent expeditions of their own").

One unexpected problem of this present go-round has been in trying to crawl back into the mind-set of "Kay Dealy," the intermediary who, at twenty-four, still lived with her parents (as was proper for unmarried "girls"). When I listen to the tapes that have been made from the original records and enhanced for me by the Archive of American Folk Song (now the Archive of Folk Culture in the American Folklife Center at the Library of Congress), I hear Kay as being more impediment than facilitator. Time and time again, Jennie pleaded, "Kay knows that" or "as I told Kay." At one point Alan Lomax had to maneuver to get Kay out of the room; she was obviously too proprietorial. But there were other limitations, too, since I tried to play the conflicting roles of proud fictive granddaughter and disinterested collector. In truth, what I have written is an "as-told-to biography," but I am character as well as narrator.

Of course, the old storyteller had her own standards, too. She always censored parts of the story of her own life to protect the mid-Victorian sensibilities of an unmarried woman. She told me about the sufferings in her marriage, but not about the joys. I regret that I could not go back, after I was married and had twice given birth, to share with her some of the "secrets" she had learned from her years on the stud farm and as a "baby-nurse." But I saw the Devlins together in their old age, and I am convinced that Jennie Devlin's embrace of life was fortified by a strong physical bond with her husband of more than fifty years.

On the other hand, while I was reticent about her personal feelings, I was aggressive in trying to get the details of her early life. In truth, my scholarly conscience played a major part in my first failure to tell this story: I had no verification of the "facts" of her birth and early years. Not that I didn't try. I wrote letters to state and local government agencies and to libraries, historical societies, newspapers, and churches in areas where "Jennie Hess" was said to have lived for the first fourteen years of her life. I never located any birth or baptismal certificates; I have nothing at all to document the stories she said she had been told. I came to agree with her: her early life was "a Chinese puzzle" with many pieces that could not be found.

Was there any truth in these "facts" she had been given? I still do not know, but this time I have decided that, in place of documentable verification, there is another category for the biographer to respect: "family lore." Such stories often begin, "I was always told," but then they grow into acceptance as "fact" by all the family. In this story that I now tell, many of the details are exactly as they were recited to me by her husband, daughter, and granddaughter. In fact, Jennie Hess Devlin's construct of her life was so rigidly formulated that I never found but one deviation: Did Mr. Stevenson shoot the rattlesnake or did he strangle it with his bare hands? This is not to say that, as an old lady, she told a straight story chronologically; most of the time it was hit-or-miss as accompaniment to her "pieces." But, sorted out, it makes a good story.

There can be a point, however, where family lore merges with folklore, or so it seems to me in regard to two stories that I have told as factual, but about which I hereby confess to some doubt. One is the newspaper account of the poor boy stopping a runaway sleigh with a rich man's family in it. As in a Horatio Alger novel, the lad was taken into the rich man's employ and succeeded well. (The significant missing detail was that a Horatio Alger rich man would have had a beautiful daughter who married the poor boy, who was then, of course, no longer poor.) But apart from that, it could have been a true story; it fits the character of "Hellfire Jack," who became Jennie's husband, and there may have been many runaway sleighs stopped by valiant lads.

The other story, about Aunt Eva getting the geese drunk, seemed out of character for such a bright and well-organized person, even when it was told to me as absolute fact by Jennie Devlin herself. I never expected to read another "true" story like it. But I have. This anecdote was told by a man who claimed that his mother had told it to him as a bedtime story: One day she and her cousin had to dump a crock in which they had been trying to make whiskey; it smelled too bad. The geese gobbled up all the mash and fell down dead drunk. But, not knowing about the mash, the grandmother believed her geese were dead and sent the girls out to pluck the down from the birds. The next morning there was a courtyard full of naked geese staggering around. In this version, the grandmother crocheted little jackets for them to wear. The real clincher to this anecdote is that I found the story in "Dear Abby" in the *Los Angeles Times* on June 11, 1985. This was about one hundred years after Aunt Eva told it in Wellsville, New York.

I had been frustrated in my first venture in not being able to locate any "hard data." This time I've discovered that I have lost something I thought I had: Jennie's wedding certificate. One night she took it off her bedroom wall, brought it downstairs, and laid it gently on the dining room table. It was such a fine treasure that I made a pencil sketch then and there. Then she carried the original reverently upstairs. I still have that crude sketch, but over all these intervening years, as the family has dispersed, that lovely certificate has disappeared. I have contacted the church where Pastor Coit married the Devlins and also the church where he was pastor years later when he sent Jennie the duplicate, the one she showed me. I have also inquired at print museums and historical societies, but all I ever got were the prosaic standard forms without engraving or colored illustration. No flowers. No doves. No angels. All these are gone, along with the fine lettering. We can still read (on my sketch) the biblical admonitions to the wife and to the husband. Their meanings are quite clear:

> She will do him good and not evil all the days of her life. [Proverbs 30:12]
> It is not good that the man should be alone. I will make him an helpmate for him. [Genesis 2:18]
> Husbands love your wives, even as Christ also loved the church and gave himself for it. [Ephesians 5:25]

At the bottom was the notation that the marriage had taken place in Wellsville "on the Thirty-First day of December in the year of Our Lord One Thousand Eight Hundred and Eighty Five." It was signed by Albert Coit, Pastor. However, in the margin below was written: "This duplicate Certificate is issued by me from my private original records. Syracuse, New York, October 17, 1900. Albert Coit, Pastor, Olivet Baptist Church." This is the only documentation of her life that I ever had.

I formally became "Katharine Newman" about the time of the Ph.D., but I abandoned Victorian studies to study and teach the totality of the literature of my own country. I created courses, compiled two anthologies, and founded MELUS, the Society for the Study of the Multi-Ethnic Literature of the United States. My professional commitment explains why I show so much interest in all the references to "Others" in the story of Jennie Devlin. Today we are apt to be smug in thinking of our ancestors as having been more bigoted than we are. Jennie Devlin's memories show that prejudice can be outgrown; she gives us some good examples of the processes of acceptance and assimilation. It is, of course, true that her life was spent in an all-white working-class society; she never knew any African Americans or other people of color. It is because of my personal interest that I have stressed the importance of African American culture as the basis for much "American" popular song, whether it was acknowledged or not, by musicians of the nineteenth and early twentieth centuries.

The most obvious differences I noted between working-class country and middle-class city people were in speech patterns and in sexual attitudes. As "Kay Dealy," I had been taken aback at learning the meanings of some of Jennie Devlin's expressions and songs. In recent years, now quite accustomed to open discussions of former taboos, I have been very shocked by discovering inane censorship lingering in folk-song collections made by academicians. I learned about it almost accidentally.

Jennie had dictated to me her long, slightly naughty "Western Courtship," and she had sung for us a total of five bawdy pieces. But when I finally got a copy of the *Check-List of Recorded Songs,* I found only one listed ("Some for the Girl"). Where were the others? I was sure that there must have been some major typographical errors made by the awesome Library of Congress. When I told D. K. Wilgus about this, he explained that the missing ones probably went into a special category, the "Delta," "Inferno," or "Big Hell" collection. "Improper material" that had been recorded, most likely by mistake when the collector was not prepared for bawdy words from a sweet-faced ballad singer, could not even be listed as being housed within the walls of the Library of Congress. This was a "secret" I never suspected.

The revelation of such censorship in a field of scholarly endeavor shocked me greatly. Why was there such prudery among so many folk-song gatherers in my time? There may have been a belief in scholarly publishing houses that such material was beneath their dignity. Or it might be that the image of the innocent folksinger was not to be sullied by inappropriate verses. Folksong was supposed to be bucolic. Tragedy was suitable; vulgarity was not.

Luckily, I have had assurance from Ed Cray, who has published his second edition of *The Erotic Muse,* that the "Delta" material in the Library of Congress is now available even though no record of those holdings has been published. Only one of the Jennie Devlin songs is in *The Erotic Muse,* but my having access to that book and to Vance Randolph's long-suppressed work *Pissing in the Snow and Other Folktales* has been liberating for me. These books have led me back to some of Jennie's "naughty" songs and sayings, for they show that Anglo-American country women enjoyed telling "indecent tales" to other women, and, more important, that women can find sex quite amusing. Without all of her songs and her piquant sayings, we would not have a true picture of Jennie Devlin, folksinger.

* * *

More than half a century has passed since I first sat at her dining room table and began to take down, word for word, the songs and poems that composed the repertoire of Jennie Devlin. As we began, I was already privileged to call her "Grandma Deb," the name her granddaughter Ellen used, and it was on such a basis of trust that she freely gave me what she called "my old pieces that I know."

As she pulled them up from her memory, the songs came embedded in the rich soil of her whole life: where she was living when she learned them, who sang them with her, who listened to her sing. And I, hearing about a world I never knew, noted every detail of that life just as solemnly as I entered the words of her songs in my notebook. I also attempted to record Grandma Deb's speech, with its many allusions, jokes, and localisms. The result was that I had a fine collection of songs and recited pieces, with her own commentary, on that night when she finally said to me, "That's the last sardine in the can!"

That was back then. Now I know that while I was trying to be a faithful recording instrument, Grandma Deb's words were permeating my own life. So now I, in my turn, have become the narrator of her story, as well as the transfer agent of her songs.

I have had to cut my pattern to suit my cloth. Now my task has been to put those pieces in order, to make creative guesses in matching parts to show connections. Some things I had to stretch a little to cover a weak spot in the fabric of the tale; some few scraps I had to throw away because they just would not fit in anywhere or because they made bulges in strange places. She gave me more — much more — about hog slaughtering than I wanted, and less — far less — about those experiences in her life that bred her robust sense of humor. She didn't tell me. I didn't ask.

There are dozens of questions I wish I could ask now, but there really is enough for a dramatic scenario: an unwanted baby, a frail foster child, an overworked hired girl, the loyal wife of a hard-drinking man, a woman who fought poverty in daily combat. Jennie Devlin became a strong woman who lived a life of quiet determination. Courageous, salty, fun loving, hard working, life accepting, she gave undemanding love to all the people who needed her. We cannot guess the conflicting powers that forge any human personality, but obviously the inner life she built out of her songs helped sustain her throughout her life.

She would apologize to me about the weakness in her voice now that she was old. "I'm no singer at all," she would say, "but I'm as good a whistler as ever puckered a lip." But there I sat waiting, with my pencil poised, and so she had to sing. You can't whistle words. And words were what mattered most. Sometimes the tune wouldn't "wake itself up" in her memory, but still the words would come. Tunes were fine, especially the old dance tunes; but the stories in "them old pieces" and even in "the junk on the radio" — these were about *real* people. These songs had to be cherished. They were her education as well as her entertainment. Her mind was so packed with stories and sayings that the words flowed out into her everyday speech.

She sang about women: women courted, seduced, betrayed; women who were faithful and endured for love's sake; women who had gotten the better of men; women who had "a little fun" on their own. She sang about old women who were wise and about good young ones who perished tragically. And she sang of women and their children: children who had lost their mothers or were saved by a mother's love — or destroyed by a mother's cruelty. She did mention men, but only in relation to women. Men were often faithless and frequently murderous. Sometimes they were faithful and docile, and — as she gleefully sang — occasionally they were the dupes of shrewd women.

She had a store of moral songs, some "hymns and pieces to teach the kiddies to do right." But she also had a store of "crazy" songs where she laughed at all the fancy airs of stuck-up people.

She never sang "worksongs" or songs about the land, even about places where she had lived at various times, such as the Erie Canal. Men sang these, working together in community. The only reflection of the world in which she lived — the world of hired girls and farmhands — was in the brief words and gay refrains of dance tunes, and in the naughty verses she "dasen't often sing aloud" but never forgot. "Some can take a joke an' see the bad side. Some can take a joke an' see the funny side. It's really no harm to it."

She had picked and she had chosen her songs on the basis of content rather than musical appeal. Believing that they were all "real," she treasured them as giving her insights into a knowledge of "real" life that she felt she never got from books or family instruction. She said, "I never sat down to learn a piece in my life. I jus' picked them up from hearing them."

Although she had spent most of her early years in the woods or on farms, she was not like those folksingers who are respected all through their lives in their own community. Instead, she lived in many places and garnered songs everywhere. Jennie Devlin had an abundance to choose from, for (as I see it) the nineteenth was the "singingest" century. The pieces that she chose to memorize cover the emotions, history, and humor of that century when sentimentalism both reigned and parodied itself. People sang freely in their homes and around their work, teaching each other the new songs. In big cities, professionals sang directly to enthusiastic audiences, and often the words went back to the folks at home on penny sheets or in songsters. The songs were shared and changed, and they became the property of everyone who loved to sing.

In her lifetime, the old ways of singing changed. The era when ordinary people had learned from each other, voice to voice, was coming to an end. While Jennie Devlin really did know this, she refused to admit it. She declared her "old pieces" to be better than anything printed in the newspapers because "more people remember them." She did not know that some of her songs were so old that very few people sang them any more, while others were popular songs of the last quarter of the nineteenth century. They were all equally old to her. She tried to explain this to me: "God knows, I hardly ever went to school. It's like living a game of Blind Man's Bluff. I don't know history or any of that. When I want to know somethin', I have to go to Ellen."

About her own history, nobody ever told her much either. "My life is a Chinese puzzle," she would say. "I try and try but I can't never fit all the pieces in." What did hold these pieces together were the songs. Some of them, such as "The Orphan Child" and "The Drunkard's Lament," even seemed to parallel her own experiences. Several others were, indeed, based on real events. She herself had visited the sites of these tragedies and had even seen the grave markers of James Bird, Martha Decker, and Miss Riot. On an Indian reservation she learned the ballad "The Old Indian." Years later, in Philadelphia, she heard the story of a prisoner who had spent "Eight Years in Cherry Hill." She sorrowed over all these tragedies.

In contrast, Jennie Devlin loved to sing (or recite) the comic numbers. When she sang bawdy ones, she got a bit embarrassed. She was sentimental over the "kiddie pieces" and earnest over the religious ones. Her voice was usually soft and worn, but it showed signs of its earlier strength when she sang dance tunes and other "crazy pieces." Jennie's songs served as a refuge, a sheltering place, all her life long. They form our bridge back to her.

Part 1

THE YEARS

"My life is a Chinese puzzle . . .
I can't get the pieces together."

1

Motherless Child, 1865–79

A ballad was bound in with the strange story of Jennie Devlin's birth, so she was told: "James Bird" had been her mother's favorite song. Years and years later, when she finally got a copy of the words and learned them, Jennie felt she had hold of something that connected her with the mother she'd never had. "That's all I have of her," she would say. "I had a mother, but I never had a mother's love." The lack of that love was a lifelong agony.

She was told that she was born on February 8, 1865, just two months before the end of "the War." "They," whoever they were, at some time or another told the child that her mother had loved a young soldier, but he had gone off to the war. That, they said, was why her mother treasured this one song; James Bird had been a soldier, too. Jennie probably never knew that two different wars were involved; James Bird had fought with Perry at the Battle of Lake Erie in 1813, but the ballad about him had been a favorite of the Union soldiers in the Civil War.

"I was born Eliza Jane Hess," she'd explain, using the nineteenth-century term for the double-S: "H-E-long S." The baby's name was changed somewhere, sometime, by somebody, into the common old nickname "Jennie." Her father, they said, was Chauncey Hess. "He was an old man who had a mill outside of Albany, New York State. Or maybe he only worked in a mill but he had enough money to get her to marry him."

Jennie was given a miraculous tale about her birth: a seven-month baby, she came into the world weighing only one and one-half pounds on the miller's scales. She was so tiny that they couldn't put clothes on her, "just the red flannel bellyband that they always put on newborns." She was fed warm milk from a medicine dropper, and she was kept in the oven in a cigar box lined with cotton. Later they moved her into a roasting pan. Naturally the oven temperature had to be carefully watched, so somebody always sat by the oven door, day and night. This loving care made her survival possible.

The next event in her life was also miraculous. Apparently Mary, her mother, had "gone out of her head" when Jennie was born. One day, the nurse came into the bedroom to see Mary about to throw the infant into the millrace. The nurse caught her just in time.

"I oughtn'ta lived, I guess. Sometimes I wish I hadn't," Jennie said matter-of-factly, seventy-two years later.

But despite these dangers, the baby did grow, and at eight months she was finally able to wear infant clothes. Afterward, having survived premature birth and a distraught mother, she was taken away from the mill, away from her birth mother. She never knew who took her away. She was positive that she never saw Mary Hess again.

"I often wondered what my mother looked like. Was she hard-hearted? They said that my hair was tow-colored, like my mother's had been, no expression to it. That's all I know about her looks. But it was my hair, so straight and light, that made people say I looked Dutch. Dutch an' dumb — as the saying goes."

It was her hair that linked her to the only memory she had of her infant days. She remembered something about a brother. "When I was little, we'd fight and one day he bit chunks out of my hair." Then he too was lost to her.

The life she was able to recall began when she awakened one morning to find herself on a hillside farm above the town of Athens, Pennsylvania. She'd been brought there during the night, although she never remembered how. The couple who had taken her in were known to her as "Uncle Charley" and "Aunty Hawkins." The fact that she called the woman only by her married name, not her first name, showed, by the naming code of the day, that this was not a "real" aunt but a "courtesy" aunt. Indeed, Jennie never found out if the Hawkinses were related to her at all or even how they had claimed her. Certainly they had not taken her in only for charity's sake. She was now a bound-out girl, obliged to work for her keep, without wages.

But at first she was too young, "not yet five years old," and too puny. She weighed only twenty-five pounds and she was racked with asthma. Years later, when she herself was a baby-nurse, she would say, "Baby may get off to a bad start if the mother was unhappy carrying her." Certainly this preemie hadn't been thriving. At that time, when babies suffered from colic, they were given a remedy called "cinder tea." Grandma Deb described this to me one night. "Take an earth cup one-half full of cold water and drop a live coal in. After it's steamed and all black, take the coal out, strain, and feed to baby."

If cinder tea could cure colic, coal dust itself might cure asthma. So Uncle Charley took the little girl to a coal mine, strapped her onto a mule, and took her down for a three-mile trip. She was choking when they set out, and her breathing got worse as she inhaled the coal dust. She passed out. Then the mule brought her back out into the fresh air.

She gave a great gasp and let out all the foul air, emptying her lungs. From then on, her asthma was cured. She grew into a large girl with a strong body and buoyant spirit.

Jennie lived there long enough to sound like a tour guide: "Athens is a twin town. The railroad runs down the main street. One side is Athens and the other is Sayre. The farms are mostly small ones, with lots of outbuildings. The crops, mostly, was hay and corn. The mountains there was not so high or so frequent as they were in Wellsville, but more wooded. It was in the Susquehanna Valley."

The Hawkinses were not rich. They worked the farm for a Mr. Thomas, and it was so hilly that "when Mr. Thomas wanted to visit, they had to send down extry horses to double up his wagon. They had cows and made firkins and tubs of butter. The September butter was always counted on for bringing in more money."

Uncle Charley was also a weaver. "You went up the back stairs — it was very cold there — then down the hall to the stairs up to the attic. There's where he had his big loom. It was for rag carpets — he also wove anything that was heavy. It had a seat and a high beam. You could hear the loom all over the house. He might have anywhere from a hundred and ten to a hundred and fifteen pounds of rags sewed into a ball. They called this a 'hit and miss' rag carpet because the pieces were all blended; he even colored the white rags to fit in. Some people called this the 'rainbow pattern.'"

This was a real home, her first. "This old-time house — all the rooms were large." She always remembered how Aunty Hawkins "made it pretty." Everything had to be very clean and in its place. In the kitchen there were "cupboards, a window with a table under it, four chairs, a sink, a boiler, and a Hoover washer [a boiler in which a plunger was used instead of a scrub board]." There was colorful linoleum on the floor and "real paper on part of the wall."

Jennie had a room of her own. "The door was just a slab, with one cross piece on the inside. The walls were whitewashed every spring. There was a chair and a chest with two big drawers and when you lifted the lid, there was a tray for ribbons. And there were curtains made of what you call Dolly Varden flowered material tacked on round sticks over the window."

The bedrooms had rope beds, that is, "ropes went lengthwise and crosswise over pegs in the frame, making squares about eight inches so it wouldn't sag. Grownups sometimes had high beds with a frill to hide the trundle beds for the little ones, y'know, and the potties underneath. In summer, there were cornhusk mattresses. Often people kep' them year to year unless children had been sleeping in them. In the winter, just put the feather beds right on the cornhusk mattresses.

And a quilt was just another feather bed. In spring the feather beds was aired, then sprinkled with tansy to keep the moths out, and hung in the loft."

Tansy and other herbs were always important. "There were pillow cases stuffed with everlasting flowers for the worst case of hay fever. Up in the garret — it was part floored and part just boards — we always had bunches of herbs hanging. We gathered them fresh every fall. Pillow cases of baby pine needles for nerves. You know you don't get a doctor for them things. Aunty Hawkins used to boil herbs every spring in a big copper kettle. Boil down, strain, then boil again. Add brandy and give one tablespoon to each person of the house each day in the spring. There wasn't the new fangdangled sicknesses there are today, and I don't mean maybe."

That Grandma Deb took the common word "newfangled" and stretched it even farther showed her contempt for doctors who apparently had concocted new illnesses just to make money. Such a rejection of modern methods was unusual for her since she pronounced many times, "You can't live in the past. You have to keep up with the times." But she had used home remedies for her children and her grandchildren, and she resented losing control of her family's health to drugstores and patent medicines.

As a child living in Athens, she learned the satiric song "Calomel," about the doctor who killed off all his patients by prescribing nothing but that laxative for all ailments. Grandma Deb sang the song with considerable satisfaction.

"This is makin' fun of the doctors, see? It goes on to say that the doctor lets the man die an' all he ever gives him is calomel. Y'know that is a laxative.

"A new doctor moved to this town where I was living with the Hawkinses. He had a great long beard and on the side of his house, he had three big pieces of muslin tacked around with wood. One said:

> My hands with blood I do not stain,
> Or poison men to ease their pain.

"Kinda struck me funny, and yet it made me feel queer, too." Her ambiguous feelings about doctors and medicines were in contrast with her usual upbeat attitudes about the changes that were made in farming and homemaking from her "young years" with Aunty Hawkins and Uncle Charley up to those very times when she was describing them to me.

"I don' remember any time when I couldn't wash dishes. They'd put a box for me to stand on to reach the zinc [sink]. Also peel apples an' potatoes — pull weeds — help with the beds — set table." And, once a year, there was candle making. "We hung strings for the wicks down from a pole that had holes in it, and we'd dip the strings in the hot tallow and let them dry. Then dip again. Dip 'n' dry. Until the candles was thick enough."

Although she was too young to weave, she was taught to sew rags for Uncle Charley, and she had her first lessons in knitting. She never mentioned having any toys, not even a rag doll to take to bed with her. What she was to the Hawkinses was a young worker being trained for adult work, but the training was gentle. "If I was bad — wherever I was living — I'd be deprived of things. I never was hit or anything like that. But I wasn't often bad. I knew I was among strangers and I had to have a home."

There was at least one time, though, that she did something wrong, but it was a mistake. "I didn't mean it to be bad. Aunty Hawkins had company an' she was going to make pancakes. So she was sittin' talking to the guests and she sent me to the kitchen to find out if the griddle was hot enough. I come back so fast that she couldn't believe it, so she asks me, 'How did you know so quick?' Says I, 'I spit on the griddle and it sizzled.' Boy, did I get Glory Hallelujah for that one! But I still have to laugh even now."

In one way she was treated as a child. In the parlor was "a little rocking chair — back covered and ruffles all around — a real child's chair. I used to sit in it a lot, especially on Sundays." And, on Sundays, they all enjoyed going to "prayer meetings in different homes — no special church. More like camp meetings today [1936]. We sang hymns, some I still know and hear people sing."

It was probably in social gatherings that she first heard the ballad about Martha Decker, the thirteen-year-old girl who had been drowned in the Chemung River in 1842. There were thirty-four stanzas — and Jennie never forgot any of them. This was probably the first ballad she ever learned. "There was never a time I couldn't sing and dance any more than I couldn't wash dishes, ever since I was so little I can't remember."

She always said that the best thing that happened to her during these years in Athens was being able to go to school. One winter, when she was about six, she was put onto a sled and taken down the hill to Mr. Thomas's house. There she stayed for three months so that she could go to school in the town. "Mr. Thomas didn't have children. He was very kind to me. One of his servants used to watch me cross over the railroad tracks to the school. It was a little schoolhouse, brownish with white trimmings and a little yard. Long benches and each class had its own apartment [sic] with boys on one side and girls on the other. The teacher was a man, youngish, with a little short goatee, like a goat's moustache, of course. He didn't whip any of us."

Jennie was learning to read and to write on her slate "that was bound in red." She may have learned some games and "kiddie pieces" like "I carried water in my glove" and other play-party songs. She was good at playing mumblety-peg. But this was all the schooling she was ever to have. She mourned the deprivation for the rest of her life. "At nights sometimes I cry. It's a terrible thing not to have an education. That's why I always told the kiddies: 'Love your teacher next to your mother. Your mother can keep you clean, but she can't give you an education. Your teacher helps you for life.' Sometimes those who've not had an education don't see what it means. I do, though. I didn't know when I was young and it was all 'do this' or 'do that' for me, but it's different now for children growing up."

Then tragedy came to the little farm on the hill. "One day an axe handle broke and the axe flew up and cut off Uncle Charley's arm. He did live, but there was only a little stub left. They got him down from the hill to the town where the doctor bound him up, but he couldn't farm anymore. Without the farm, they couldn't keep me."

She never forgot them: the house, the teacher, the ballad of "Martha Decker," or the buckwheat "white as snow" when the fields were ripe. But she could never remember what happened to her in the months — perhaps years — after she had to leave Uncle Charley and Aunty Hawkins. "My life was all mixed up like a nightmare."

Was it her singing and dancing that won for Jennie her next home? She never knew. There seemed little other reason for the Stevensons, a family of basketmakers, to want a little girl to work for them. They were, it is true, very kind to her, and the new life was exciting, but frequently Jennie felt that she was living nightmares by day as well as by night. The little group traveled in a wagon from one desolate house or abandoned shack to another, staying an indefinite time in each location. It was an incredibly difficult existence, nomadic and rigorous. She went from the security of the established farm, the settled community, the little brown schoolhouse, into the backwoods. It was as though she had been dropped back in time; she had been taken from reading to memorizing, knowing that she had to keep her ears open to learn whatever she could. This was her time of education through folksong. Basketmakers — like umbrella menders, watch repairers, knife sharpeners, peddlers, and tinkers — were the Johnny Appleseeds of American folksong. As these itinerant workers carried their wares and their skills from town to town, they also carried songs. They knew the old songs that had come over from England or Scotland, and they sang them to the people living inland. When their memories failed or played tricks with the words or the tunes, variant forms were created.

Their hearers, in trade, offered them the new songs of America, the comic songs and the ballads about local events.

Among these travelers, the Stevensons were very effective song-bearers because they accompanied themselves on musical instruments. Amos Stevenson played first violin and was caller for dancers; his wife and his brother played second fiddle. And Jennie Hess danced and sang.

It is possible that the basketmakers were putting on these entertainments primarily to sell their goods. But, again, they may have bartered for food. Certainly they needed payment of some sort. Grandma Deb first denied this — "I never saw no money" — but her own function clearly was as a solo entertainer. For these appearances she had one of the finest outfits she ever had in her entire life. She had "a Dolly Varden dress with a little hoop at the bottom an' calfskin boots to do my little steps in. Hair clear down to my knees. Flaxen hair, tow head, no expression to it, but she braided it and tied bows of ribbons, bright ribbons."

Mrs. Stevenson taught Jennie little dance steps and the words of the old folksongs; she gave her a special ditty to sing at the conclusion of her performance. When she sang this to me, she explained: "I'd sing this and I'd curtsy. Like Mrs. Stevenson had taught me. And I had a little basket to pass, too. That's what I'd sing, see, when I was singin' at a party. I'd curtsy an' then they'd drop pennies in my basket. That's when the Stevensons would dress me up."

During these years with the basketmakers, the little girl was a true folksinger with an audience that applauded her enthusiastically. From this experience, Jennie may have developed some of her personal identity, seeing herself as more than a motherless, bound-out child. She was beginning to have knowledge of other women's lives as she pondered their actions in her songs. She tried to understand worlds far beyond the woods.

Making and selling their baskets and giving their dances, the Stevensons moved so often that Jennie was never able to put into any order the names of all the places along the border between New York and Pennsylvania where she traveled with them: "Fort Erie, Troy, Bradford, up into Canada, and Tidioute." She was sure only that this part of her life finally ended in Ithaca. She had one strong recollection of Troy, New York. "That's one of the places the Stevensons took me. They'd go to these places, playing — I can't remember — but they'd always take me along."

In Troy, she learned the ballad of "Miss Riot" [actually "Miss Wyatt"]. The story told how a young man, Henry Green, who lived there in 1845, poisoned his bride of two weeks, Mary Ann Wyatt, and was hanged for his crime. The Stevensons may have taken Jennie to see the double grave; it was a popular attraction. Jennie memorized the twenty stanzas of the ballad, which was still being sung in Troy, thirty years after the grisly event. Ever afterward, this made-in-America ballad occupied a special place in her mind, along with "Martha Decker."

While she still had never heard anyone sing "James Bird," the ballad that her mother was said to have loved, little Jennie did come in contact with the James Bird legend while she was with the Stevensons. "One day I was gathering catnip for my little kitten down near the shore at Fort Erie. There was this wooden slab, painted old style. There was two men there and they said it was the grave of James Bird. They said he was a great hero along with Perry. But he was shot like a deserter. Jus' jealousy."

There was a revealing little detail in this story: she mentions having a little kitten for her own pet. This and other anecdotes seem to indicate that the Stevensons were as indulgent to her as was possible in their world. She had vivid recollections about dogs. "The Stevensons always kep' two or three hounds. One day, one of them had babies." Since it was a cold night, the puppies were moved to a warm place: under the step stove. ("A step stove was a high stove. It had a reservoir to hold six, eight buckets of water so it didn't freeze," she explained.) Jennie thought that was a good idea, and she crept under the stove, too, and was allowed to sleep with the puppies all night.

She was given a little dog of her own, "Curly, with white ringlets in his hair." One day he ran into the woods, and Jennie went after him. "He was gone two, three days and they had to hunt me a-hunting for him. When I found him, he was all covered with needles from porcupines. He must have fought a whole family. The men took him into the basket shop and put me out while they pulled all those quills out. Some they had to cut out, he was stuck so bad. I cried my eyes out."

There was a curious relationship between Jennie and the Stevensons. She never used the courtesy titles of "Uncle" and "Aunt" with them. She always referred to them as Mr. and Mrs. Stevenson. Yet "at serious times" she called him "Dad" and Mrs. Stevenson "Mother." These were the only people in her whole life whom she was allowed to name as though they were her parents. They remained sharp in her memory, especially this "mother" with whom she worked side by side.

Mrs. Stevenson was "dark, had a brown complexion. Her coloring was light. She was plump, not fat, actually a delicate, frail little woman, not very strong. Any little thing would upset her." But she worked very hard and Jennie, of course, had to work hard, too. Some of the places where they stayed were little better than shacks that they tried to make habitable. They swept and they scrubbed. Often they had to carry heavy buckets of water from the pump or from nearby streams. When the two Stevenson men unloaded the wagon, the women set up and re- corded the beds and put the quilts on. They did all the cooking and washing, planted vegetables, and made or mended the clothing. By the time she was eight, Jennie was knitting the wristlets, gloves, and muf- flers that they all needed for living in the cold woods.

"There never was any time to fix up any of the places where we lived, we moved so much, always after fresh wood. The big baskets were made only with oak: red, white, or scribblin' oak. Or ash. Hickory baskets don't last and it didn't pay to make them. We always had to live near a woods, set up the shop, and then make the baskets. Then Mr. Stevenson'd be gone two, three days at a time selling the baskets. The men could only use trees three, four years old. So when a stand of oak was all finished, we'd have to pack up everything and go in the wagon somewhere else. One time we had to move even sooner because there was a fire in the woods. Mr. Stevenson thought it had been started by somebody who was jealous of him having that special wood."

Jennie may have conjectured that such a firebrand would be as jealous of the finished product as of the wood. She regarded Mr. Stev- enson as a master craftsman. She was fascinated by every step in the process.

"Preparin' the splints was much harder than weaving the baskets later. The first thing was to cut down the tree on a diagonal. Then Mr. Stevenson'd take his maul and beat it into the tree with his hammer. That made the tree split into layers. Next he took a sharp moving knife, held the layers 'uphill' so it kep' straight, and cut the splints perfect: one-half inch thick by one and one-half inches wide. It was an art. Mr. Stevenson was very, very good at it.

"The wood could only be used when it was moist, so the men—Mr. Stevenson and his brother—could only cut enough for one day at a time. Sometimes they'd find a clay pit and put it in that." When there was no easier way to do it, Mrs. Stevenson and Jennie carried buckets of water to pour over the wood.

"When they was workin' hard, the men could make six, eight bushel baskets a day. They made some smaller sizes: half-bushel and peck, too. Some had heavy handles out of two long splints coming up from the bottom. Big baskets for the fields sometimes had runners tacked on the bottom.

"Sometimes, when there was willow or hickory in the woods, they'd make other baskets, different shapes and sizes, like square ones or clothes baskets. Sometimes the fancy baskets was in colors. Mrs.

Stevenson and me, we collected the inkberries and boiled them, and the splints was steeped in that. An' we dyed some splints with bluing — that was sumac tea that we had boiled. An' Mr. Stevenson would put two rows of ordinary splints, then blue, red, and plain, and repeat that to the top; even the little handles had color."

There were lots of wild animals in the woods, but they usually did not bother the woodcutters. However, "sometimes, foxes would come down and eat the vegetables that we had planted. I wasn't afraid of foxes. But the food had to be saved. So the men would go fox hunting. They wore double-lined coats and went on foot like they'd go after hare. They'd track them and hunt quietly around, and then shoot them. I see pictures now of fox hunters on their horses and think, 'My, ain't that a cinch. They darn near know where he's at after they let him loose like that.' It wasn't a game back then."

Their life was never a game. They worked hard, traveled far, sold all they made, and had nothing to show for all their work. One day Mr. Stevenson decided to take them all to Canada. He went up first and found a house, the only one he could get near a good stand of trees. The owner told him that the house was haunted, but Mr. Stevenson did not care. But he didn't tell his wife, either.

"One day, after we was settled, there was a great rainstorm and the wind blew and blew and blew. There was a jog in the house and a tree there — it was hit by lightning and splintered. The bottom was all slivers and the whole top was taken off."

Mr. Stevenson, standing by the window, watched it all, and he heard "the wind humming through the tree stump." He knew that was the ghost sound that was supposed to be haunting the house.

"That night at dinner he told Mrs. Stevenson that. She was upset. 'I wouldn't have come if I'd known there was a ghost,' she said. He said he didn't never believe in ghosts. And so they never did pay no rent there."

There was one gain in Canada; they got a "Canuck heifer." "Canuck" was a very small breed. And a "heifer," in Grandma Deb's vocabulary, always meant a young cow that already had a calf and therefore was a continuing milk supplier. They named this one Lily, and she was Jennie's special pet. But everything else was hard, very hard, and they were so poor that they had to leave Canada.

The trip down was truly a nightmare. "The Stevensons never took no strangers in and never asked leave to stay at nobody's. So on the trip down — it took eight or nine days — we slept like Gypsies in the covered wagon. Lily's feet bled, and she couldn't stand. The men had to hold her up to milk her. So then they strapped her and wrapped her and laid her in the wagon during the days. Afterwards, when we was settled again, I was allowed to milk Lily and I cared for her."

The next place they settled was worse; in fact, it was the worst place of all. It was in Tidioute, Pennsylvania: "a slab house, with just a big slab for a door. There was an abyss between the house and the basket shop. There was a terrible odor of snakes from there, like rotten potatoes.

"Mr. Stevenson and his brother would go out in the mornings and shoot the gun to chase the snakes away from trees and rocks in the woods before they could begin cutting. Rattlers and long black runners could climb trees as well as rocks. And the men took strips from the timber part of the white ash bark and tied them around the dog's neck and around my ankles and legs so as to scare away the snakes.

"The worst was that the snakes could get into the house because the slab door wasn't tight. I always slept in the trundle bed. One night Mr. Stevenson woke up, looked over, and there was a rattlesnake coiled at my feet! He was so scared he didn't think. He just reached for his gun and blew the snake's head off.

"It was a terrible, terrible time — and then Mr. Stevenson was taken. In those days people didn't call them strokes — I don't remember just what they did call it — apoplexy, I think. Anyhow, his brother went for the doctor. He had to go down this path that wound around the stones. We had to wait an eternity for the doctor. They bled him after the doctor got up the hill. Back of the ears. He was unconscious but he came to. But it was too late. He'd been unconscious too long and he didn't live."

Mrs. Stevenson wanted to go back to her family in Ithaca, so Mr. Stevenson's brother took care of selling everything, to get her the money. Everything was sold. Even Lily. "When the day came that we went down the hill, to go to Ithaca, Mrs. Stevenson looked back and said, 'We're leaving this terrible hill at last! Thank God!'

"On the way to Ithaca, we had to change trains. Mrs. Stevenson carried her money in her bosom. We had to stay overnight some place. The landlord or some other man carried me up many flights of stairs, with Mrs. Stevenson behind us. Then the man come into our room, and afterwards he came back two or three times that night, rapping on the door. He said it was 'to see if she wanted anything.' Mrs. Stevenson got nervous and cried. She thought he was going to rob her.

"In Ithaca we lived in a valley. Up on the hill was this big school. It was a college — not a school — in Ithaca; it had high walls along the river. We lived near there."

But not for long. Although Mrs. Stevenson was only middle-aged, she was "never strong. She was worn out with all the hard work. And her heart was broken. He died in the summer. By the fall, she was dead. "I thought that all I had was gone."

$$* \quad * \quad *$$

Where she was, where she lived for the next "two, three years," Jennie could never remember. One thing she did remember was having her ears pierced — by somebody, somewhere. "The holes was drilled in my ears after they numbed the lobe by pinching it. Then they put a cork firmly against it and pushed a waxed needle threaded with silk through. The silk stayed there and they pulled it back and forth for a few days." She also recalled that "one time I was on a farm in the Alleghenies, a farm so stony that in one year I wore out eleven pair of shoes and two pair of rubbers." But where was that farm? She had no idea.

It is not to be wondered at that she could recall so little of these years. This must have been a period of terror: she had no job, no means of supporting herself, and nobody to turn to for love and advice. It must have been a period of pain and loss: twice tragedy had swept her away from women whom she had trusted to take care of her, women who were substitutes for the mother she had never known. She had worked as hard as any child could, but she had lost two homes. Now, as she was entering her teens, she was being handed from family to family, a stranger to all of them. She was homeless. Motherless. A nobody.

Then, "It was like Athens. The same thing happened to me. I woke up one morning and I was in Wellsville." But now there was a great change. No longer was she a "bound-out girl" as she had been for most of her life. She now worked for wages. She did the housework and took care of a little boy named Matt in the home of Mr. W. P. Decker, who was in the wholesale whiskey business. She remembered chiefly that Mrs. Decker did not know the value of money. But Jennie herself certainly did. With her own money she could buy all her own clothes. She went to a shoestore: "High everyday shoes, laced up. For years Sunday shoes were low, button." Her clothes were made by a professional dressmaker in Wellsville. "We wore hoop skirts." She also went into a store to purchase her own stockings and underwear. "We used to wear our underwear for one week, and then had another set to put on. Heavies in winter we wore for two weeks." She enjoyed gaining this much control over her own life.

In 1879, at fourteen, when she considered herself "free," a great challenge came to her. A Mrs. Ed Bentley sought her out and offered Jennie better wages than she was getting from the Deckers. Jennie left a position as a maid in a fine house in town to go to work as a hired girl on a farm. "I went of my own free will. Only because of the money."

But with this, her first independent decision, she had bought into a home and a family that would always be hers. Finally.

2

Hired Girl, 1879–85

Grandma Deb loved "true stories" as much as she loved story-ballads. She relished describing every step in any process that she had been part of. These, too, were "real stories" that she wanted to pass on. It was ironic that this bright woman had so little knowledge of historical time yet understood the value of the past and her own function in transmitting it.

The story of the creation of the Bentley farm was her favorite tale, and we spent many hours together on this topic. What made it important for her—and for me as the recorder—was that in this long story, she herself had played a major role. This was the way it went:

Edwin and Eva Bentley were very strong people, strong in body and even stronger in will power. They knew what they wanted in life, and they eventually got it: a large, successful dairy farm. But it took years and years. The price they paid was constant worrying, skimping, and hard, hard work: their own—and Jennie's. "Them days, farmin' was not like today. You *worked*."

Their story began when Edwin Bentley, the county superintendent of schools, met young Eva Clemens at the Teacher's Institute in Wellsville, New York. She taught only one year. When they married, he resigned his position and they opened "a dairy store on Jefferson Street. Then they bought this big piece of land, 'Sandy Flats Farm.'" That was a contradictory name because it was "hilly and almost all in woods. In fact, that's how he got it so cheap. It wasn't a farm at all."

The Bentleys rented a little brown house across the tracks and lived in it for a few years. They hired men to cut down the trees and rented a portable sawmill to cut the lumber for the barn and silo. "The farm soil was mostly clay, but there were beds of marl—that's like black sand. He sold that for buildings in Wellsville." When Uncle Ed began to build the new house, "every part of it came from the land: the stones, the sand used in the cement, and the wood. Everything else he bought came from selling off the extry lumber and the marl."

They started by digging a great cistern, "six foot deep by eight foot wide," that ran under the whole side of the house, under what was to be the storeroom and Aunt Eva's room. They dug four other cellars, put up the house frame, and put on the roof. Not much more could be done until the plantings were established. The pastures and the orchards were being cultivated; corn and grain were stored up. Then they could buy their first cows. "Uncle Ed always had jus' Holsteins and Jerseys." It was at this point that Eva Bentley sought out and hired Jennie Hess. It seemed a good business deal for both of them—and it was—but it was far more than that.

Jennie's relationship with the Bentleys was different from the others. From the start, she always called them "Aunt" and "Uncle" with never any need to use their last name as she had with Aunty Hawkins. She didn't call them "Mother" and "Dad" either, as she had the Stevensons. Uncle Ed and Aunt Eva seemed like real relatives, but Aunt Eva would never define that relationship. She never ended it, either. Years and years later, she still sent letters and Christmas cards; once she even made the journey from Wellsville to visit Jennie in Gloucester City, New Jersey.

"Was she blood-kin? She would never say, one way or the other. I used to think, 'Why me? Why did she come after me to work for her?'"

Aunt Eva was only seven years older than Jennie, but she seemed very much older, being educated and a settled married woman, with her family living in the area; there did not seem anything in her history to relate her to Jennie or to Mary Hess. Yet one day, when the girl complained about her tired feet, Aunt Eva unexpectedly retorted, "You're going to have feet like your mother. Hers were so flattened an' blistered an' sore, she went barefoot even after she was married, even when she went down to the town." But when Jennie asked for more information, "Aunt Eva wouldn't tell me no more and neither would anybody else. When I tried to find out, I was always told, 'Don't ask questions,' or else, 'Jus' get on with your work.' So, y'see, I can't give you my ancestors."

Besides her bitterness at being denied the information about her own identity to which she had a right, Jennie carried lifelong resentment against the Bentleys for another reason: their failure to help her become better educated. They themselves "read the *Wellsville Reporter* every day and took the Sunday paper too," but there were no discussions around Jennie of what they had read. They seemed to think that there was no need to teach a hired girl. How could two people who had been professional educators not see that this bright girl in their own home had not had even a primary-school education? All she got from them were instructions about the right way to do her tasks on the farm or in the house—and Aunt Eva's strict training in manners, morals, and cleanliness.

"Many's the night I cried myself to sleep through tiredness. That an' not having an education and not knowing who my mother was."

She was overworked, and she felt that she was underpaid. Instead of working alongside the woman in the house, as she had always done, she now had to follow the orders of both Aunt Eva and Uncle Ed. They made her work outdoors as well as in. They got her up at 4:00 in the morning, 4:30 at the latest, so that every day she milked some of the cows, sometimes as many as twenty-eight of them. There were times she had to get the whole herd back from the pasture at night, too. "Uncle Ed had a dog he'd send: 'Go ahead, Shep. Go get them.'" Sometimes a hired man would go if Shep didn't bring them back, but often it was Jennie who had to go if the cows were stubborn.

On Sundays she often had to do all the barn work because it was the hired men's day off. She had to milk all the cows—the entire herd numbered about ninety—and carry the pails to the milk cellar, then come back, take the pitchfork, and shovel the droppings out the window onto the manure pile. It was hard work, and in summer "them flies bite thunderin' hard."

Sometimes she had to take the place of an animal. "In the shed behind the kitchen there was the butter churn; it was built on a slope. They'd catch a loose calf and put him on the milk treads, up on the slope with crosspieces for his feet so's he wouldn't slip when he was trying to get off. If they didn't catch a calf, then they'd use a dog. But if there wasn't no dog, then I had to work the churn. And, at the same time, Aunt Eva was wantin' me to do work in the kitchen.

"One day he sent me across to another field with a message. I was so tired, I climbed onto a harrow, just to get a ride. Uncle Ed threw a clod that knocked me right off. 'You little fool!' he yelled. 'Want to lose your legs?'"

She was exhausted most of the time, and she did not have much pleasure in spending money. She was earning more than she had gotten as a housemaid, but she spent more for boots and dresses.

"My wages was two dollars a month, but it was charged against my clothes. It would take me two, three weeks to earn the material, and another two weeks to pay Aunt Eva for makin' the dress. No, she never taught me to sew, neither. Just to darn stockings, put on patches and buttons, that sort of thing. Of course, we always cut off the buttons and used them on dress after dress; they cost a lot of money. I always saved the buttons. I still have a button box."

"Once, I had malaria. They cut off all my hair. It was down to my boot-tops. And Uncle Ed sold it. I have no idea if I got the money or not. I don't think I did. That was when my hair was white, like straw.

When it come in again, it was yellow and softer. I wore it in plaits as soon as it got long again."

She was grateful for the way Aunt Eva nursed her all through this illness. Actually, this kindness was a demonstration of the dual relationship they had: she was part hired girl and part family member. A room labeled "Jennie's room" was drawn on the plan for the new house, indicating that she was intended to make her home with the Bentleys. Located near the front porch, right off the parlor, with sunny windows on three sides, this was to be a room appropriate for a young relative.

But when they moved out of the little rented house and into the one that was being built, they did not move into a real home. It was a workplace, a necessary farm building. "None of the rooms was papered, jus' white plaster, waiting for the house to settle, but not even that much was done in Aunt Eva's room and the parlor. Them walls was jus' studs for years. Doing it this way was very inconvenient. It took several years to really get settled."

Jennie had to sleep in the parlor for a year or two. "I hanged my clothes on the pegs in my own room only after the cold cellar was done, and the men put the milk pails down there after they was scrubbed each day. My best clothes was in Aunt Eva's room before that."

When she finally moved into it, Jennie's room had a few pegs on the walls, enough to hang her clothes on, a small bed, a chair, and a small chest with a mirror on it. The room, being exposed on three sides, was the coldest of all the bedrooms. "Many's the time I took hot bricks to bed. People today thinks it's a joke, but we did crochet lids for our potties. Otherwise they might crack in the cold."

It wasn't the cold that Aunt Eva had worried about when she planned to put the girl at a distance from the rooms where the men were—the storeroom, kitchen, and dining room. It was the men. She had drawn the plans for the house so that, when the men went up to their five big bedrooms on the second floor, they must use the only "pair of stairs" in the house—just outside Aunt Eva's room. Aunt Eva liked to know what was going on in her house. In the summer, when there might be "anywheres from nineteen to twenty-two hired men on the farm, all the doors was kep' open so that there was no chance of 'funny business.'"

So the three big common rooms were finished first. Actually they were in use even before there was a water supply. "The walls of the cistern was stone and cement, and they wasn't completely dry, so we all ran around with every sort of receptacle to catch the water when it rained. Afterwards, the rain water ran through pipes to the cistern: it filled up from the bottom. We pumped water up into the kitchen zinc. And the water from the zinc then went down outside and drained through the ground back into the cistern so that hardly a drop was lost."

When finally there was water in the house, some of it was hand-carried in pails from the kitchen into the storeroom because that was where everybody got washed. Each person had his own towel and washrag hanging there. "Aunt Eva always made the hired men leave their muddy work boots outside in the shed an' put on old shoes to come into the storeroom. She made everybody wash up before they came to the table. Aunt Eva was very strict about this."

Of course there was no bathroom. "It was outdoors. You wouldn't want it indoors. At a distance from the house. Uncle Ed was very fussy about keeping the privy clean. He used a strong plank box and hauled it away back up into the woods every spring and fall and made a new box."

To keep the men comfortable, Aunt Eva furnished the storeroom and the dining room with "settees" with padded backs and cushions covered with flowered material, "like Dolly Varden pattern, with ruffles and all." These were washable, of course, since the men sat in both of these rooms in their dirty clothes. The dining room held about thirty people; "the hired men all sat down at once to their meals."

Jennie had thorough training in both preparing and preserving food. The men ate three huge meals a day. "Long griddles set in the center of the kitchen stove. We made six or eight pancakes at a time. We'd have to have two-foot stacks of pancakes piled on three plates before the men was called for breakfast. We'd bake twenty, twenty-five pies at once. In cold weather, I'd have to carry extrys up to the loft, especially mince and pumpkin pies. And put them on a long carpenter's bench up there. Often the pies'd freeze, but when they was wanted, they'd be brought down, put in the oven, thawed, warmed — and *good!* In summer there was an old woman hired to help, but in the winter, there was only Aunt Eva and me."

Aunt Eva's cellars were planned to keep food at different temperatures. One was for vegetables that were grown on the farm, and for apples, several kinds of apples; these were all stored in bins near the middle of the cellar so that they did not get too cold. Another cellar was for the preserves. With the help of Jennie and the extra woman hired each summer, Aunt Eva would put up two hundred to three hundred jars of fruit. The preserves were "stored on shelves put up in the earth sides, and it was lined with wood and double doors, so that they didn't freeze."

The third cellar was for the food that could freeze. The food — "stuff like mincemeat and sausage and thick slices of tomatoes frozen in the fat they'd been fried in" — was put into crocks, jars, and firkins. "Them crocks was so heavy that the men had to carry them down the stairs."

The fourth was the cold-cellar. "It was heavy lined, under the front rooms, but the entry to it was always awkward, between the store-room and the front parlor. At that time we hung a blanket over the opening because Uncle Ed didn't want a door until it was all finished. That hung there for years." That was typical of the way things were for the first years: "It was hard enough to do regular work without having the confusion of an unsettled house being built around us."

During these early years, the chief source of income was the daily milk route. "Uncle Ed knew what to do when he got for himself. He had worked on a farm earlier. His big milk can he got in Alfred Center. It had another can in the center which held ice, so the milk was nice and cold by the time he got to town. The big can — it was forty gallon — was on a platform. It was an open wagon. He only sold to restaurants and hotels, not door to door. People who wanted milk would come to the house, to the door with their pails, not buckets. Anything with a bail (that's a handle) was a pail.

"They sold eggs at the door, too, for eight to ten cents a dozen, but they gave them away free to poor people. Sometimes Aunt Eva would exchange eggs at the store for granulated sugar, like rich people used.

"Soured milk we made into cottage cheese. Sometimes we thinned it with cream and sold it for five or ten cents a bowl (depending on the size of the bowl) for table use, to the people who came to the house. Some of her cottage cheese we made into balls. That's the way Aunt Eva got her piano — from the extry milk money."

In winter Uncle Ed had to have the wagon put on runners. "On cold, frosty nights or afternoons, you could hear the snow squeak and the sleigh bells for an hour before the wagon come over the hill. Any-body worth a cent always had sleigh bells. Once, one year, you could put a sleigh on the roads for ninety-one days straight." At the Bent-leys, "cutters with sleigh bells and all were covered with blankets and hoisted to the rafters of the barn when the snow and ice ended, not left cluttering up the place in the summer like some lazy farmers did."

Each success only led the Bentleys to look for another target, an-other way of making money. When they had more than enough apples for themselves, they began to ship them to places like New York City. They slaughtered hogs and butchered the meat, curing the hams and bacon. With the help of the womenfolk — especially Jennie — they made sausage, scrapple, head cheese, and even pickled pigs' feet. "We used everythin', skin an' all, excep' the eyes," she explained.

"The first harvest of the year was always the ice cutting." Next came lambing. "Uncle Ed usually bought a new ram each year at the county fair. Sometimes he'd pick out a ram from last year's flock, but he didn't usually think much about inbreeding. One year we had twenty-three sheep and we got twenty-two sets of twins." A great source of fun was "sheep day. The men wore only overalls. They drove the sheep into a pen in the river. Then they'd use lots of white soft soap on them. The water'd get so dirty that they'd drive the sheep in the stream away from the suds and then back to the pasture to the shearers."

After that the wool went to Alfred Center to be carded. Much of it was sold, but Aunt Eva always took several sacks out to her mother's home at Shiloh. Grandmom Clemens's husband was "Mark Twain's own cousin." (This generic term could mean any blood relative such as a second or even third cousin.) Grandmom Clemens had a spinning wheel and a loom, and Aunt Eva, of course, could use both, so by the end of the visit there was cloth for the entire Bentley household, including Jennie. "The coarsest wool we made into petticoats. I wore two or three of them, with a sateen one over the cotton underwear. An' in winter, I had a quilted one with cotton wadding from above the knees to the ankle. That kep' you good an' warm."

Aunt Eva and Jennie would dye the wool, too, in red and blue, so the dresses were always in stripes, year after year — "no checks." And "we used the same colors for the wool to make mittens, pulse warmers, men's Sunday suspenders." Aunt Eva used the same style over and over for Jennie's dresses: "a Garibaldi waist, that was, the yoke and the waist was shirred onto the skirt," and long sleeves. "You could wear a dress like that for four or five years in winters." It was like having to wear the same uniform all the time, just in larger sizes.

The house was nearly finished. Aunt Eva had a bed with metal springs and a factory-built mattress. In the parlor there was a store carpet and the new upright piano. Kerosene lamps had taken the place of the old candles. This definitely was an improvement, but filling the lamps, trimming the wicks, and washing the globes every week was another messy chore for Jennie. On the other hand, there was only one wood-burning stove. That was in the parlor, but that was the company room, not for every day, so she did not have much of a problem in taking out the ashes. When the house was finished, there was "natural gas, with gas stoves in the kitchen, the storeroom, and the dining room. Of course there was no heat in any of the bedrooms, downstairs or up."

On the whole, Jennie was proud to be in a family that "knew how to do things right." As the years of work added up, there was a "hen-house, smokehouse, pig pens, red hay barn with a place for sheep underneath. There were stables, also, underneath. We had cows and horses, our own paddock for the horses, a windmill for the troughs. Cucumber logs were bored out; they brought water from the mountain down into the milk cellar."

The Bentleys had cause to be proud of their farm. According to the local history, there was a population of 4,247 in Wellsville in 1875, "at which time there were 957 cows in the town, and the milk of 231 was taken to the factory and made into cheese." Among so many milk-producing farms, the Bentleys' record was outstanding. They had about one-tenth of the area's cow population within a few years of this census. The irony was that, while they had given up the life of educators to become farmers, their hired girl yearned for the life they had left.

"Of course, there never was a chance to go to church on Sunday mornings, with the milking and the chores, but we did almost always go to town to Sunday school — the Bentleys was Episcopal." Then, "when we'd come home, I hated to take the dress off as soon as we got back from Sunday school. It was the beautifullest dress. I would stand in front of the mirror and look at it. I had a craving to wear nice dresses every day.

"I used to think I'd like to be a teacher and go to school. I wanted — I always wanted — to be Somebody."

* * *

What happened to the little folksinger? Had she disappeared into the person of this sturdy farm girl? Even seeing itinerants did not seem to awaken any memories of the Stevensons, perhaps because these travelers brought no songs with them to Wellsville.

"The clock man came fairly often, the umbrella man once in a great while. Clothes baskets of willow were sold by a traveling man, too." The most fun was the china man. "No! He wasn't Chinese! He had a bell on a stick in the front of his wagon; he'd strike it every now and then. Aunt Eva bought her big crocks at the store in Wellsville, but she bought dishes from the china man. He had platters, plates, and bowls, but all seconds. Once or twice the china man stayed overnight at our house."

Aunt Eva never cared about the old English ballads and songs as the people in the backwoods had. She knew many of the pieces that Jennie knew, but she was not one to sing at her work. Moreover, she preferred hymns and the new sheet music she bought after she got her piano. Of course, Jennie, always on the alert, picked up these new songs. One of them, "Pretty Pond Lilies," illustrates the change. There is no real story to it, just "a pretty tune" that could allow a pianist to dominate over the singer.

So it happened that Jennie's old songs that had bonded her with the Stevenson family were no longer communal but strictly her own, her secret cache of "real" stories that she kept to herself. The whole torrent of song was released when her work was the hardest: doing the milking on Sunday mornings when she was by herself, hour after hour. "I sung to the cows every piece I'd ever learned, at the top of my lungs." It was the only audience she could find.

Of course she could whistle softly or hum to herself as she moved about house or farm, doing the mundane chores that meant so little to her and so much to the ambitious Bentleys. It is probable that she was now constructing the house without walls in her imagination, the secret place where, through all her days, she could take refuge. Here she shunted aside the conditions of her own life and pondered the questions of the "real people" in her songs. Why did the Lady of York murder her babies, and why did Henry Green poison Miss Riot? Why didn't some of the heroines in the old ballads recognize their sweethearts when they returned? Did the Old Indian ever see his sweetheart again, and did the Orphan Child ever find her father? Jennie entertained herself with these questions, but she also loved the actions in the stories themselves, and she enjoyed both words and tunes. Her songs taught her and sustained her, and nobody, not even those working beside her, could guess where Jennie Hess's mind was.

Singing with others was now a party activity, and there were lots of parties because that was the way that farm people shared work. There were purposes, hours, and customs associated with the women's parties and another set for the "night parties," which were chiefly for the young people. Jennie got to take part in the work and the fun of all the parties.

The women's parties, in spite of their titles, required hard work, either in quilting or rug sewing, from one to four o'clock. Then they had refreshments. When they came to the Bentleys' house after it was finished, "Aunt Eva served her own biscuits with maple syrup, and she had real granulated sugar for their tea." As the ladies sat in her parlor, Aunt Eva played her piano, and they all sang.

The quilting parties on the farms were not like those where intricate patterns are worked out and slowly pieced together. Such "Sunday quilts" made "by some old women in tiny, perfect stitches" were used only on the family beds. Women like Aunt Eva who had to furnish beds for many hired men had to have dozens of heavy, warm quilts, and, of course, these quilts had to be kept clean.

In the spring, "the knots were cut so that the quilt could be taken apart. The cotton was taken outside, under the apple trees, and beaten lightly with a carriage whip, and sunned until it was light and clean." The case was washed thoroughly and dried, then the cotton was put back inside. It was when these quilts were all refilled that the neighboring women came to tie each quilt "in a diamond pattern either in red and green, or red and blue, or just black thread. Heavy winter quilts were tied again, in the center of the diamond."

Rug sewing was much harder. "Every two years you unravel the rag rugs 'cause they was too heavy to wash whole. To scrub rugs we used to put the rug in one tub an' keep pulling it over the bench and scrubbing the part that's on the bench with plenty of soap suds and a scrub brush, and then piling it up in the tub on the other side. When the whole rug was over the bench and in the second tub, we'd turn it over and scrub the other side the same way. When both sides was done, we'd get fresh water in the tubs an' rinse an' rinse till there wasn't a bit of soap come out. Then we'd get the menfolks to put it around the line, looped over because it was all so heavy.

"Then the women would come to each other's houses and re-sew them. And in another two weeks you'd go to some other woman's house."

These parties were an important part of Jennie's education, for the women swapped recipes, home medicine, and bits of folklore, such as "The Shoe Charm":

> Wear on ball, spend all.
> Wear on heel, spend a good deal.
> Wear on toe, spend as you go.

They retold local gossip, family stories, and ghost stories. Some of the woman-stories were even a bit romantic, like this one:

"Once a girl had two suitors; she liked them both and they were both crazy for her. She got one needle in a pack that had no eye. She sent it as a test to one fellow. She told him that the one that could thread it, she'd marry. The following Wednesday he returned it, disgusted. She was anxious but sent it to the other fellow, who she really liked better. No word from him for a week — afraid she'd lost him. She wondered why she had ever suggested such a thing. Still on Wednesday he didn't come, but on Friday he did and he kissed her. She was surprised and asked about the needle. He unwound a tissue package — there lay the threaded needle. He'd sent it away and had an eye drilled in. Wasn't that clever of him!"

Another such tale was a ghost story set in Wellsville itself. "On one other day a woman asked if the pond had froze this year near the black iron swan. It hadn't. It never did. Y'see this here swan was on a pond on a big estate near Wellsville and two sisters had lived there. The one sister was engaged to a fellow, but before they was married, she overheard her sister an' him kissin'. Her heart was broke, but her sister felt even worse 'n' she throwed herself into this here pond by the swan. An' the other wouldn't marry the fellow. She kinda went out of her mind. So he disappeared an' she lived there alone for years an' years till she too died. But never, from that day the one sister was drowned, never did the pond freeze over in that spot. I've saw that."

The story that was laughed over most was one that Aunt Eva told about herself: "Once a bunch of geese on our farm got drunk on some wild cherries that had fermented. I was sick when I seen them in the yard. I thought they was dead. But then some was staggerin', some on their backs, some on their sides. I got even the hired men to help pluck the feathers because we all thought that the geese had been poisoned or strickened in some way, an' we wanted to save the feathers at least. The men had plucked out the pins and some of the down before the birds surprised us all by reviving. So they lived—but they was naked!"

Besides entertaining the other farm women, Aunt Eva would sometimes bake a cake, especially a Jersey City cake for birthdays. Perhaps it was for Jennie's birthday that Aunt Eva gave the first real party the girl had ever known. During the afternoon she cooked maple sap to syrup. Then, when the young people came that night, she "had each one pack a pan with the snow outside and march past her. Aunt Eva dropped a ladle full of lukewarm syrup onto the snow in strands, and when it hit the snow, it hardened and could be pulled like taffy. A taffy pull was always great fun with the boys."

"Havin' fun" was a new part of Jennie's life. She had grown into a tall, well-developed, energetic, and attractive young woman. She could do all the hard work on the farm; she could make pies "blindfolded" and do all the cooking for a large hungry crowd; but she could also sing and she could dance, hour after hour. Aunt Eva could keep her in a safe room at night, but Jennie liked to "fool around some" during the day and at parties with the hired men, most of whom were farmers' sons themselves. She was getting feisty.

One Sunday she got into a terrific snowball fight with a hired man. She got "Glory Hallelujah" for that escapade—but the reprimand was delivered in Aunt Eva's own style. "There was never an argument. Any discussions or blame was done in your own room, not with others around. And no words wasted. About any problem, Aunt Eva always said: 'Ask it once, not twice. You should know the second time.'"

Uncle Ed's way was different. He would yell and at times even curse. Once, when Jennie was about seventeen, Uncle Ed became furious because he said Jennie had let the heifer go dry (from not milking her). Jennie got angry, too, declaring it was not her fault. She demanded that Uncle Ed fire the hired man who was really the culprit. This display of temper amazed the Bentleys, used as they were to Jennie's compliance. They had to believe her. The hired man was not discharged, but Jennie was not in trouble any more. Years later, Aunt Eva told the story as another "Jennie joke."

The night parties were entirely different from the women's afternoon parties. These were corn huskings in the barns or apple-paring parties in the kitchens. At the Bentleys', there was great need for help when the apple crop was picked. The young people worked from eight to ten at night, competing with each other to see who could core, pare, slice, and string the apples fastest. When they were finished, long strings of apples were ready to hang in the kitchen and storeroom to dry out, some for the winter's pies and others ready for market.

From ten to midnight they danced, and then they had a big feast, including hard cider. When they came to the Bentleys', "Aunt Eva played piano. When they went to other houses, people played violin, Jew's harp, and mouth organs." Jennie never had violin lessons but she did "pick up" the way to play the Jew's harp and the mouth organ, practicing in her room at home.

When they went to other houses, there were more jokes, riddles, and funny sayings. For example, the boys would tease: "What's the difference between a lamb and a woman? Lamb tongues are delicious, but you couldn't eat a woman's tongue. It was too tough from wagging so much."

She learned punning: "How can you ask for 'mo-lasses' when you haven't had any yet?"

"'This is the last 'n' awl,' said the shoemaker, as he threw them at his wife."

"Don't ask for a wheelbarrow, that is, borrow a wheel, when you really want to use the whole barrow."

"What did Adam and Eve do when they found out the difference between them? They raised Cain. And they did it again when they got Abel."

Perhaps the hard cider had some effect, because the boys did enjoy the bawdy songs that she'd never dare sing around Aunt Eva. It was "all part of the fun." But best of all was the dancing. "I can't remember the time when I didn't have a foot for dancin' and a fellow to follow it." Her love for dancing blocked out her love for singing. Now she didn't bother to learn all the words of a dance song. She wanted to know only as much as the others did as they spun through the dances. It was tune and time that mattered, not the sad story of some other woman.

During the dances, laughing and flirting with the boys made her life enjoyable.

She made friends with the other farm girls. They told her about sex ("behind the barn") and they talked and talked about the coming of sweethearts and love making — after marriage, of course. The girls knew rituals and charms:

"Put two round seeds, wet by spittle, on your eyelids. Name each for a beau. Open your eyes, and the seed which stays on longer is the faithful one." Or, "at the time of the new moon, look over your right shoulder and say:

New moon new
Please let me see
Who my husband
Is to be.

The color of his hair,
And the clothes he's to wear,
And the happy day
When he'll wed me.

Young people always loved ghost stories, and, of course, the stories were most "scary on Hallow Even. If you walk upstairs backward with a lighted candle and your own mirror in your hand, you'll see your future husband. On Hallow Even you did things then you'd be afraid to do any other time of year."

But none of these charms worked for Jennie until one night when she went to another girl's house and they used apple peelings to see whom they would marry. The other girl tossed the curling over her shoulder and it landed in the fire. "I ain't going to get a husband," she lamented. Then Jennie's peeling fell in the shape of a "D."

"I'm goin' to marry the Big D! I'm goin' to marry the Devil!" she laughed. But when she retold this story in old age, the brightness of memory would die out of her face, and she'd say, "An' many a time I thought I had."

Now it became apparent that Jennie attracted the boys. The Bentleys thought they had good reason to be very worried when her first serious beau asked permission to take her out. He was the son of the town butcher. His family was considered well-off, or, as Jennie said, "they had the chinks." She never forgot the interview when Aunt Eva came to her room and closed the door.

"'You must not go out alone with him,' she told me. 'Rich boys never take poor girls out for any good.' I said he could see how innocent I was.

"'Yes,' she said. 'He knows you're green. And the only thing you have in the world is your character.'

"Now wasn't that selfish? She knew I was a good worker, and she didn't want to risk losing me."

Jennie had often sung the old ballad "The Butcher's Boy," about a girl who had been seduced and abandoned. It seemed that Aunt Eva was warning that the ballad could come true in Jennie's own life. She was stunned. She did not dare disobey Aunt Eva, so she never went out alone with Otto Weaver. But she became angry. This was one more way that being poor and motherless was cheating her.

By now she knew her own worth. No other farm girl in the area equaled her because nobody else had been trained by Aunt Eva. She could go elsewhere and get better wages with easier work. But she didn't go. "I worked like a little slavey, not 'cause of the money but 'cause I wanted to stay with people who were some relation to me and made me feel I had a home. It was my wantin' a home so bad that bound me to them then."

* * *

Paradoxically, it was the Bentleys who took Jennie outside of the white Protestant culture in which she had always lived. Now, as the work pressure was lessening, Uncle Ed would bring around the democrat wagon on Sunday afternoons, and often he and Aunt Eva would take Jennie with them on their rides. The beautiful red wagon had "a canopy top and a four-inch fringe that was held on with brass tacks on the trimming. It had three seats across, so that made room for six people."

Sometimes the Bentleys drove out to the Indian reservation at Salamanca (some people called it Indiantown). People often went there to have their fortunes told or to see the "war dances." Jennie understood that these weren't real war dances; she also suspected that Uncle Ed paid the Indians to dance for the whites. But it certainly was impressive to see dancing so solemn, so different from the farm style. Uncle Ed seemed to be very sympathetic to the Indians. He told Jennie: "By rights every bit of land around here should belong to the Indians. The agent asked them did they want a reservation thirty square miles or thirty miles square an' the chiefs didn't see no difference, so today the whole reservation runs round the state forest, just one mile wide and thirty miles long. An' the Indians aren't allowed to buy anything for themselves; the agent buys for them."

The evil created by white people's hatred toward Indians was forever fastened in Jennie's mind by the ballad "The Old Indian," which she associated with Salamanca. It was the story of a doomed interracial love, and Jennie was entirely sympathetic. She did think, though, that Indians should be Christians like everyone else, so when she heard a missionary sing "The Converted Indian Maid," she asked for a copy of the words; she memorized them as well as the tune.

One day, "a whole car full of Italians was brought out here to build a road to Salamanca. They was so dark and spoke a different language so people used to drive out in their carriages to see them. It was a long time before the women came. The men lived in shanties, had corn husks jus' thrown loose on the floor for beds, kicked 'em up with their feet. The women, when they come, worked very hard." But the men offended Jennie's standards for "decent living." It was not the language difference that mattered to her; it was the sleeping arrangements.

These first looks at "strangers" were probably with Uncle Ed and Aunt Eva in 1882 or 1883. But she came to know many immigrants from the Old World, and she merrily sang many of the popular ditties about "the greenhorns." Within a few years she herself married into another non-English culture. She was fascinated by the culture clashes, sources of good stories and happy songs. She never doubted that the new-comers would be good citizens. She found the best example of this in the family she gained by marriage. By the 1920s she would proudly usher her grandchildren into the handsome city dwelling of their new cousin-by-marriage, the very popular Italian-American soprano Jessica Dragonette.

The widening of her experience led to some new independent thoughts, especially about the prejudice against the Jewish people, although she never saw a Jew until she moved to Philadelphia years later. She reasoned: "The Jews were God's chosen people. Our Savior was a Jew. He was 'circumskized,' showing people how to be clean."

Although she was born in the year that the Civil War ended, Jennie, apparently, never knew any African Americans. She believed, of course, that it was against Christian morality for one person to own another. She had heard about plantation brutalities, although she did not see an enactment of *Uncle Tom's Cabin* until she herself was already "emancipated" by marriage. She could not have realized how terrible life was in the South for the ex-slaves after the Civil War. What Jennie Hess meant when she said that she was being worked like a "slavey" was that she was not being treated with proper respect for her worth as an individual; she was being treated as even less than other hired girls who could leave at any time since they had families to go home to. Slavery meant being bound to the farm.

* * *

An encounter of a very new kind greatly changed her focus in life. Even farm work was more meaningful to Jennie when Aunt Eva had her first baby, a boy, in 1883. From the moment that Jennie first held

Ora ("Orrie") Bentley in her arms, she loved him, and, after him, every baby that she ever met. She became "a baby woman." Men were often attracted to her, but Jennie, from now on, would rather be "singin' to the kiddies" than flirting with the boys. She now added another type of song to her collection: "I learned to sing and say all the little pieces out of an old book Aunt Eva had, of songs for kiddies. And I sang him all the old pieces I knew."

One day when Orrie was still in baby dresses, he was crawling in the house and fell down into the cold-cellar, that fourth cellar that still had no door. Luckily his father was working down there. "The floor was packed in sawdust—so Orrie wasn't hurt, jus' scared. Uncle Ed jus' picked him up and threw Orrie right back upstairs to me without even a look to see if the baby was hurt.

"'Damn you, Jennie,' he yelled. 'You're supposed to be minding him. You go to hell!'

"'I don't go to your house when you ain't home,' I yelled right back. I was saucy! But I couldn't be too fresh; this was the only home I had. But they expected me to keep care of him and do all my regular kitchen work too. I was runnin' on about it, I was so upset, and Orrie was cryin'. Aunt Eva come and shook him and slapped him. She said Orrie an' me was 'sissies' for cryin'. Them Bentleys sure wasn't!"

3

Hellfire Jack's Sweetheart, 1883–85

One day a young man, "the handsomest man" Jennie Hess had ever seen, came to the farm to buy milk and eggs. With his wavy black hair, heavy moustache, and strong blue eyes, he looked very different from the farm boys. He was, in fact, different in many ways. His name was John Joseph Devlin, and he was an Irishman from Philadelphia. In Wellsville he had a very good reputation for taking care of the thirty-two horses in the livery stable. Some of these horses he rented out, but most belonged to important men in the town, such as Colonel Scott, the owner of the *Wellsville Reporter*, and Enos Barnes, its chief editor.

"Johnny" continued to come to buy at the farm — and Uncle Ed became more and more worried. This young man was not, by Bentley standards, so rich that he was above Jennie in class, as the butcher's son had been. But Uncle Ed at once recognized him as a threat and always invented some errand to send Jennie out of the way whenever Johnny came to the farm door. "He's Irish and a *Catholic*" was all Uncle Ed had to say. In Wellsville there was a gulf between the Anglo-Scots middle-class people and all newcomers, as there was throughout the country. Moreover, Johnny Devlin was the son of an Irish immigrant, which would mean he practiced a religion that was taboo. The Irish were Catholic, believers in "Popery" and "idolatry." No good Protestant girl would marry a Catholic boy, so there was no good to be gained by going out with one.

Yet Uncle Ed could think of no excuse to use when Johnny politely asked permission to take Jennie to a band concert at the Salvation Army barracks in town. Obviously he was not "R.C.," because Roman Catholics would not attend Salvation Army services. Johnny agreed to have her home by ten o'clock. He kept his word — and so he could not be denied the same permission when he requested it, time after time.

Now, at last, Jennie was free to enjoy some of the events in town. Up to this time she had been able to attend the Episcopal Sunday School, but the Bentleys usually joined Wellsville social activities only twice a year: on Memorial Day when they went to the cemetery to decorate the soldiers' graves, and on the Fourth of July when they watched the parade.

Only occasionally had Jennie even seen the Salvation Army parade before its meetings. The "Army" was a powerful revival organization. Its converts were recruited, enrolled, and trained in military fashion. It was famous for its uniformed band and for its hymnals, which included not only the Army's own songs but some of those made popular by revivals, those great religious events that could arouse an entire community for weeks or even months. Some of the most dramatic songs in the Salvation Army song books came from the famous evangelical team of Sankey and Moody.

Jennie's greatest musical treat was going to the Town Hall when the Hutchinson Family Singers appeared in concert. These famous singers, who always appeared in elegant evening attire, including full dress suits for even the smallest boys, "was really one fam'ly. Nine boys and one or two girls toured and gave concerts. When one might die, another would take his place, so they kep' on for years and years." They were noted for their genteel deportment, high moral standards, and enthusiastic singing.

The Hutchinson Family had been abolitionists before the Civil War. Afterward, with slavery abolished, they were deeply concerned with the ravages of "the drink," and they always included temperance songs in their concerts. What delighted Jennie most, however, was their rendition of the old comic song "Calomel," which she had learned when she lived with the Hawkinses.

Besides espousing inflammatory causes, the Hutchinsons put full power into promoting music suitable for families like their own. One example that they sang was "Katie Lee and Willie Gray." Apparently Jennie Hess did not hear them sing this bucolic piece for she never tried to sing it to me. She did know all the words, however, and recited them with glee.

Sometimes Johnny brought around a buggy on Sunday afternoons, and Jennie was allowed to go for a ride with him. When they were out on the road by themselves, they sang. They liked the songs they had heard in Wellsville — the Salvation Army hymns, the "renditions" of the Hutchinson Family — and finally Johnny taught her some of the Irish songs that his family sang in Philadelphia. In return, she taught him the songs that she knew. He had a fine voice. He loved to sing, and he sang with Jennie as nobody else ever had — or ever did.

Although she never did learn why he had come to Wellsville and become a livery stable man, she did hear how he had become a horse trainer, starting as a stable boy, and how he had gotten the nickname of "Hellfire Jack." Years later, on December 1, 1937, he told the same story to a reporter for the Camden, New Jersey, *Courier-Post:* "I started taking care of horses through an accident. I was a youngster down around Broad and Fitzwater streets down in Philly, where I was born, and in the winter, we kids always went to Fairmount Park to see the brushes.

"All the big sports were on hand, and all drove 'singles' and 'doubles' to sleighs. I was standing in the crowd one day when I heard somebody cry, 'Runaway!'

"I looked out, and I saw a team of horses come tearing along the speedway. In the sleigh was a man, several women, and a couple of youngsters. I sprang out to the road, grabbed the bridle of one of the horses and brought the sleigh to a stop.

"The man in the sleigh was Jim McCartney, who once managed the Hotel Majestic, while the others were the family of William Singerly who owned the *Philadelphia Record* and raced both trotters and runners. The family thanked me, and Singerly looked me up and asked me if I wanted a job.

"I told him I did, so he put me at work in his stables. That's how I got started in this business."

This was only one of the many exploits that caused other men to admire him as Hellfire Jack. But when Jennie thought about that "Hell" in his nickname, plus the fact that his last name began with "D," she decided that the prophecy of the apple peel she had thrown into the air years before was being confirmed. She *was* going to marry the Devil! Johnny was always impulsive, always unpredictable, always gambling on his "luck," and always—for good or bad—exciting. In the staid, boring world of the Bentleys, Hellfire Jack captivated her.

Once again Aunt Eva came to her room for a talk. She must have sensed Jennie's feelings and decided it was time to warn the young woman more forcefully. She pointed out that nobody in Wellsville knew very much about this Irishman who was not a native, not somebody whose family was known, not somebody who could be counted on as a husband. Jennie listened, but she had already learned one rule of life: "Tell some and keep some." She had known Johnny for two years. He had treated her with courtesy and attention such as she had never known before. And she loved him. She did not tell this to Aunt Eva. Actually she knew more about the horses Johnny had trained and the racetracks where he had worked than she did about his personal history. She never knew how hard his early life had been until she went to Philadelphia herself many years later.

Soon Johnny fulfilled one of Jennie's dearest dreams: he took her to the circus. Over the years she had seen the wonderful posters all over town when Forepaugh's Circus was coming. A few times she had even managed to see the circus parade itself. But, of course, she never got to go inside the tents and see the actual performance. "I had no money and wouldn't have been allowed to, anyway."

Jennie and Johnny spent a lot of time in the animal tent that night. Although she was scared of the animals, she was very curious and wanted to see everything. "Some of the monkeys was comic, but some was indecent," she recalled. "Wasn't I the greenie!"

"Some fellows who took care of the horses and knew him in Philadelphia come up and they said, 'Why, Hellfire Jack, what are you doing here?' He introduced me to them and said something about he hoped I'd be a nearer relative some day. It was the first time he said anything like that."

They were driving home from the circus without talking when Johnny suddenly spoke. "What say we get married, Jennie?"

She replied, "All right, Johnny."

In the first week of January 1886, the *Wellsville Reporter* summed up the major New Year's Eve festivities: "Wellsville Friday night turned out three big audiences, one at the rink, another at the Salvation Army barracks, and still another at the opera house. The crowd at the opera was the largest ever assembled in this city to witness any hall entertainment where an admission was charged."

Jennie had permission to go to the Salvation Army barracks with Johnny. She did not go there—she never intended to. She put on her best clothes: her "shirtwaist was black with soutache braiding on and the skirt was black jersey. It had a little bustle; women was wearin' them then. They was all the clothes I had to be married in. I was told to be home by 10 o'clock. I got there at 10:30, but I was a married woman."

4

Johnny's Wife, 1885–99

Johnny met Enos Barnes, the editor of the Wellsville newspaper, on the street on New Year's Day. He always loved to describe the conversation:

"'Hey, Johnny, Pastor Coit says you got married last night.'

"'Yes,' said I.

"'What you got to say for the paper?'

"'No Cards, No Cakes, and Nobody's Business,' said I."

That was the headline on the story the next day in the *Wellsville Reporter*; Jennie Hess was mentioned as the bride. Johnny carried that clipping in his wallet for the rest of his life.

But it *was* somebody's business — at least Uncle Ed thought so. When Jennie showed the beautiful wedding "sistificat" signed by Pastor Coit, at the breakfast table on New Year's Day, Uncle Ed was furious. He swore that Johnny would never set foot on the farm again. Jennie said to herself, "He knows he'll have to get a new hired girl. Him and me both know how much trouble he'd have gettin' someone to do all the farmwork and all the housework too, like I done." It was two weeks before Uncle Ed gave in and Johnny came to his bride. He paid board for both of them, and he and Jennie started married life in one of the upstairs bedrooms in the farmhouse. Johnny's first gift to her was a "gold pin shaped like a horsewhip with three little horseshoes on it for luck." He gave little Orrie, who adored him, a pair of little red boots with red tassels. Gradually he was accepted as a member of the family, as Jennie's husband, although Aunt Eva always considered him a "harum-scarum."

Johnny and Jennie had their wedding pictures taken in the clothes they had been married in (except that Jennie was wearing the new gold pin). Then Johnny found a few rooms near the livery stable and they moved into them, considering this as only a temporary home. Aunt Eva came and helped Jennie cord the bedstead; she gave her an old blanket to put on before they put down the thick cornhusk mattress. Jennie made sheets and towels out of some of the old flour and sugar sacks on the farm, and Aunt Eva gave them food — food that Jennie herself had helped preserve just last summer and fall. Now Jennie cooked only for one other person, her husband, and he did not require much. "Even in them days Johnny'd only eat two meals a day." After all her years of catering to a large group of hungry men, this cooking was child's play to her.

There was time for other play: watching Johnny take care of the horses and riding with him on his errands. One day they drove to Angelica to see John L. Sullivan train for a fight. Johnny told this anecdote: "Jennie and me killed jack rabbits jus' by stunning them with a horsewhip." That was fun, an adventure they both remembered when they were old. These were "the happiest days of my life," she'd say wistfully.

She came to realize that her husband was "very stern." He said his wife would not work for money; he would take care of her. She was to behave in a ladylike way. They had different views about the proper behavior of women, as is revealed in the way each recited an old nursery rhyme:

Johnny: "A whistlin' girl
          And a crowin' hen
          Never comes
          To any good end."

Jennie: "A girl that whistles
          And a hen that crows
          Can make their livin'
          Wherever they goes."

The easy times were soon over. Jennie got pregnant. Since Aunt Eva's mother, Grandmom Clemens, was a midwife, it was arranged that Jennie would go out to Shiloh when "her time came" to have the baby. When she went into labor, Johnny did get her out there all right, but it was a race with storm as well as stork, for this event, so momentous for them, took place during a great blizzard.

In later years she would tell her story to other women. "It was forty degrees below and the snow was so bad they couldn't see the road to the barn over the snow banks. But you could drive right over the crust of the snow, carry heavy loads on it.

"Aunt Eva got there, too, of course. But they had to send for two doctors. I was in labor from two o'clock Sunday till between seven and eight o'clock on Friday. Johnny was a wild man. They wouldn't let him touch me, and me cryin' all the time. But he wouldn't let them use forceps to get the baby.

"So they sent him out to get coal oil, and he was so excited he never realized that there was a barrel of it in the corncrib. Poor Johnny went over that snow all the way to town and back.

"The two doctors folded quilts to keep me warm before the fire and lay me down there. The bed was too high and yielding. Then they took the baby. When Johnny got back and didn't hear the crying any more, he rushed in. He thought I'd died. I wasn't moaning because the pain was gone. Then he laughed and cried and said he was so glad it was a boy."

They named the baby Eddie. This was their way of showing their gratitude and that Johnny accepted Uncle Ed and Aunt Eva as Jennie's family. Now, too, they saw each other in new roles: as "Mama" and "Papa" to their children; later they were "Grandma and Grandpa Deb" (for Devlin). But they never sank their own relationship into using such generic terms to each other. They always used their first names, "Jennie" and "Johnny," whether they were tender or raging. But when she talked to me, as she would to another woman, Grandma Deb called him "Pop." I must confess that I often thought of Grandpa Deb as "Hellfire Jack" after I learned more about his life apart from his family.

Fatherhood did not stabilize Johnny. "He had said that he was glad it was a boy. But he wasn't. He wanted a girl. Each time it was a boy, the same thing happened—he wouldn't save money. Drank it all away or gambled it all away on the horses. He never fooled with no other woman, but horses and liquor sure raised the devil with my married life."

Johnny's conduct changed radically. He was fired from the job at the livery stable, and he told Jennie angrily, as though she were to blame, "I told you I wasn't a liv'ry stable man. I'm a colt man." He had been paying board for her and the baby out at Grandmom Clemens's, but now since there was no more money, they had to go back to the Bentley farm. Jennie tried to work "twice as hard as ever," because the farm was the only home for her, her baby, and her husband. Now she had a family—and greater trouble than she had ever imagined marriage could bring. "Out of the frying pan into the fire." Or, as she often said, "Live trouble is the worst."

Her greatest trouble was that "the boy wasn't perfect. I was so small-boned inside that the baby's eyes had rolled back in its head. We never saw his pupils until he was three months old. By that time we was back living on the farm and Aunt Eva was takin' care of the baby— she was crazy about him—and one day, when I was skimming milk, Aunt Eva began screaming. I rushed to her.

"'My baby! What's happened?'

" 'He'll see! He'll see!'

"It was just like the moon coming up. The doctor had put a tight bandage around his head — the bone was separated — the band made it all knit together, and every third day we'd let it out a hole like an eyelet as the eyes came up.

"He was a Spanish doctor, an old man. He saved my boy. He put this band on after a month, after we was back home in Wellsville."

When Eddie was eight months old, Johnny found a good job taking care of the colts on a stud farm. After spending the first two years of married life in Wellsville, the Devlins spent the next two years in Elmira, on the Babcock Stock Farm.

"They called it a 'stock farm,' but it really was a stud farm. Stud horse is the boy. People from far and near come to have their mares served. Pop was the colt man, but he also exercised the mares while they was there. They foal the mare in the fall so the colt is out of the way by next spring and the mare was some good again then.

"Mr. Babcock was the boss. He had at least twenty-five, sometimes thirty, men on the farm all the time. If the mare was served, all right. But if she didn't, the men had to stay overnight."

Usually these men joined the group of residents at Mrs. Eli Berry's boardinghouse. Here the Devlin family lived for two years, a period when Jennie, with very little work to do, spent her days taking care of Eddie and enjoying this life, so different from anything she had known before. There was always a large crowd at Mrs. Berry's dining tables, and that meant a lot of "joshing" and raucous storytelling, in keeping with the sexual process that had brought them all to the stud farm.

One man who brought his mare to be serviced was the leader of a troupe of actors. He was "E. O. Rogers, the first man that ever produced *Uncle Tom's Cabin*. They went through the country in covered wagons. P. T. Barnum was using covered wagons then, too. Rogers had regular bloodhounds and would get real ice. Eliza would be barefoot, with a doll for her baby and a shawl. Used a canopy for the audience. Later he used halls, but now it was like a circus tent with a platform. His company was together for a long time.

"E. O. Rogers was a dandy chap, and so was his uncle (same name). E. O. Senior was Legree, swung his whip and cracked it. He really was a kind man but he could swing a whip! E. O. Junior was also in the play. He was St. Clair. It was just the regular play. No singin', no dancin' in between or any such foolishness. The woman who played Liza had a sister who took Little Eva's part.

"Well, anyways, E. O. Rogers, Senior, brought his mare one day and he had to stay over. He was fifty years old, and he'd just married a young girl about twenty. And the boys was teasing him. Y'know, like men on a stud farm would tease:

"'Don't you feel guilty?'

"'Well,' he said. 'I'll tell you the truth. It takes me a little longer, but I don't begrudge the time.'"

That tag line became a favorite expression of the people at Mrs. Berry's dining table, the women as well as the men. Time after time, when somebody was describing a task, the joke would clinch it: "It takes me a little longer, but I don't begrudge the time." The memory delighted Grandma Deb in her old age chiefly because, when she'd mutter the phrase as she was shuffling around the house, nobody understood the sexual implication (except me, after she knew me well enough to tell me the whole anecdote). Such joking was not uncommon among the fourteen women who lived at Mrs. Berry's. They were "a wild bunch, all devils, not afraid to say anything." They loved to tease Jennie for being such a "greenie," right from the farm.

The women had their own female-oriented jokes and stories, too. One concerned bustles, which were then very fashionable, even though expensive. A steel or whalebone frame was stitched into a dress; it folded like an accordion when the woman sat down. But poor women who couldn't afford the frames would still make the same pouch in the back panel so that the skirt would be full "back there," and then they would fill it with newspaper. "Well, one day a lady was out in a boat with a man and they got adrift. They needed to signal for help, but they didn't have anything they could use for a flare. So she asked him not to look, and then she gave him the newspaper. He had matches and so they were rescued. But when she got out of the boat, she sure was embarrassed because she was so flat in the back."

These wild women sang a lot. Many of them had been taken to minstrel shows, those family entertainments where the songs were sentimental and pure and the jokes were clean. Some of these daring women had even gone with their husbands to the music halls, which were considered the focal points for night life in places like New York City. In these halls the fun was fast and rowdy—and the songs that were brought back to the farms included parodies, dialect pieces, and the "crazy nonsense" songs that Jennie called "them monkey be-doodle things."

One day these women took Jennie to the Elmira County Fair. First they went to the exhibits. "There was stock, chicken, fruits, vegetables . . . the largest this an' the largest that. Bed quilts, too. And there was some tightrope walkers an' horse racing.

"A man was selling penny sheets. I bought one. It was 'Western Courtship,' no tune, jus' words. But I learned to say it. It's about this

poor fellow—the preacher was supposed to come to marry them in
their new house, but he didn't come and so this fellow, he had to sleep
all night lookin' at his sweetheart through a chair she'd put up between
them. Or else, he didn't sleep, at all:

> He peeped and he sighed,
> And he sighed and he peeped,
> And he felt that no mortal
> Was ever so tried.

"And in the morning the girl left him because he hadn't moved the
chair! That was funny, all right.

"Some men were handing out pamphlets—and one had a naughty
piece on. On the other side was something worse. I burnt it before I
came to Pop's folks.

"This one special pamphlet was an advertisement for Tulip Soap.
There was a circus girl on a tightrope across blue waters above a picture of the Elmira Bridge. She had a big ape monkey on the rope behind her, and she's leading him. She had on a full short skirt and bare
legs. On the card was printed:

> If I succeed
> In crossing this rope,
> I'll wash my monkey
> With Tulip Soap.

"Them women had lots of fun laughing. And I said, 'I don't see
what's wrong. She has her monkey with her.' How those women
laughed! They was with Mrs. Eli Berry, the landlady, and she thought
they was talkin' terrible! There was a slang meaning to 'monkey,' jus'
like 'bird's nest' and 'black kitty.' Made fun of me for bein' a country
girl!"

Despite the easy time she had living in a boardinghouse—or perhaps just because it was too easy—Jennie got restless. She was worried about Eddie, who was not growing up in a "real" home, and she
saw that Johnny was drinking again. When he got too drunk one day,
"Pop told Mr. Babcock what he thought of him for the way he treated
the horses' feet, an' he quit the job." They went back to Wellsville, to
the Bentleys' Sandy Flats Farm, again without money.

Hellfire Jack did get another job quite soon, and even Aunt Eva
approved of it. He was in charge of hiring out seven horses to oil men
when they came through, and he was also training racehorses for Judson H. Clark. "Clark was in oil and he was seven times a millionaire.
He had paid $40,000 for 'General Wellington,' a horse imported from
California, not a native horse. Clark also paid $51,000, the highest price
ever paid for a horse up to that time, for 'Bell Boy.'"

It was at this time that Hellfire Jack had his greatest triumph. Years later, he told the newspaper reporter who was doing a feature article on him: "The thing that pleases me most is that I trained the first mustang that ever trotted. His name was 'Samuel J. Tilden,' and the owner, William J. Becker, of Wellsville, New York, picked him up in the West somewhere. I took that mustang green, broke him to harness, trained him, and saw him win the first heat in the first race ever trotted under electric light in this country. That horse ran a one-mile heat in 2:36." Jennie was so proud of this feat that she could recite the data to me many years later.

Judson Clark was so rich that he was a pioneer in another way: he had a bathroom in his mansion at Genesee Valley Farms. In the town of Wellsville there was "a bathhouse with six private baths, but they were rented out, twenty-five cents a visit, and only to men." Nobody in the area had a bathtub and an indoor toilet until Clark did.

Jennie took little Eddie up to see this remarkable room, but she failed to notice that her little boy was playing with the faucets. "We went back downstairs, and pretty soon the water commenced coming down too. Eddie was only about three years old, so Mr. Clark was very nice about the damage to his rugs."

Since Johnny was now paying some board to the Bentleys for the three of them, Jennie, while still working as she always had in the farmhouse, did not feel pressed to "slave" as she had before. In fact, she was more like Aunt Eva's younger sister now that she was a married woman and no longer the hired girl.

They went together to the women's parties—the same sewing tasks still had to be done—and heard the latest stories. At last, after years of wondering, Jennie heard some entertaining stories about Mary Hess, her own mother—or, at least, she learned about her mother's second husband. "He was named Thomas. He was a Welshman from the old country and came over here. He couldn't talk right. Instead of saying 'You good girl' or 'good boy,' he'd say 'Titty-ma.' I don't know what that means."

At some other time, she heard the story of her stepfather's death: "He died in a dive. He struck the water flat. Split himself open. They buried him in a tar-lined coffin so he wouldn't purge through it."

Bizarre as these stories were, even more amazing is the fact that Jennie did not realize, in 1890, that these were local stories and that Mary Hess herself was living in Wellsville at that very time. She learned this fact only years later when it was much too late.

In 1892, Jennie was "caught" again. This time she knew what to expect and what a woman who was "feeding two" should or should not do, according to woman lore. One taboo dealt with the fear of having a baby choke on the umbilical cord. To prevent this tragedy, a pregnant woman should never hang clothes on the line. Other women or even her husband should do this for her.

Another prohibition dealt with handling raw beef. "Dried beef is okay if you have to touch it. In them days we took fresh beef, soaked it in salt water, two, three days. Then used molasses and salt, pepper and pickled it. Then hung it up to dry. One day a string broke and a piece of beef fell right down on me, hit me on the arm. I worried an' worried all the rest of my time, that the piece might have been spoiled. Maybe somebody touched it had bloody hands.

"Madeline was all right when she was born, but she did have a mark like a string of dried beef across her upper right arm. Has it to this day."

Was Jennie right in her belief that having this girl made Johnny more of a family man, or was it just coincidental that he soon saw a chance to get his family on its own, away from the Bentleys? There was a notice in the *Elmira Telegraph* that a "Mr. Whinney would give fifty dollars for a pair of matched mares for Zebulon Reed Brockway's coach." Now Johnny knew, from his time on the stud farm, where there were "two grey mares with huge tails." He answered the letter, and I. P. Whinney came to Wellsville. Johnny met him and took him to the next town to see the horses.

"Mr. Whinney liked the horses, but he wanted them broke. They'd always bite each other. Pop put a heavy piece of wood through their two mouths so they couldn't turn their heads to get at each other. Then he hitched them to a sulky and drove them to Elmira. When Z. R. Brockway saw it, he said, 'You're an Irish lad, aren't you?'

"Pop said, 'My father was Irish, so I guess I am.' Brockway said, 'Which would you rather have, the fifty dollars or a job?'

"'A job.'

"Z. R. Brockway was the superintendent of the Reformatory for Men in Elmira, and Whinney was assistant superintendent. Mr. Whinney was nice, but Z. R. Brockway was very cruel to his prisoners." But he kept his word to the Devlins. After Johnny started work, Mr. Brockway sent a beautiful baby coach. "In three, four weeks, there came a draft of money; he paid for us to come to Elmira from Wellsville by train."

Jennie was relieved. Her baby girl was just three weeks old when Johnny got this job. Now they rented a little house at the foot of the reformatory hill. It was small and old but "the roof didn't leak. There was a little flower garden in front and a grape arbor and a cherry tree in the back." Jennie happily began to furnish it. It was their first real house, although they had been married for six years. She brought with her what was her personal equivalent of a dowry: "two hundred and some odd balls of rags sewn for carpets." She had been saving the scraps of material ever since Aunt Eva had finished carpeting the big farmhouse. ("Old overalls made the strongest rugs.") But now she sold them in Elmira and bought a real rug because they were supposed to buy everything from the reformatory while Johnny worked there.

The women on the stud farm had teased her immoderately when they learned that she had never seen a bedspread before, and that she was so afraid of mussing the one she now had that she used to take it off the bed and fold it carefully each night. At first, too, she had not understood about the pillow shams that went on top of the pillowcases, but she had been delighted when her friends taught her how to embroider. "I had one pair with pictures embroidered on in red: 'Good Night' and 'Good Morning.' In one the woman was asleep, and the other, jus' waking up." Now Jennie Hess Devlin had a white bedspread and her pretty embroidered pillow shams on the new bed in Elmira.

There was money at first since Johnny had two jobs at the reformatory. He always wore a uniform, blue with brass buttons, when he was a guard. He was also assistant coachman, and when he drove he wore the same outfit but a different cap. As guard, one of his jobs was marching a work detail to the railroad yard. The men had to shovel the coal for the reformatory onto the big wagons. The prison burnt twenty-four tons a day. Johnny never had trouble with his group — ten to twelve prisoners — because he always marched them past his house and Jennie would give them cookies.

"When he was a coachman, he sometimes got to drive the coach with those same matched gray mares that he'd tamed in Wellsville. Twice he drove into Elmira to get Mark Twain, who was living there with his wife's family. Pop brought him out to the reformatory to speak to the boys. It made Pop proud to do this, you bet.

"He also was stable boss. To see that the parole men took good care of the horses, he slept at the prison seven nights a week and then slept home for seven nights. But he got all his clothes and his meals at the prison."

Jennie was very happy now, with but one problem: they had no name for their baby girl. "Pop had insisted he was going to name her himself, and he kept lookin' and lookin' for names. She was three months old before she had a name. Then one day he rushed in all excited. 'I've got it! Y'know, the man who's president of Elmira Bank, Z. R. Brockway's son-in-law? Well, his last name is Blossom. And his wife's name is Madeline. Madeline Blossom Devlin!'" And so it was settled. Jennie loved the name, and she shared with Johnny the satisfaction of having their children named for special, important people.

All this time, Aunt Eva had kept in touch with Jennie, often sending gifts of food from the farm. Once it was ten pounds of dried corn. "One cup dried makes three cups cooked, it swells so, so we had corn all that winter." One Christmas, Aunt Eva herself came, bringing a twenty-eight-pound turkey gobbler. Before she left, though, she broke down and cried, begging Jennie to come back to the farm. She said she had never found anybody who could do the work that Jennie could. It was startling—and it was upsetting to Jennie to see her stern mentor so humbled. But, at the same time, it was like getting special recognition.

This was a peaceful time in Jennie's life. Johnny liked his job, and she liked her house, her babies, and the steady income. She innocently thought life in the reformatory was pleasant, designed to reform, not punish, wrongdoers.

But it was Jennie's innocence that almost cost them the whole situation. To make some extra money she used to show visitors around the reformatory. One day she noticed a blanket hanging down outside of one cell, with stockinged feet showing beneath the curtain. Her curiosity got the better of her; after the visitors had gone on, she returned and pulled the blanket aside. She found herself staring directly into the face of a man who was lashed to the bars by his outstretched arms. She could not be silent. "What are you tied up like that for?" she whispered. He was embarrassed. "For beating my dummy," he whispered back. She dropped the curtain and hurried to catch up with the visitors, hoping that no one had overheard.

That night when she asked Johnny what "beating a dummy" meant, he laughed at her for being a "greenie." But Jennie cried. She declared that the man was being tortured. So Johnny had to tell her about a male's need to practice self-control. He also told her that she was too soft-hearted. There were worse punishments than that man got, he said. When prisoners at the reformatory were beaten, the guards used "a lash two feet long and eight inches wide what had been soaked in water." That made it cut just that much harder.

"Then Pop got serious an' told me that it was lucky none of the other guards had been around jus' at that time 'cause if they had reported it to Z. R. Brockway, Brockway would have fired him." So Johnny forbade her ever showing people around the prison again. In fact, he didn't want her to come inside again, the matter seemed that serious to him. So she lost those extra quarters she had been earning, but she gained some knowledge of male sexuality and male cruelty.

The Devlins lived in Elmira for five years and eight months. Toward the end of that time, another boy was born. Johnny named him Lewis Cass Devlin, after the American general and statesman who had been one of his heroes since childhood. So this child also was named for a special person, as his siblings had been. (But he was always called "Lou," and later on he spelled it "Louis.")

As before, Johnny was unhappy after he got another son. His heavy drinking increased, and he indulged in self-pity. He told his wife that he was *not* a mere prison guard or even an assistant coachman. "I'm a colt man!"

He coupled this declaration with complaints of homesickness. He lamented that he had not seen his family in Philadelphia in twelve years. He may not have been totally honest about his "homesickness," for the fact was that there were racetracks in Philadelphia and, across the Delaware River, in Gloucester, New Jersey. Some of the colts that Hellfire Jack had trained were running on those tracks. He was sure that he could make money by placing his bets right.

So the job at the reformatory was gone. The money was gone, and Jennie's home was "sold out from under" her. She had only enough money to get herself and her three little children back to the farm. All she owned was their clothes. She was back to working for Aunt Eva again—this time in humiliation and gratitude.

"He had a good job there, kid," Grandma Deb said, thirty-eight years and several homes later. "The one mistake of our life was that we left Elmira."

She was very worried that Johnny would not send for them to join him in Philadelphia, and she was relieved when he did send money. She never gave me a hint about the source of that money, but the 1937 newspaper account reveals that Hellfire Jack had won $2,500 on a hundred-to-one shot about this time. Undoubtedly most of this money, like most of his other winnings, went right back to the bookies. He was a colt man by trade and a devoted gambler all his days. At intervals, he was also a family man.

When Jennie received the money for the fares, she left Sandy Flats Farm for the last time. She remembered that day as one of the "very worst" days of her life. "Eddie was about nine, Madeline five, and Lou a babe in arms." She had to handle all their baggage and change trains three times during the day-long trip. "I didn't know Pop's people or how they would take us in. I was nervous as a hen on a hot griddle." Then at last they were in Philadelphia. "And there was Aunt Mary, Pop's sister, at the station with Pop, and she took me and loved me for the rest of her life."

Jennie got to know her husband better when she came to know his family. They were "Neckers," which, in Philadelphia, meant people living in the narrow area where the Schuylkill and Delaware rivers converge. They were exuberantly life-loving, clannish Irish Catholics, even though the mother, "Wee Sallie Ward," was Scottish by birth. James Devlin had been her first husband. He was the one who was Irish — indeed, he had emigrated from Ireland — and had made a good beginning of a life in the new country. He had been boss stoker at the Point Breeze Gas Works, and he had bought the house where they lived, 2029 South Tenth Street, in a totally Irish-American community. They had four daughters but just this one son: John Joseph Devlin, born March 6, 1860, and baptized a Catholic at St. Theresa's Church at Broad and Catherine streets. One of his sisters had a picture taken of Johnny, a bright and handsome child, sitting in a little rocking chair. The picture represented a secure home, but that was suddenly lost when James Devlin died at the age of thirty-seven.

The family did not want to talk much about the years after James Devlin's death, but Jennie learned some of the details from a neighbor and pieced the story together: "There were some relatives, the Lewises. They offered Johnny's mother a little shop, a notion store, so that she could have supported all these children she'd had by Devlin. But, instead, she took up with this Charlie Smith, a policy writer. She married him legal, but he beat her and got drunk and she did too, and so the Lewises wouldn't have any more to do with her."

The Lewises had continued to look after the Devlin children for a while. "They put Johnny in St. John's Home in West Philly where he got all the schooling he ever had. After Mary — she was the oldest — got married to Hugh Tinney, she took Johnny out of school to help Hugh in his stables."

When Jennie learned that Johnny, like herself, hadn't had his chance at an education, she was shocked. "It wasn't fair!" she declared. That Johnny himself felt deprived was revealed years later in his advice to his grandchildren: "Learn all you can. Nobody can take away what you put in your head."

Much as they disapproved of Sallie's life, the adult Devlin children did not abandon their mother. "The family would never call her 'Smith' nor use her second husband's name at all. They jus' talked about 'Wee Sallie Ward.' She had children by Smith all the time, like puppies, but they all died excep' Charlie, who lives in Atlantic City.

"Over the years, Grandma Ward became fond of me, and me of her. Once, when we was in Woodbury, they brought her over for me to take care of her — her face, her neck — all black and blue because she fell down a flight of stairs when she was drunk. She looked terrible, but I could see she'd once been lovely.

"Seein' what his mother was like — knowin' now that he'd been cheated out of an education by his own family" — made Jennie realize that "it was a miracle that Pop was as good as he was."

At first, being in Philadelphia was like a miracle, too. Now Jennie had permanent family relationships without any ambiguity. When she spoke to her children about "Aunt Mary," she meant their *real* aunt, not a courtesy one. The three little Devlins now had many cousins, the children of Aunt Mary and Uncle Hugh Tinney, and those of Uncle Lou Morris and his wife, Aunt Sally. Aunt Sally really was the aunt of the Morris children; but after her sister died, Sally married the widower and, according to Jennie, was "a very good stepmother."

It was with Aunt Sally and Uncle Lou that Jennie and her children first stayed in Philadelphia, apparently in an apartment house. "Bells and knobs and house numbers confused me though Sally showed me at once. I couldn't tell their flat from the others so I just turned the mat up outside the front door. When Lou and Sally got on to that, how they laughed! Sally had lived in that place eight years and didn't even know her next-door neighbor.

"One day I missed my baby. Sally's stepchildren were just crazy about my little Lou and had been playing with him. Then he disappeared. He was across the hall in a neighbor's apartment, gone after her dog. Then the woman kept him awhile. When she brought him back, we was friendly. But Sally was furious — she still didn't even want to know this neighbor. She told me never to go over to visit her again — but I went anyhow. The woman was child-hungry."

Lou Morris was prosperous; he was in the wholesale butter and egg business. To a woman fresh from the farm, it was astonishing to hear that cheese was sold for a dollar a pound. One day Sally suggested that Jennie take Eddie down to see Lou's store. So Jennie set out, carrying little Lou. "I walked an' I walked. When I saw the train station, I knew I was lost. 'Oh, my God!' I said, an' I was crying. A policeman come up an' pretended not to notice me cryin'. He jus' said to Eddie, 'You're a great big boy.' That gave me some time. Then he said to me, 'What's the matter, lady? You a stranger?'

" 'Yes, sir,' says I, very meek and real low.

" 'Where are you going?'

"I could only give him Lou Morris's name. But he knew Lou so he said he'd take us there. The store was eight blocks away, but I wouldn't let him carry the baby — too afraid he might steal it. At the store, he went in and told the story to Lou Morris. Him and Sally laughed at me!"

While staying with the Morrises, Jennie had other adventures that she had never had before. One special treat was being taken to the Eden Museum, a Philadelphia theater. "Five dollars a seat! I'd like to pass out! An' saw *Shore Acres* — cried over that. An' walked in the park every Sunday.

"Never saw a Jew before we come to Philadelphia. Never saw a woman drunk before that, either. Saw this tall, thin, red-haired woman carryin' a kettle of beer. I was speechless. Tried to tell Aunt Sally 'bout it, and Johnny, too, soon's he come home. They wasn't surprised. I was."

Being laughed at and treated like this prevented Jennie from loving Sally as much as she did her husband's other sister, Aunt Mary. She admitted that Sally was a good person, but she was such a selfish woman that, as Jennie lamented, "she took my love from her."

Johnny did not like the situation either. "No more home than a rabbit," he would intone, with all his depths of self-pity. Then Aunt Mary fixed up a little house for her brother's family, near hers, close to the Tinney stables, and Johnny worked the entire winter on a horse-drawn truck down at the wharf, bringing home regular wages. It looked like the beginning of a good new life. But when spring came, Johnny left Philadelphia for a job training colts in Iron Hill, Maryland. He left Jennie with the children and without a cent.

From then on, it was the same thing over and over. He'd come home, sober or drunk; he'd be kind; he'd make a fuss over Madeline — and he'd leave again. "He'd be gone, usually with just one colt, maybe a year at a time. . . . London, Ohio, one year; Alexandria, Virginia. . . . Sometimes we wouldn't even know where he was."

For the first time in her life, Jennie was destitute. She could not take her children back to the farm in Wellsville, where her work would pay for their board and keep. Johnny had burnt that bridge behind her. Nor could she expect her husband's family in Philadelphia to support them. Johnny had failed to keep his vow that his wife would never work. He had not supported her. Now the time had come. She had to turn over the care of her children to Aunt Mary and go out to find work.

Aunt Mary was totally sympathetic. What was a husband good for, if his wife had to go to work? Her summation was: "No use keepin' a dog an' doin' the barking yourself."

Jennie Hess Devlin, January 1886.

John Joseph Devlin,
January 1886.

Farmlands, Athens, Pennsylvania.

Narrows of the Chemung River, where Martha Decker drowned.

Martha Decker's grave, East Waverly Cemetery, New York.

Farmland and harrow, outside of Wellsville, New York.

Indian house, Red House
Reservation, New York,
near Wellsville.

Young Indian man posing at Katharine Dealy's car, Red House Reservation.

Below: Perry's flagship, the *Niagara*, had been raised from the bottom of Lake Erie and was being restored by the WPA in 1937.

Grave of James Bird, Bird family burial plot, Forty Fort Cemetery,
Wilkes Barre, Pennsylvania. Photographed on Memorial Day, 1936.

Home of Ed and Eva Bentley, Sandy Flats Farm, 1937.
The porch awning is obviously a later addition.

Johnny ("Hellfire Jack") Devlin driving "Sam Tilden,"
a trotting horse, Wellsville, New York, ca. 1890.

Jennie Devlin, boardinghouse manager, Gloucester, New Jersey, ca. 1908.

Family party on the *Maid of the Mist*, Niagara Falls, with Ellen and Charles Arthur ("Bud") Eaves as children.

Confirmation Day for "Grandma Deb" and Ellen, 1924.

Johnny Devlin *(center)* with friends at the racetrack.

Parents and grandparents with the college students, Bud and Ellen Eaves.

"Aunt Jennie," the baby-nurse,
in Gloucester, New Jersey.

Kay Dealy, 1938.

Madeline and Arthur Eaves with her parents.

Jennie and Johnny Devlin and next door neighbor, Mrs. Shindle.

"Grandma Deb" and her great-granddaughter, Hilary Henneke, 1940.

5

Working Woman, 1899–1930

"My children is my very life. They're all I got," Jennie told herself resolutely as she applied for a job as second cook at Lit Brothers Department Store, at Eighth and Market streets in central Philadelphia. She was hired to work for a Mrs. Ryan, preparing and serving the daily hot meal to all the employees "at long tables in the restaurant itself, after it was closed each day." When she brought her first wages home in her handbag, Mary was there to encourage her: "God bless that Almighty dollar! Love yourself an' you're sure of it."

It was embarrassing to go out to work. It was also a blow to her pride that her children had to wear their cousins' hand-me-downs. Since Aunt Eva had never taught her to use a pattern or to sew new clothes, Jennie felt helpless. Then Aunt Mary, always her friend, lent her a sewing machine, and "a lady who lived next door to Aunt Mary" taught her to use it. Jennie even mastered the intricacies of shirts for her boys as well as simple dresses for Madeline.

For the two years that they lived in the little house, Jennie made the trip uptown and back on horse-drawn cars six days a week in all the varieties of tough Philadelphia weather. Sometimes Johnny would come home, and sometimes he brought money. But only sometimes.

Even this meager lifestyle was threatened when Lou became seriously ill with "some sort of internal hemorrhages." The doctor said the child needed country air. That meant Jennie would have to give up her job and move away from Mary, her chief source of emotional support. Johnny, who was home just then and in one of his optimistic moods, proposed a dubious solution. He told Jennie that the answer was for her to bring the family to Woodbury, New Jersey. He promised he would stay home, that he would bring his wages home. He would work at the racetrack where some of the colts he'd trained were now running. All would be well.

In accordance with his promise, he rented them a house at "49 Packer Street, a short distance from Broadway, opposite the school." They could afford the rent because the house was run-down. It must have been a fine house in its day. On the first floor there was a wide

hallway with folding doors that opened to the parlor on one side and
the dining room on the other. Upstairs there were four bedrooms and
an inside toilet. A ladder led to a large attic. Into all this spaciousness
the Devlins brought only "a few shabby sticks of furniture." Jennie's
single wall decoration was her framed wedding certificate.

Of course, there was very little money. Very soon Hellfire Jack was
drinking and boasting that he would soon make the family rich by a
lucky bet on a horse he fancied. "Luck" was always a key word for
him. All his life he counted on "good luck omens" not only for winning at the track but for getting any kind of job at any time.

Jennie, who believed that "your luck is what you make it," began to
work for the rent money, "takin' in washin' an' bakin' fancy cakes for
rich people." She was furious with her husband and frightened about
the future. It seemed that he came home only to "lay down the law"
for her and the children. Her patience was at an end. One day she
screamed at him: "You're so perfect, God Almighty's overcoat
wouldn't make you a vest! An' still you're the only drunkard in
Woodbury!"

He went completely wild. He grabbed her treasured wedding "sistificat" from the wall, broke the frame, tore the paper into pieces, and
threw them all in the fire.

"Now," he yelled. "Now you got your wish. You ain't got no husband, not even a drunk one. Get another father for your kids!" Then
he was gone. This time it was for a year. Jennie was overwhelmed by
shame and fear.

"I'd always tried to hold my head high and my nose clean. But now
I didn't have a husband. And I didn't know, was my kids illegitimate? I
didn't want them to know, nor the neighbors neither.

"Luckily, because we was new in town, the minister came to call. I
asked him: 'What makes a marriage legal?' And he says, 'The license.'
'Not the sistificat?' And he laughed at me. He says, 'Why, I imagine
half the women in Woodbury don't know where theirs are, right this
minute. What matters is the license. A license is in the files where you
was married.'

"So I cried and I told him what had happened. He asked questions
and took some notes and—bless that man!—in a few weeks he
stopped by and gave me this beautiful sistificat. He'd found Elder Coit
even though he'd moved from Wellsville to Syracuse, and he had just
the same form he'd had before, too. And now I know Pop can't just get
a divorce on his own, that way." Jennie knew that he might stay away
but he'd always have to come back.

At Woodbury, for the first time in her life, Jennie went hungry. On
the farms there had always been plenty of food. Even with the itiner-

ant Stevensons there had been vegetables from their own garden, rabbits caught in the woods, and staples bought in stores with cash from selling their baskets and the pennies from Jennie's singing. In Philadelphia there were the visits to the food-laden tables of the Devlin clan, and lots of leftovers to bring home. But now Jennie felt more than physical hunger. She suffered especially because she had no food to give to her children.

She and the children now counted on Aunt Mary's Sunday morning visits. "She would come all the way from South Philly to Woodbury by horsecar, ferry, and another horsecar, just to see us. And most often she brought us food. I was tryin' to make every penny to do the work of two in them days, and she knowed it."

Preparing special food treats at the holidays, especially Christmas and Easter, challenged Jennie's ingenuity. For Christmas, she and the children would get any small tree or bush that they could bring indoors; they could not afford a traditional tree. Then they would string cranberries and popcorn and make cotton puffs for snow on the branches. Jennie made other ornaments, too: gingerbread boys with raisin eyes and raisin buttons on their fronts; engaging gingerbread turtles with raisins for eyes and cloves for legs and tail, "with the bristly part of the clove out in front for his head." From regular pie dough she made "babies" to hang on the tree. The last touch, on Christmas Eve, was to deep-fry "doughnuts that looked like squirrels or little doggies when they was all puffed up." Of course, in the days after Christmas all the ornaments were devoured.

At Easter, although she did not have money to buy the traditional Easter ham, she more than compensated by her creativity in dyeing eggs. For this project she saved scraps of cloth all year. "A dress that fades makes good egg dye, and a plaid makes a real pretty one. Wrap them [the eggs] very, very tightly in boiling water for fifteen to twenty minutes. Then cool completely before you untie. Even where the string was, there'd be a nice rolling mark. And another way was to dye with onion water. Pare onions for the Easter dinner, cook the skins, and you could make three shades of dye — dark maroon, deep orange, and pretty bright lemon, according to the time you let the hard-boiled eggs lie in the hot water."

Then, on Easter afternoon, Madeline would take her Easter basket out to show her friends. When she came home to report that other mothers wanted to know how Mrs. Devlin got those beautiful effects, Jennie was an artist triumphant. She bragged a bit: "Maybe they wasn't pretty, too, all together!" For her sons, the decorations on the eggs were of secondary importance. For them, Jennie had boiled all of the eggs long and slowly so that they were as hard as possible for

Pecky-upper, an Easter game the boys played with their friends. It was quite simple: the boy who yelled "Pecky-upper" first got to be "on top"; that is, he held his egg tightly in his fist above his opponent's egg and smashed it down as hard as he could. The trick was to break that egg without cracking your own. A cracked egg was captured — and brought home by the winner. Eddie and Lou Devlin were very good at Pecky-upper. They had great motivation because eggs cost money, and they were playing for their own food. "The boys played real good, and they'd win lots of eggs from other kids, so we'd have maybe twice as many eggs to eat as we'd started with."

* * *

Jennie and her children felt themselves to be part of the community of Woodbury. They had their own friends, and she exchanged news, recipes, and home remedies with the neighbors. Lou had recovered from his intestinal disease, and none of the family was affected when an epidemic of diphtheria hit Woodbury. But people that they knew were sick. Jennie accepted one cure that was being tried then: "People caught frogs, split them open, and that saved a couple people's lives. Bound the frogs on the throat and drew out the poison."

She knew several methods to draw out ordinary colds and fevers. One was to use a dirty stocking — "tie around the neck of the sick person the sole of a stocking that hasn't been washed. Sounds 'fasible,' don't it? Onion poultices for fever — on soles of the feet, on wrists, and the chest — that was wonderful. If you thought you was likely to catch cold: tansy tea, hot tansy foot baths, then into bed with hot bricks. Or catnip tea for a cold. Had to put some honey in it to make the children take it. Little babies are given it to keep their strength till their mothers can feed them."

She said that she didn't believe in spells, signs, or witchcraft — "That's all hooey" — but she did believe in natural remedies. "Take strips of fat bacon or salt pork if the bacon's running lean, laid on your neck from ear to ear, and bound round with flannel. Then put another piece of flannel up around your head to hold it tight. The worst sore throat — feelin' like you're going to get diphtheria — will be better by morning. There'll be all little yellow pimples like, out on your throat. That's the poison that it's drawed. Sometimes it's only red there.

"For a stubborn chest cold, use a spice poultice. Cut out a piece of flannel to fit your neck and just go around the chest. Then spread it with lard, thin. Put all the ground spices you got in the house on this lard and put the ginger on last. You'd think that'd burn, but it don't, not a bit. Then you put a double thickness of flannel on top so as not to stain your nightgown 'cause the heat of the body will melt the fat.

"'You smell just like a cake,' children used to say. I made my children wear them, maybe two or three weeks at a time in the bitter cold weather. I'd put one on just as soon as the other one had dried. They dry out quick, maybe in a day or two. Even in the cradle my children had spice poultices, and they never got down sick like other children for two or three weeks every year."

The most important advice she gave to other women (as I learned later) was about birth control in the days before the Pill. "Stick a piece of oiled silk up as far as you can possibly go. And afterwards, use a douche. But if there isn't time beforehand, then get a clean rag, dip it in lard, and rub and rub and rub, as hard as you can . . . because y'know, a greased egg never hatches."

She was concerned about her children's minds and their spirits, as well as their bodies. Despite the fact that they had far more schooling than she had ever had, she spent time each day "tryin' to teach them all I knew." At night they would sing together and tell jokes and riddles.

Some of the riddles sounded as though they were very, very old. In particular there were two real puzzlers very much alike. First she told the riddle. Then she gave the children time to guess. When they couldn't, she would explain that, supposedly, the riddles had been made up by a young girl in prison who had been sentenced to death; she was promised that she would be saved if she could tell a riddle that nobody could guess. This was the first one:

> As I went out and in again,
> From the dead the living came.
> Six there were and seven shall be,
> And that will set the virgin free.

The answer was that the girl had found an animal's skull in which a bird had built a nest. There were six little birds in it, but the girl knew that when the mother bird came home, there would be seven.

The other riddle was even harder to guess:

> Oh, riddle, oh, riddle, oh, write:
> Where was I last Friday night?
> The winds did blow
> And the cock did crow,
> And the leaves did shake
> And my heart did ache,
> To see what a hole the fox did make
> And covered it over with green ivy.

The girl had been in prison "last Friday night," so the judges could not guess. Actually she had climbed into a tree in the prison yard and had seen the men digging what was supposed to be her grave. Then they covered it over with leaves until the time she was going to be killed. Of course she never was.

There were two conundrums about Philadelphia. One asked, "If Billy Penn fell off of City Hall and into a molasses cask, what flower would he represent?" The answer was "Sweet William." To enjoy this the children had to know that "Billy Penn" was the statue of the city's founder, the Quaker William Penn. For many generations his eminence was protected by a local law that said that no building in downtown Philadelphia could be constructed to top Billy Penn.

The other Philadelphia riddle posed this question: "If John Wanamaker got tired and sat down, and sat on a pin, what flower would he represent?" "Johnny-jump-up" was the answer. Wanamaker was the "merchant prince" who developed the first successful department store in America. The favorite place for Philadelphians to meet was "at the Eagle," the large statue of the national bird in the middle of the Great Court in Wanamaker's.

Jennie's own pleasure in various forms of wordplay was apparent. She loved tongue twisters and hidden-word tricks. She never blinked over the conclusion to the nursery rhyme about the three dogs . . . and a bitch named Witch. As she explained: "Helps the kiddies think, y'know." But she had a deeper reason: "Bring the kiddies any little happiness you can. God knows they'll find unhappiness enough for theirselves. I believe in filling their little minds with good thoughts. All them pieces I know I used to teach them. But the first rule with a child is love them."

Wanting to make it up to her children for other pleasures they lacked, Jennie violated the rules of good housewifery. "I let my kiddies write with chalk on the big wood doors; they wrote their lessons and made drawings like them doors was a black board."

Her children told their friends about what they were allowed to do. "Then I started to get other kiddies to come in by the day. Their mothers paid me. And they chalked on the doors and the floor just the same as my children did. They made lines to play 'Red Rover, Red Rover' and games like that. At night I'd have a laugh over their funny drawings. And at night I'd scrub the doors and the floor so that the kiddies had fun doin' it all over again next day." Thus, she had accidentally created a new business that brought in some of the money she needed so much.

"And I always was singin' to them, every song I could think of, teachin' them to say prayers at night, teachin' them to stop fightin'. I can still hear the kiddies singin' all of them songs together. It used to sound funny."

Her day-care program grew to include evening care also. "I've had as many as thirty children left with me at a time, when there was a big party somewhere in town. I'd put 'em all to sleep somewheres . . . even if only on pillows and blankets on the floor in the parlor and the dining room.

"The kiddies got afraid of 'Now I lay me down to sleep' because they were scared that they would be caught dead in the morning, since it said 'If I should die before I wake' . . . so I taught 'em this prayer to say too — that they would have another day:

> When I, dear Lord,
> Arise from sleep,
> This day my heart
> From evil keep.
> Precious Saviour, come and stay
> With your loving child, I pray.

"An' when the parents'd come and want to see how I managed the first time after they brought their kids, I'd say, 'Information costs a dollar an ounce. Come and see for yourselves.' And they'd have to laugh, too, seein' how the kiddies all was asleep."

She was always afraid that Johnny would come home drunk some night when the neighbors' children were there, although she knew the children would not be frightened. Johnny had always loved all little children, and he could get them to laugh and sing. They would think he was funny. But the parents, if they found out, would certainly take their children away. Such a confrontation never happened. Luck was with her.

That the family was actually living a hand-to-mouth existence was revealed by Madeline years later. She had never forgotten how her brothers, first thing in the morning, would take their cart and go to the neighbors' houses to pick up the laundry baskets filled with dirty clothes. Their mother would wash the clothes and hang them on the line while the children were in school. When they came home, they would sit on the back step and wait for the clothes to dry. They hurried to deliver them and rushed back home with the money so that their mother could go to the store to buy food for their supper.

One day Jennie received a pathetic letter from Aunt Eva, pleading with Jennie to let her adopt Madeline. Aunt Eva had given birth to a second son, but she never got the daughter she wanted. Jennie, who often feared that she would not be able to feed her own children, now hugged Madeline tightly and had her write a gentle letter to Aunt Eva, turning down the offer. So they lived day to day for years. There were times when Johnny was home, sometimes not. There were times, amid all these years of poverty, when he did come home with big winnings at the track. Then there would be grand purchases: store-bought Christmas tree ornaments, a Wheeler and Wilson ("that's a real good sewing machine"), some pieces of fine furniture, and, finally, a piano for Madeline and money for lessons.

Johnny always treated his "Madeline Blossom" with tenderness, but this partiality did not protect her from suffering when she witnessed his quarrels with her mother and brothers. Jennie would often fight back, screaming at him, while Madeline ran and hid. His fights with his sons got more violent as the boys got older. From their first days in Woodbury they had tried to help with the rent by shoveling snow, cutting grass, or asking the neighbors for any other chores. It was embarrassing for everyone to know they were so poor. Every day they more and more resented going hungry while their father was spending his wages on drink.

Even among men, Johnny Devlin's belligerence cost him respect. The best friends that Hellfire Jack had in Woodbury were the horses. He was never mean to a horse in his life, whether it was a splendid racehorse or a plodding workhorse. Every horse he ever trained remained an individual in his memory, and apparently horses felt the same way. Years later, when he was watching a parade in Philadelphia, he recognized one of the firehorses he had trained in Woodbury; the horse knew Hellfire Jack, too—he came out of the parade and over to the curb to nuzzle his old trainer.

But training firehorses was only one of several jobs Johnny had drunk himself out of by 1906. There was not enough money to pay the rent. Once more he made promises. He was not penitent, but he was cajoling. He would hold a job and bring his wages home, if Jennie would just move to Gloucester. There were shipyards there with openings for men—and there was the Gloucester racetrack. Eddie was willing to give his father another chance. So, after six years in Woodbury, Jennie "had my home sold out from under me." Again.

* * *

On February 28, 1906, the Devlins moved to Gloucester, to 25 North Broadway. It was a real home, but it was also the place where Jennie herself could make a living for her family. She served meals for regular boarders and took in lodgers during the fifteen years that they lived there. Now there was always money to pay the rent each month. Her children never went hungry again.

Since there were no restaurants in Gloucester, people ate in boardinghouses, and Mrs. Devlin's was regarded as one of the best. Many working people came just for lunch, day after day. Others returned for the evening meal, as well. From the first, Jennie had to call on all the skills that Aunt Eva had taught her for cooking and baking for a large group of hungry people, and on her own experiences in setting and waiting on tables at Lit's Department Store. In fact, she often had more people to cook for and more personalities to contend with than Aunt Eva ever had with her farmhands. Still, she enforced Aunt Eva's rules: "No bad language or drinking allowed. Everybody was expected to come to the table cleaned up."

It was a big three-story house they now occupied. There were rooms for Jennie's family and several for "paying guests." The smallest group she ever had staying in the house consisted of nine women who worked at the local factory that manufactured Welsbach mantles for gas-lit chandeliers. Usually there were many more lodgers than that. To furnish all these rooms, Jennie Devlin finally had the money to order bureaus, chairs, and beds with springs and sturdy mattresses from the Sears Roebuck catalog or from the Philadelphia department stores.

In one way she departed greatly from Aunt Eva's practice: she honored her own family. After her boarders left the dining room at night, a separate table was set, with a good tablecloth and her best china dishes, for the family and the permanent lodgers. After supper they went into the parlor where Madeline's treasured piano was, and they "all laughed and sang a lot," chiefly the newest songs, which the lodgers and her sons especially liked. But always they also sang the old pieces that did not have any printed words or music; these they sang just as Jennie had taught them.

Johnny wasn't traveling so much but he still was drinking a lot. The children used to say that they never knew when he was going to come home having drunk "out of the singing bottle" and when "out of the fighting bottle." Sometimes he stayed with the singers in the parlor all evening. On other nights he came in later, bringing some "friend" he had met in the bar, usually somebody who was down on his luck. Hellfire Jack would throw open the front door with his most expansive gesture and, according to his mood or his last bottle, he would sing out to his new friend, "Come in! Come in! Welcome to Hotel de Bum" or "Come in! Come in! Liberty Hall!" If he saw his wife frown slightly, he would know that provisions were low, and he'd chortle, "To hell with poverty! Put on another herring!"

The family tensions were particularly nerve-wracking to Madeline, who was just fourteen when they moved to Gloucester. She blamed her mother for provoking her father's temper, so Madeline used to watch for his homecoming. When she saw that he was "a little the worse for wear," she would come running: "Mama! Mama! Papa's coming. Don't say anything to him, Mama, please! Don't get him started."

One day he didn't come at the time Madeline was expecting him, so she anxiously asked her mother, "Where's Pop?"

"I guess he's down sittin' in front of the barber shop."

"What's he doing there?"

"Dryin' out."

Then Jennie confessed. "Well, he come home drunk and started bein' nasty. I was tired. I was scrubbin' clothes. So I jus' up with the tub of suds and dumped it on him."

These years marked the climax of the battles between Hellfire Jack and his high-spirited sons. As soon as the family settled in Gloucester, Eddie went to work in the shipbuilding industry, but, disgusted with his father, he left home in a few years. He settled in Buffalo and continued to keep in touch with his mother, but he refused to come home again.

Lou, who was only nine when they moved to Gloucester, seethed for years over his father's drunken abuse of his mother and over the physical beatings he himself endured. One night when he was about eighteen, he went into a murderous rage in the dining room. Art Eaves, who by then had married Madeline, was there, and he managed to wrest a chair out of Lou's hands in time to prevent him from killing his father. Two days later, Lou also left home.

In contrast to these painful separations from her sons, Jennie gained a good son-in-law. This was one of the best things that ever happened to her. In 1911, when Madeline was about eighteen, she asked permission to go over to Philadelphia on the ferry, to go to a "hurdy-gurdy dance." Art Eaves brought her home. And that was that. They loved each other. Art was apprenticed to a bookbinder and was not yet making a living. His mother had made Art leave school and learn a trade, against his own wishes. Jennie was sympathetic, classing Art Eaves with Johnny and herself as people deprived of the education they deserved.

Art learned his trade well, and in later years he held good positions in the paper industry. His family never knew want. As soon as he finished his apprenticeship, he and Madeline were married. She was only nineteen, even younger than Jennie had been, but it was a good marriage for all their lives. And, over the years, it became a strong support for both sets of their parents.

Soon, to everyone's delight, Madeline gave birth to a daughter, Ellen. The name, according to the Devlins, was a combination of "Ella" for Johnny's sister, who had died, and "Eliza" from Jennie's birth name. The Eaveses' side also claimed "Ellen" as a name in their family. So everyone was satisfied except the mother — she who had the flowery name of Madeline Blossom. She insisted on adding "Mae," to give her daughter's name a more elegant touch. Two years later there was "Bud," or Charles Arthur Eaves, Jr. These two children were the delight of all four grandparents.

Ellen developed especially strong bonds with "Grandma Deb," as she began calling her Grandmother Devlin. She had her own little rolling pin and knew "how to bake a cherry pie," singing the right words from "Billy Boy" as she did so. In fact, as she trotted around the house with Grandma Deb, the child learned all the old songs — that is, all that were fit for a little girl to hear. Thus, the old ballads had been handed down to yet another generation, in the folksong tradition.

Somewhere around 1918, Madeline and Art rented a little house and took Ellen and Bud to their own home. When all of her own children were gone, leaving empty rooms, and with more and more people coming to Gloucester as the demands on the shipbuilding yards increased in World War I, Grandma Deb took in more long-term lodgers and many more boarders. "At noon there'd be as many as fifty-five — maybe even fifty-seven — sailors and marines from the Immigration Station. Other men, shipyard workers, come in for their meals, too. Maybe one hundred twenty different men in all, in a week. We set up three big tables for lunch."

Of course she employed help, but she herself managed the menu planning, food buying, and money collection. She was overseer of the kitchen and the dining room. At night she made all the pastry for the next day, somehow maintaining her energy with only a few hours' sleep.

This was, beyond a doubt, the most successful time of her life. At midlife, she still had the physical strength derived from milking cows and scrubbing clothes. Now, moreover, she had the self-confidence of a woman who had built an independent business. After years in a quagmire of poverty created by a partner who was under the influences of impulse and alcohol, she was finally free from dependency on him or anyone else.

At this time, perhaps at the request of her children, Grandma Deb went to a professional photographer. Surprisingly, the picture reflects neither physical power nor an assertive personality. Rather, the words "gentility," "sensitivity," and "thoughtfulness" best describe her. Looking at the photograph, did she ever remember the teenage girl studying herself in the mirror on the Bentley farm, wishing she did not have to take the pretty dress off, wishing she could be a teacher? She looks like one here, with her rimless glasses and her right hand hidden, ironically, behind a pile of books, the photographer's props. In truth, although she never realized it, she *was* a teacher, teaching first her own children, then the "kiddies" at Woodbury, then her grand-children, and finally — in her old age — teaching me, with patient love, the old songs and the old ways of life.

There is one other significant detail in this undated portrait. On her left hand she wears a large stone ring. It was from her husband. Some-how, in spite of his drinking and gambling, Grandpa Deb managed at last to accumulate enough money to do something he had dreamt of for years: he bought his wife a "very good diamond," a ring such as most girls received when they became engaged. This ring was given — and received — with pride and with love, thirty years after the begin-ning of this tempestuous marriage.

Jennie deserved such a ring. She had been a good wife. She had raged and argued, but she had never rejected him. Instead she had forgiven him and encouraged him to give himself another chance. There were times when he came home in despair when he was out of work. Invariably he blamed his joblessness on his "bad luck," but she always scoffed at superstition. She tried to replace his depression with hope. One day he was "terribly down" because a man had offered him only a half-day's work. He wasn't going to take it, but Grandma Deb had a "present'ment," or what she called "a first thought." "First thoughts are the best," an old fortuneteller had told her once, and she agreed. "I told Pop to take the job, even for the half day. An' he did. He come home at noon, and at two o'clock he got a call to the shipyard and he worked there for seven years as a crane operator. Even though he was still drinking, he kep' that job."

After the war ended, the shipyard slowed down and he lost the job. He was frightened. When he broke a mirror one day, he moaned, "It's seven years' bad luck!" "Pshaw!" she told him. "That's not so." To me she explained, "An' sure enough, the next morning he got a full-time job with a movin' company, so breakin' the mirror hadn't meant a thing."

The connections between superstitions and witchcraft continued to fascinate Grandma Deb. Although she herself didn't really believe in witchcraft, she admitted that she followed some superstitions, like knocking on wood when boasting of good luck. She also recalled, "'If you put your undergarments on inside out, don't turn them right until they are washed agin, or evil will come.' That's what they used to say, and I still do that with slips. Not that there's witches, no, jus' superstitions.

"Don't hang your cap on a door; that's a sure sign of death. Don't put three chairs in a row; that means a funeral. Those are just old Irish ways of teaching children. Same as in the song 'Shoo Fly,' you taught them how to make a house neat, jus' by singin' about it.

"Some things you jus' do, because everybody says so, like 'Fold bills toward you as the Jews do; this folds your luck towards you and you'll always have money.'

"Some things look silly, but they work, like rubbin' warts with the juice of milkweed. This worked for me. But a woman on the other side of the hill used to powwow and take warts off in Wellsville. There's two or three of them in Gloucester now. They claim that they say a prayer, but I think — I think that's hooey.

"On the farm we had a young cow — had one calf. We put it in a swing — but it went down. Wasted away. People said an old witch did it. But no such thing. She died jus' like people die. Any other ways, that wouldn't be a just God."

However, the ways of a just God were hard for many people to understand when the influenza epidemic of 1918-19 swept over the country. Now, instead of the usual full obituaries, newspapers just listed the names and addresses of the dead — page after page. When the epidemic reached her boardinghouse, Grandma Deb tried to serve as nurse as well as cook. None of her lodgers died, but one boy nearly did. She got a reward for his care years later.

"Y'know, all my life I've wanted to be Somebody — and that's why I enjoyed going to Lock Haven with Madeline to visit some people, the Winters. They are my staunch friends, an' they showed it in the way they acted toward me, even though Madeline and Art did most of the visiting. Their boy had the flu very bad when he was a sailor and was boarding with me during the war. I nursed him night and day for three weeks. I sent for his parents and when they come, they got two nurses. I got sick myself then. But they always thought I had saved his life. I was Somebody to them Winters."

During the war years, Grandma Deb worried about her own sons, Ed in the navy and Lou in the army. As soon as the war was over, Ed left the service to go back to Buffalo, but Lou stayed in the regular army. He wrote to his mother that he became "an orderly to Colonel Scott. Lou wrote and told me how kind and good Colonel Scott was."

"Once there was a picture with Lou in it in the paper. In a barouche with the top down, Lou in his uniform there beside the Colonel, and Colonel Scott laughing to break his heart at the things Lou was saying. This was in a parade. Lou Morris, Jr., saw the picture in a Philadelphia paper and he told Aunt Sally, his stepmother, 'I never felt so proud of our family before as when I saw that.' Our Lou always was a devil." But no matter how proud she was of Lou, his mother always had a cause for grief; like his brother, Lou never came back to the big house.

After the war, the Devlins themselves were not doing very well. Grandma Deb's wonderful health had been undermined by the flu, and she suffered a loss of energy for the first time since her early teens, when she'd had malaria. Her spirits were depressed even more as her boarders left and as the group of nine women who had made Welsbach mantles finally disbanded. She could no longer maintain her home without help.

Johnny continued to follow the proscriptions of his "Lady Luck" theories. "Pop wouldn't cross a house, y'know, go in one door and out the next. He always went out the same door." But luck was not operational for a man over sixty years old. Sometimes he would get a job, and he'd spend the money with a flourish: "Turkey today, bones tomorrow" was his summing up. Too often it was only "bones."

He was attempting to control his drinking, hoping to get work. Grandma Deb was selling off the furniture, slowly breaking up her home. Both of them were frightened. Hellfire Jack's career had sputtered out. His forlorn condition reminded Grandma Deb of a story from the old days of the temperance movement. It was called "The Man Who Reformed for Cherries."

"There was this man who was always spending his time and his money in a bar. He loved cherries and there was always a lot in a bowl on the bar. Nothing could stop him from drink — not wife nor children nor nobody. One day he's spent all his money for liquor. He wanted some cherries, and the barmaid (that's what they called the wife of the man who has the saloon), she said he couldn't have any cherries without paying for them. So he said, 'All right. If that's the kind of friends drink makes, I won't drink.' So he stopped.

"That's what happened to Pop. Nobody wanted him, and we couldn't keep the house going after the war. So I lost my last home. This one I'd lived in for fifteen years. We had to go live with Madeline and Art."

Grandpa Deb, who had always gotten along well with his son-in-law, accepted this hospitality by making the best payment he could. He told Art, "After I come to live with you, I'll never touch another drop."

"And he never did."

He had given Madeline the gift she had wanted ever since she was a little girl: a peaceful life with her parents.

6

Aunt Jennie/Grandma Deb, 1921–36

"We had to accept charity from Art Eaves." That sentence tolled in Grandma Deb's heart through all the years that followed. She had never had to accept charity before. She had always earned her keep. She struggled to escape from dependency. "I'm always tryin' to figure out a way to pay Daddy [Art Eaves] back. It's the only thing Madeline an' me ever quarrel over."

The reason for this "quarrel" was that Art and Madeline did not see their invitation as an act of charity. After all, they themselves had lived with the Devlins for six years when they were first married. They believed that it was the duty of children to care for their aging parents. Art's parents, too, needed a home. So he and Madeline put aside their dreams of a little brick house, bought a large frame house with four bedrooms at 312 Market Street in Gloucester, and settled everybody down. The year was 1921.

Grandma and Grandpa Deb never took this humiliation lightly. They could accept the fact that they had to live with Art, but they wanted to pay him for their board. They became quiet, almost conspiratorial, partners sharing their hopes. One time Johnny got a night job; Jennie would keep his evening meal hot and serve him when he got home. During the day she bathed his feet in alum water so as to toughen the skin. But, like all the other jobs, this too was only temporary, and they could "pay back" very little.

Age was now a major hindrance in Johnny's search for work. He came to depend more than ever on dreams of "winning big" on the horses. He was "a handicapper," figuring the horses on every track in the country. Hope kept his mind alert and his spirits up. He had enough successes to command the admiration of other men in the corner cigar store who also liked to "play the horses." Hellfire Jack went out every afternoon "to see the boys," to offer tips, and — if he had the money — to place a bet himself. Occasionally he won a substantial amount on a race and gave the money to Madeline, to Jennie's pleasure. When he won smaller amounts, his invariable rule was to "split it down the middle" with his wife. If he won only five dollars, he gave her two dollars and fifty cents so they would both have spending money. They were partners as they never had been before.

From their own big three-story house, they had come down to one room in a house not their own. During the day they were subdued. When Grandma Deb was not working, she moved about the house, helping Madeline, singing softly to herself. Grandpa Deb no longer could roar out his "Welcome to Hotel de Bum! Come in, come in to Liberty Hall!" He had never been "much of a talker," except about horses, and now he seldom spoke, even at mealtimes.

Only at night in their own room did Johnny and Jennie have any privacy. Long after they'd gone to bed, they'd whisper together over the day's hurts or laugh over the absurdities that they had watched with carefully held sober faces.

They were closer now than they had ever been in their entire married life, so when Grandma Deb got a chance to work outside the home, there was no resentment against her husband. Instead she had the satisfaction of being able to contribute to what they both wanted: money for Madeline.

This new career was the perfect one for her: baby-nurse. Along with it came a new name: "Aunt Jennie." This courtesy title, reminiscent of the way she had referred to the good women who had befriended her—Aunty Hawkins, Aunt Eva, Aunt Mary—reveals the warmth and affection that her patients felt for her.

She was willing to accept all the hard work, the lack of sleep, and the burden of responsibility in exchange for the rapture of holding a newborn. "Bless the baby" had been a favorite expression of hers since the day she first held Orrie Bentley. Now, she could exult as she recalled each birth, each a wonderful story in itself. She counted the babies she'd helped deliver, and for years, the grateful mothers kept in touch with her, so that Aunt Jennie could watch "her" babies grow up.

Fifty-one times she was sent for by a phone call or by a messenger rushing frantically into the Eaveses' house. She would be ready and would hurry to the woman who was in labor. Frequently Aunt Jennie got there before the doctor. She'd check that everything was ready, reassure the woman, and be at the doctor's side during the delivery. He'd turn the baby over to her to bathe, diaper, wrap in the cotton blanket, and take to the mother to nurse. If it was a first child, Aunt Jennie would show the mother how to hold it and how to help it suck. Then she'd clean up the bed, burn the afterbirth and the bed pads, wash the mother, and, finally, do whatever the rest of the family needed. Since women had to stay in bed for two weeks after delivery, Aunt Jennie often lived in the house until the mother was strong and able to care for her family again. Of course, these babies heard their first lullabies when Aunt Jennie rocked them to let their mothers get some rest.

There were some difficult cases over the years. "Mrs. Roberts's baby come early. When the little girl come to get me, I was out, but Madeline promised to send me right away. But the kid got another woman. In five minutes I was there, but this other nurse got the case.

"Mrs. Roberts was crying that she was going to die. 'Ain't no such thing,' I told her.

"'My baby's dead.'

"'You ain't lost none yet, and I don' believe this one's goin' to be either.' She'd had fourteen children before. I thought she was delirious.

"The other nurse was a-standin' there, doin' nothin', so I laid back the covers, and there was its little feet and legs sticking out but no head and only one arm. It was come feet first. He wasn't blue yet. The chin was caught under the pelvic bone. Well, I couldn't see where it'd do no harm, so I reached in with my thumb and forefinger an' eased that bone apart a little an' out he popped, as easy as you please, and I laid him on the towel there, but I left everything else for the doctor for I knowed he'd be right there.

"The other nurse raised a fuss; said she got there first and it was her case and I went against the law when I touched the woman, an' she was goin' to report me and have me 'rested. But I didn't care. The baby was okay. And the doctor applauded what I'd done, an' the other woman hadn't done one thing. She never reported it, neither, though she talked it up all around town."

Another time, a patient died within three days because she had waited too long to call the doctor. Aunt Jennie nursed her, as best she could, and afterward the patient's sister gave her the dead woman's sewing basket. It was a "treasure: a gourd to use as a darner, and lots of spools of thread, and blindman's needles and needle threaders." In talking to me about the woman's dying, Grandma Deb mimicked other people. "They say, 'I knew we was goin' to have a death in the neighborhood. I heard So-and-So's dog howl last night.' Or else they say, 'If a pigeon lights on the window and pecks on the glass, that's a sure sign of death.' That's tommyrot. When it's your time, you die."

Grandma Deb's career as a baby-nurse ended with her fifty-first case. When she went ahead of her patient's due date to meet her client and get familiar with the house where she would live for two weeks, she felt uneasy. The house itself "was of a cheap construction. It looked as though the second floor had been added by someone who didn't know much about building. The steps went right straight up into the back wall. There was no landing. You just had to step sideways, reach out and open the door toward you as you perched there, and then step into whichever room. There was a room on each side at the top.

"Well, the baby come all right and everything was going fine, until the middle of the night when I got up to go over to the other bedroom and bring the baby to the mother to nurse. I opened the door to my room. I stepped out and I reached for the door to the opposite room. And I fell down the entire flight. I heard that woman moan, 'Another one! Everybody's fell down them terrible stairs!'

"And that was all I ever got 'in pay or pity' from that family."

* * *

This injury was the most devastating of a set of three that had incapacitated her over the years. The first one had been the most bizarre. It may well have been connected with those incredible stories of her infancy. "Some time before 1929," she suffered "terrible pain" in the left side of her face. She thought it was "facical" neuralgia, but Madeline took her to a doctor who saw that she was losing her sight in one eye and advised an operation at the world-famous Wills Eye Hospital in Philadelphia.

Grandma Deb did not understand the procedure. As she explained it, the doctor rolled her left eyeball out of the socket and rested it on her cheek. He found there was too much damage to the socket and he could not save her sight in that eye, so he stitched the eyeball back into place. He told Madeline that he feared that part of her mother's face would be paralyzed, but actually he had maneuvered the muscles and the nerves so competently that this eye always moved with the right one. Most people never realized that Grandma Deb was blind in one eye.

But the doctor had found something very strange: a "cobweb net" behind the eyeball. He had never seen anything like it. It looked like scar tissue, such as results from a burn. When he asked Grandma Deb about her medical history, she told him about having been a premature baby who had been kept in the oven. The surgeon speculated that some of the women who sat by that oven had not been careful enough and the eyeball actually had been burned during this critical time of the baby's development.

A second serious accident occurred while she was still working. She injured her spine in a heavy fall off the back porch. As a result she had such bad leg cramps that often she could not sleep through the night. Sometimes she would have to get out of bed and lie on the floor. Then Grandpa would get up too, bring wet rags from the bathroom, and kneel beside her, rubbing her legs until the cramps were gone. "He never complained and was as gentle as could be. God bless him!" she would say.

The worst injury, though, was this third one, the result of her fall down "them terrible stairs." She fractured five vertebrae and was in Philadelphia's Jefferson Hospital, flat on her back, for months.

"And every Saturday, regardless of the weather, that whole time, Madeline came over to Philadelphia to see me and brought me a pear, because she knew I was partial to pears. She did that even when pears was out of season and costing ten cents apiece."

Finally they brought her home from the hospital and carried her upstairs to her own bed. Accidentally she overheard Dr. Connell telling Madeline that "Aunt Jennie" would not walk again. Later, when Madeline came upstairs with her mother's supper tray, she pretended to be cheerful, and Grandma Deb responded with the same fake optimism.

But she was resolute. She had a desperate plan that she intended to undertake no matter the cost. As soon as Madeline left, Grandma Deb put her feet tightly together so that her body was rigid, and then, using her strong arms on the bedframe, she pulled herself to the edge of the bed and slowly lowered herself onto the floor. After a short rest, she wriggled to the bathroom. There was a wall radiator there, with horizontal metal pipes. She reached up and grabbed the lowest pipe. The pain was excruciating, but it was still not as devastating as the doctor's verdict. She hung on. Then she reached for the next higher pipe. Again she rested, shaking with the agony. Then she grasped the next one. And the next. She pushed herself harder, knowing that her time was limited. If she failed, she would be watched and prevented from trying again. She did not fail. When Madeline came to get her supper tray, she found her mother almost upright. She kept on practicing, now with Madeline's encouragement. And she did walk again, although never again could she go out as a baby-nurse. She always had what she described as "fever" in her feet—and her back was bent—but she could do her share of work in the house for many years to come.

These physical disabilities intensified the major losses she sustained between 1921 and 1936: loss of independence, income, home, physical strength, and pride. She might have become a melancholy or bitter old woman. She had not had much luck in her life, and now here she was, once again working for another woman, working for her board and keep. But Jennie Hess Devlin did not think like that. Nobody heard her complain aloud, though she did show an ingrained habit from her earlier years of dependency. Her granddaughter remembered: "All her life she was sensitive, easily hurt, but never apt to strike back with words. She was never sulky. But when her feelings were too strong, she would withdraw." There had only been one person in her life with whom she could safely expose her anger: her husband. Now he was her best friend. So she choked back her tears and took refuge in her old ways of living within herself.

Safely ensconced in the kitchen, she found her own drama, her own jokes, her own competence. Friday was often the high point of her week, when Madeline returned with the supply of meats, chickens, and vegetables from the Italian market in South Philadelphia. As a frequent visitor to her cousins in "the Neck," Madeline knew that the food was cheaper and fresher there. When she brought it home, Grandma Deb had the happy task of unpacking it and storing it in the big touch-bar refrigerator. "Sometimes, rememberin' what we had on the farm, I jus' hug that refrigerator," she confessed.

She had a way of individualizing objects in her life. Although she hugged the refrigerator, and admired the new pink gas stove, she swore "Shit!" when it didn't light fast enough and the match burnt out. She had a personal involvement with the soups, the pies, the cakes, even the chickens she cooked, comparing them with their predecessors, blaming them if they didn't meet her standards.

She did not mind spending all day to make a pot of soup. "It might take a little longer, but I don't begrudge the time," she'd say slyly, relishing the old joke from the stud farm. "After I saw the bones all apart, I put the thyme into a bag. I don't like it floating in the soup like little pine trees." Then she'd smile at her own whimsy: "It's only a matter of mind."

Grandma Deb amused herself with her comments: "I'm not settin' the table with any fancy doodle-le-dums tonight — the food's good and everything's clean." "This butter is as hard as Phareo's heart." "Tonight when I was emptyin' the 'gerbage' I saw ev'ry star like a kite with a light on it."

Madeline got her mother out of the house and into a life of her own by persuading her to join a lodge, a chapter of a secret fraternal order. Madeline saw to it that Jennie had the money for the dues, and a white dress to wear to the meetings. Jennie Devlin became a "Shepherd," a member of the Gloucester lodge of the Shepherds of Bethlehem. Like other fraternal organizations, this lodge collected weekly dues that included sick benefits and a burial policy, matters of great concern to people facing old age in the years before Social Security.

But the Shepherds meant much more than that. They were a women's support group, an example of "female bonding." Attendance at the weekly meetings was requisite. Members who were not able to be present were expected to notify the "chair," the elected head of the group. The women called for each other and went to "lodge" in small groups. They were bound together in ceremonies conducted with patriotic and religious fervor. Grandma Deb enjoyed all these rituals, but one gave her personal pleasure: "The march that they played at lodge was the same one we marched to when I went to school in Athens, only there the teacher played it on the melodeon. I loved to think about that."

As a member of the Gloucester lodge, she gained a new status. She was "Aunt Jennie" to all the "sisters," and thus the name of the baby-nurse became even more familiar in Gloucester homes. There were visits back and forth between lodges in different towns, and beyond that level were the state meetings attended by officers from each lodge. Aunt Jennie, despite her educational handicap, was able to "go through the chairs," meaning that she held each of the elective positions all the way to the head of the lodge. She was held in high esteem by her lodge sisters, not only locally but throughout the state of New Jersey. Although she had no car and could not drive, she was always sure of a ride to all meetings.

When she had completed all these steps, she chose what she wanted as a permanent position: scribe. Each week, as her part in the program, she sang what she considered an appropriate song. Thus, once again she was a folksinger, with a reputation for it in her own community. Later, when she herself decided that her singing voice was gone, she spoke the words of her songs or recited other pieces she had collected just for this function. Her lodge sisters' tribute to her was that when she was absent — sick or working — nobody ever took her place. There was never any scribe but Aunt Jennie.

Aunt Jennie won this respect by obeying her own precept: "It takes two to make a quarrel but only one to make it up. An' I'm going to be that one." This was the same lesson that was in the ditties she had taught children to recite: "Let dogs delight to bark and bite / But children must not do so," and "Birds in their little nests agree." Adults could not be taught this openly, so she used humor as the best path to reconciliation. But her message always was clear: people should live in dignity and harmony.

One of her efforts was to get her lodge sisters to appreciate a love story being acted out before their eyes. They were cold-hearted and narrow-minded, she felt, in their attitude toward one meek little sister in their own lodge. This is the story of Edith.

"An orphan — little underfed thing, taken from a home by an aunt during the war because boarders were plentiful and lots of work. Worked the poor thing near to death. It affected her mind, too — she ain't quite bright. 'Course she left there when she could but she's never known nothing but work. Has a room and goes out by the day; does any kind of work, scrubbing floors or anything. Work's the only thing she's ever known — no home nor consideration. Now she's thirty-four and this fellow wants to marry her and some of the old busybodies up at the lodge wants to break it up and tell her that he's had goodness knows how many other wives though he wasn't married to them. What do they want to do that for? It ain't any of their business and the poor girl couldn't be no worse off.

"Anyways he's about seven years older than what she is and his mother just died a while back so he's lonely and he says, 'Edith, we're both alone.' She's got a nice little ring — oh, maybe it only cost thirty, forty dollars but it's a nice cut and they're going to be married in a week or so.

"Now she had got so she drank because of all her troubles. He found out about it and he said, 'Edith, I understand you take a drink of beer now and then. Is it just beer?' 'Yes, only beer.' 'Well, that's all right but when we're married, when you want a beer, we'll go together.' Same with lodge and all other events, he always says, 'We'll go together.' She says it seems too good to be true. Now why should anybody want to stop her?

"And, you know, there ain't a thing inside her — she's had everything taken out. She told him, too. She says it took her two, three weeks to 'screw herself up together' — that's the way she talks — to tell him. And she waited till they was out on the porch. He said, 'Let's go in,' but she held back. She knew she couldn't tell him in the face of the light.

"So she said, 'You know I haven't a thing to offer you. I had an operation and I can never have no children.'

"'Oh, is that all you wanted to tell me? I knew that and it don't make a bit of difference to me, Edith. What we haven't had we'll never miss.'

"He probably thinks of her as a child herself. I tell her I think they'll do okay, and I tell that to the other women in the lodge, too. How can they judge them two people's chances?"

Aunt Jennie expressed herself quite strongly about Edith's story to other Shepherds who came to sit in her kitchen for an afternoon visit, to gossip or to ask her advice. Because of the vicissitudes of her own life, she had great powers of empathy that made many people confide their troubles to her. They were all working people whose lives she respected. She seldom gave advice. She did not see herself as any wiser than they, just as a person who had lived longer and perhaps experienced more than they had.

One frequent visitor was "Uncle Billy," a widower who needed a friendly listener. One morning, right after Grandpa had had to rub her legs, I watched Grandma Deb hobble down the stairs to greet Uncle Billy with a cheerful "How are you today?" She gave him no hint of her pain while he told her all of his.

In gratitude, Uncle Billy sometimes brought her candy. Art teased her by saying that Uncle Billy was "her beau." Grandma Deb was not amused. She was living with the only man she ever loved. She saw Uncle Billy not as a suitor but as a person in distress. Art seemed to think that Grandma Deb should have cried when this "beau" died. But she was not one to cry when any of her friends were freed from their suffering. Her faith sustained her in the presence of death.

Many other kinds of people came to the house: Art's brothers, Hell-fire Johnny's betting cronies, Madeline's friends, and neighbors who went to the markets with her on Fridays. Mrs. Shindle, the next-door neighbor, would sit in the kitchen, enjoying a "nice cup of tea," while Grandma Deb pored over Mrs. Shindle's box of poems clipped from the newspapers, occasionally selecting a new one to read to the Shepherds.

Frequent visitors, of course, were the mothers showing off the babies that Aunt Jennie had helped bring into the world. Then there were children who lived in the neighborhood and knew a good place to get cookies. When they had new clothes, the children would rush in to get praise. When one girl pirouetted around with a whole new Easter outfit, from hat to shoes, Madeline and Ellen admired it all—but Aunt Jennie, remembering how expensive buttons had been back when she used to have to pay Aunt Eva to make her dresses, had only one laudatory comment: "My! Ain't the buttons beautiful!" How they teased her for that. Another time a little girl came in to show off a new dress, and Grandma Deb reported, "Gracie's a cute kid. Wears her dresses clear up to her behind."

Best of all were the visits from Grandpa's family: Aunt Mary Tinney and her children, Aunt Sally Morris and her stepchildren. Sometimes the Gloucester people went to parties in Philadelphia. And, as Grandma Deb had learned years before, "all of Johnny's relatives met at family funerals."

Grandma Deb helped with two funerals at home, those of Art's parents, who had lived with them for several years before they died. "Poor Grandma Eaves had diabetes and she had to have a leg amputated. Art paid for the operation and for the wooden leg, too. When she died, the leg was buried in the coffin with her, so that she looked right for the viewing."

Funerals, hospitals, clothes, trips, and food on the table — all were at Art's expense. Yet he and Madeline were proud that there was always money in the front of her bureau drawer to meet emergencies or to give their children an extra treat. He earned good money; she managed it well.

Grandma Deb was very excited when Art and Madeline got a car. She was very willing to go for a ride whenever she was invited. "Pop won't set foot in a car if he can help it," she explained. "Horses was his trade all his life. And he says that the Bible says that the last time the world was destroyed by water and this time it'll be by fire, and ain't that so? Look at all the electricity around now. The Welsbach plant is closed now. Everybody's got electricity even in the kitchens. It's jus' the easiest thing to believe. Say what you like, you have to keep up with the times. Me — I'd like to go up in an aeroplane, as long as somebody was with me."

In fact, these were the years when, as Grandma Deb, she relished being part of Madeline's family, especially watching her grandchildren Bud and Ellen grow up. Often the best part of her day was when they came into her kitchen after school, to show her their papers. Year by year, they grew and succeeded. Bud was not often in the house, but Ellen loved to help around the kitchen, singing along with Grandma Deb, telling her own anecdotes of the day, or appreciating her grandmother's stories of the old days.

It came about naturally that, when it was time for Ellen to be confirmed, Grandma Deb went to catechism class too. They studied together, and, in 1924, Ellen Eaves and Jennie Hess Devlin were both confirmed in the Episcopal Church of the Ascension in Gloucester, New Jersey. "It was the same as the Bentleys. They was Episcopal, too, same as the Eaveses, but they never had much time for it."

Later, she explained to me, "Here in Gloucester I went regular, but not any more. My knees are too bad. I hope God understands."

* * *

In these days there was more than one great blessing in her life. As soon as Grandpa Deb began his efforts to stop drinking, he made up with his sons. They were willing to "forgive and forget," and Grandma Deb saw both of her boys again.

Sometimes Ed would send the money for Grandma Deb to come to Buffalo; at other times, he would send for his father. (Ed usually could not afford railroad fare for both of them at once.) Hellfire Jack, when he went, was always hoping to find work in the city. On one big trip,

Art, Madeline, Bud, and Ellen traveled to Buffalo by train when both Devlin grandparents were there, and, with Clara, Ed's wife, they took a ride under Niagara Falls in the *Maid of the Mist*.

The most momentous visit for Ellen took place when she was about nine. Grandma Deb took her to Buffalo for a treat after she finished fourth grade. Ed, at that time, had taken on an extra job as chauffeur to a rich woman, and Ellen had an experience only the richest person could have: she rode in a Rolls Royce.

Ed shared his father's "hot-headed derring-do adventure streak." In the late 1920s, his quest for excitement led him to become a volunteer policeman in his spare time. One night, as they were charging up the stairs after a suspect, Ed rushed ahead of the regular officer and was shot to death. His likeness to his father—the old "Hellfire" spirit—had led Ed Devlin to his death.

His brother also lived a life of adventure. From the time that he left home, Lou wrote to his mother occasionally to tell her about his special army assignments, which took him around the globe. "He was in Europe, California, the Philippines, all over." Once he managed to visit her after she was living in Madeline's house. He had only an hour's visit, so he slipped a check for thirty dollars into his mother's apron pocket so that she'd have the fare to come to him at once if he ever got leave nearby again.

She used the money later when he telegraphed that he was going to be in Buffalo. She rushed to take a train up there but he was transferred that same night, before she arrived, and she never saw Lou again.

He continued to write. Then, shortly after Ed died, Lou's letters stopped. It looked as though both sons were dead. She could not accept it. For years, Grandma Deb continued to carry a Metropolitan insurance policy that she had taken out on Lou's life. Finally she gave up hope of his being alive and decided to cash it in.

The company said they'd put a tracer on him. She thought that "that was a gag, just to keep me paying, but they told me not to stop. Then their salesman came to report: Lou was working for them—for the very same company! And he lived in Huntington Park, California. They told him to write to his mother or be fired.

"He wrote ten pages at once. He'd thought I was dead, and since he never did get along well with Madeline, he figured why write?

"His wife, Bernice, was in the hospital at that moment, expecting their child. And when she got out, the first letter Bernice wrote was to 'Dear Mother.' She told me about the new baby, Mary Ellen. Lou gave her the middle name of 'Ellen' since he remembered his niece so well. Bernice typed on account of my one eye gone.

"Once she wrote 'I've been turning collars and cuffs on Lou's shirts today, trying to get them done before I have to go for Mary Ellen.' She must be a good wife to be so thrifty. I told Madeline to tell her so when she wrote to her again, and Bernice wrote back and said that Lou said, 'That sounds just like Mother.' Everybody from Gloucester who goes to California goes to see them. Lou can't get only two weeks' vacation, so he can't get here. Other mothers go see their children every year, even if they go on the bus. But Pop an' me, we don't have the money.

"Lou wrote to Madeline once and said, 'You've had Mother and Dad all this time. Now let me have them for the last lap.' Madeline was so mad, she saw red. She sent him a special delivery back. He wanted to send for me one month and Pop the next because it costs a lot of money for train fare. She said, 'You always was Lou's fav'rite and you're supposed to go first. But jus' suppose you and Lou's wife don't hit it off or you get homesick in a month or two. It'd be all right if Lou'd guarantee your money home again. Then I'd have nothing to say. But you're not going out there and not be able to leave if you want.'

"So Madeline wrote right back to him, and then she drove up to Philadelphia where I was nursing our Mary, who was dying, and all these letters were sent before I even knew anything about it at all. And Lou never mentioned it again.

"I said to Pop, 'There goes our chances of ever seeing California.' Though I do say every night, 'And, dear God, if it be Thy will, may I see Bernice and my granddaughter and Lou again before I die.'

"But I mustn't complain. We've got a good home here. But I do wonder what was in that letter that Madeline sent. I'd give a lot to know. You know I only had my own home three times in my life. Every time we run out of money and I was sold out. All my things. If only I still could! There's a little house — really only one room, out back here. . . . It'd be jus' right for Pop an' me." But even that wasn't possible.

7

Folksinger Discovered, 1936–38

It was my friend Ellen Eaves who forged the partnership between her grandmother and me. Visiting at my parents' home one day in 1936, Ellen sang "Little Birdies" to my small nephew. He was enchanted. "Kay," she said, "you really ought to take down my grandmother's songs. You could make a book of them for Bobby."

So, the next time I visited Gloucester, I did ask. Of course, Grandma Deb was happy to dictate to me her "pieces to sing to the kiddies." I planned to paste them in a notebook, with pictures cut from magazines. These were still Depression times and I did not often buy books.

At first I felt no personal attachment to Grandma Deb. She was just Ellen's grandmother, an old woman who knew a lot of songs that I wanted. I certainly was not looking for a replacement grandmother for myself, nor did she correspond at all with my image of a grandmother. I had much to unlearn.

My own long-dead grandmothers had worn black taffeta dresses, not cotton wash dresses like a housemaid. They wore high-laced black shoes, not Daniel Green comfy slippers. They had stiff coiffures, ringlets around the face, curls on top of the head held in place by tortoise shell combs decorated with pearls. Grandma Deb usually wore her long silver hair pulled back tightly into a bun.

My grandmothers had been "ladies." They had not had to stoop to menial tasks. They had had hired girls, usually Irish immigrants, who lived in and went up to their bedrooms by the back kitchen stairs. Grandma Deb herself had been a hired girl, and even now she slaved away in the kitchen, all day long, not leaving until the last dinner dish was washed, dried, and put away.

I also found Grandma Deb's constant comments strange; I can still hear her expression of doubt as she'd turn a cake out on a plate: "If this cake ain't good, God bless the boat that brought me over." If she was not satisfied with the icing after she'd put it on the cake, she'd mutter, "This looks like a homemade patch. They'll never know whose cat messed that up."

Later I learned that "bless the boat that brought me over" was a common expression in the Eaveses' home, probably borrowed from their Irish relatives. Her concern about the cake icing was a professional's judgment based on her years of baking fancy cakes for rich people in Woodbury.

I sometimes thought her expressions a bit vulgar, too. This soft-spoken, sweet-faced old lady would shuffle about, getting all the crumbs off the dining room table, working all the creases out of the tablecloth, and yet saying, "I don't like things all buggered up."

In truth, I did not see her clearly. She had her standards and she was keeping them, even in old age. I could not then appreciate her physical anguish: the swollen finger joints, the stiff knees that were liable to buckle any time, the severe back pains, and the leg cramps that shocked her into wakefulness at night. But I did begin to appreciate her determination one evening as I watched her cautiously lift each foot in turn and then slide it onto the next step, as she toiled upstairs to the linen closet. One of the men wanted to wash up in the kitchen, and Grandma Deb simply would not let him use a dirty towel. "On the farm, we always made the hired men keep clean," she said. "Ye' can't expect much if you give him a dirty towel."

I visualized her as a Cinderella whose prince had never freed her from the kitchen hearth. But at least he had come. He was that subdued old man with the large shaggy moustache, smacking his tea-flavored milk and then going meekly back to their bedroom upstairs. He had been the dashing young hero, once upon a time, who had borne her off from the farm where she was an overworked servant. But he had carried her into poverty. For fifty-one years she had never taken off her plain gold wedding ring. She had stuck it out with Hellfire Jack. And this was where it was ending.

Now she waited on all of us because she was self-driven by love, by habit, and by stubborn pride. Despite all she had been through, she taught us to find the world funny as well as fascinating. No wonder so many people loved her. I did, too.

As often as I could, I would drive over from Philadelphia to the hospitable little house in Gloucester — in time for dinner, of course. Afterward I would visit with Ellen or sit in the kitchen with Grandma Deb. I have no recollection of ever drying a dish there. She certainly spoiled me, in the best grandmotherly tradition.

One weekend I was the only one in the house besides her and Grandpa. She greeted me with one of her private little jokes: "If you would have came earlier, then I'd have had a freer foot and a fellow for it." The implication was that our time together had been shortened by my late arrival, but the actuality was that we had an entire leisurely weekend ahead of us. The saying obviously had come from the farm dances of her youth. It made a very awkward fit here. Certainly she had not denied herself a free foot. She had been planning for my visit for several days; all we had to do was eat and talk—certainly my idea of a good time. My notes recorded my pleasure: "Apple pie (Saturday), lemon custard pie (Sunday), Jersey City cake with another little one baked just for me. The big cake was not iced until I came. Then she used the chocolate icing that she had saved in a mayonnaise jar from the last cake especially for this one. The leftover icing was also spread between graham crackers, just for me." It was all—every bit of it—just for me. I'd never had such pampering. When I tried to thank her, I got a "kiddie" speech: "When the cat's away, the mice will play, and by heck, who cares if they squeal a bit?" With Madeline and Art gone, Grandma Deb may have felt, for a time, as though she were entertaining in her own home again.

* * *

When she first sang "Little Birdies" for me to take home to my nephew Bobby, I was just the adoring aunt, eager to learn other "kiddie pieces." But Grandma Deb thought that all of her old pieces, treasured through the years since her own childhood, would help kiddies understand life. So she next recited the ghost story of two "babes" who had been murdered by their cruel mother and who then returned to haunt her. She was giving me—and I wrote it all down in great astonishment—the old English ballad that she called "Lady of York." How could a seventy-two-year-old woman, in a crowded little house in the shipbuilding town of Gloucester, New Jersey, know a Child ballad? I knew about these ballads, of course. I had an M.A. in English literature. But here Grandma Deb, a woman with almost no schooling, was reciting stanza after stanza (eleven in all, plus the refrain), from memory.

"Wherever did you learn these pieces?" I begged her.

"I growed up with them. Whether it was this year or that year, I jus' couldn't tell you. I've known 'em all my life. 'Where does the birdie learn to fly?'"

It was hard to believe—but what an incredible stroke of luck for me. I was instantly snared, by the songs and by the singer. I wrote down on pieces of paper all that she dictated to me that night. After that, I always brought a notebook. "I'm all finished and buttoned up," she would say, wiping her hands on the kitchen towel. Then we'd go to work, I with my pencil, Grandma Deb with mending or sock darning. She would chat a bit as we settled into place. "I can't sew fancy,

like a whole dress," she would say. "But I can darn like a kite." She
gave me hour upon hour, with all the "pieces" she knew, and riddles,
charms, nursery rhymes, "true life" stories, and anecdotes about her
own life, even some she had never remembered to tell Ellen.

I wanted everything. Sometimes a poem would come "in the wink
of an eye," but sometimes it was only "on the tip of the tongue," so
that she would have to put down her work while she struggled to
"consecrate." But at other times, pieces "woke themselves up right
when I was in the kitchen."

Since she had always been a conscientious person, she took me and
my notebook seriously. Sometimes, she would open a session apolo-
getically: "The other night in bed I remembered one and, thinks I, 'that
would be a nice one for Kay to have.' But it's all gone now, every word.
You know, dear, sometimes when I can't sleep, I lay thinkin' 'bout
these pieces for you. I can think then better than when there's so much
to do in the daytime. I wish I could remember that darn thing now."

But she really could not understand what I was doing. The old, old
pieces, and the newer "pretty pieces," the funny ones, and the ones
for the kiddies — she herself had learned them from other people, and
she had taught them to her daughter, Madeline, and to her grandchildren and other kiddies — what was so remarkable about them?

I saw how puzzled she was about me one night when a neighbor
came in, as the neighbors were always doing, and Grandma Deb tried
to explain who I was. "She's a bird," she said. Then she grew apologe-
tic and added, "in a gilded cage." Did she really know that song? If so,
did she see how incongruous the comparison was? "To be a bird"
meant to be an eccentric, an unconventional person, hardly a description of me at that time. But how else could she explain what I was
doing in the Eaveses' house? I thought that she made it worse by saying "in a gilded cage," the rest of the title of a late-nineteenth-century
song, since that meant a kept woman. We all laughed and that moment passed. I am sure the neighbor would not have understood what
I was doing either.

Grandma Deb said to Ellen one day, "God love Kay! But I don't see
what she wants all these old pieces for." After Ellen explained that I
wanted to put them in a book, she tried even harder, trying to recall
words long stored in memory. Finally came the night when her memory was emptied. I was bewildered by the wealth I had been given.

Everything was safe in my notebooks — but there was one lack that
I had discovered when I was studying the research of other collectors.

"Gran," I said, a bit plaintively, "Gran, don't *any* of these pieces
have tunes?"

"'Course. They all do."

"Why didn't you tell me this before?"

"I didn't think you'd want to be bothered with any more of this old junk."

Junk! With the addition of music the significance of the whole collection became much more exciting, but it also became a matter of greater scholarly responsibility. I now had a *real* folksinger, a true inheritor of the oral tradition, and I believed that I had a duty to transmit these gems in my turn. I was a "Child-and-other collector." I dearly prized the pieces like "Lady of York" and the four others that carried the pedigree of a number in the scholarly collection of ballads made by Professor Francis James Child at Harvard. Night after night, as Grandma Deb had dictated her pieces to me, I dreamt that at least one more — maybe even two or three — Child ballads would wake themselves in her memory. It would add to my glory. I concealed my disappointment when we got scraps of some songs I myself knew, such as the exuberant "Pop Goes the Weasel." Doggedly, though, I took everything. Now, fifty years later, I rejoice in that spread; we wouldn't see Jennie Devlin so well if all we had were the songs she learned as a little girl.

* * *

The next step in our project was Ellen's bringing Janet Grimler, a high-school music teacher, to meet Grandma Deb. Janet too was enthralled by the old songs. Now it was she who sat opposite Grandma Deb at the dining room table. But besides demonstrating that she could write down music, Janet impressed Grandma Deb with a surprising tidbit of domestic news that I heard her later repeat to several other people.

"Janet says her mother only cleans house once a year. In the fall. Janet says everybody in Newark does that — takes down the curtains and wipes off the fingermarks. But with the windows open all summer, no use cleaning good in the spring, jus' the fall!"

Art Eaves, once again looking for a joke, teased Ellen and me that Janet had "stolen our thunder" with Grandma Deb. This teasing she wouldn't let pass.

"Now, Daddy," she ruffled up, "them two're good and you know it. It isn't many can do what Janet can. 'Little hands must do what they can,' same as the hymn says. That's what I always taught the kiddies."

I noticed that Grandma Deb did not attempt any mending while Janet was there. She sat still or absentmindedly folded and refolded a dinner napkin. It was hard work for both of them. They worked out a process. Janet had my copies of the lyrics. Gran would sing through a piece once. Then Janet would get out her pitch pipe, and they'd hum to each other. Janet would write the tune down on the ruled music paper that she brought, and then she would sing it back. Grandma Deb's ear was so good that she noticed at once whenever Janet had a problem. "It don't come in right, does it?" They'd go over it again and again.

"I don' care how many times I sing it, jus' so I please," she would say. I prefer Janet's notation to the transcription from the recordings (made later that same year) because Gran was so relaxed, accepting Janet as another of Ellen's friends, and they worked over each song, hour after hour, until Grandma Deb felt satisfied. One night Gran surprised us by producing a Jew's harp, which she put in her mouth and twanged, making a metallic tune. We three, her "girls," laughed with her. She even shuffled a few steps in her carpet slippers, giving us a glimpse of how she had danced as a young girl.

My notes show that she ended one session with a phrase I didn't know at that time, but it sounded cute and quaint: "That winds up 'the little ball of yarn.'" "Huh?" I said. She sedately said, "That's all for tonight." Later I was allowed to learn that song; it was quite jaunty — and quite bawdy. I realized then that Grandma Deb had not considered this as appropriate for Janet's ears. All that our conscientious musician had been given was a tune without words. Those sessions with Janet went so well that she has left us a legacy of forty-four melodies. I have a letter from her, unfortunately undated, written when she sent me the set of tunes that she had finished. At that time she was hoping to put accompaniments to them. But, like me, Janet did not get back to the project after she married, and, in intervening years, she has passed away.

The most significant part of Janet's letter deals with the song "Pretty Pond Lilies": "I have two endings to the chorus and I have a distinct recollection that she sang both at different times. When we tried to check on it, we got the second version (no words), but another time we might have gotten the first page. It might bear re-checking." In the second part of this book, I have printed all that Janet had taken down; the question about "Pretty Pond Lilies" must remain a puzzle.

*   *   *

Although Grandma Deb was now my fictive grandmother, I never stopped being a researcher and a collector. On school vacations I took long field trips; first, I drove to the great libraries: the Library of Congress, New York Public Library, and, after a heavy snowstorm, Harvard College Library, where, by previously granted permission, I was allowed to see the manuscript notes left over from Child's monumental work. I could read very little of his handwriting.

Much more exciting were my visits to places where Grandma Deb had lived. Although I found no one still singing their stories, I did locate the graves of both Martha Decker and James Bird and knelt on the ground before them, taking photographs.

I also went to Wellsville and met — and was thoroughly intimidated by — "Aunt Eva" Bentley, who was obviously very guarded. She was willing to hear song titles and indicate which ones she herself had known when Jennie came to her, and which ones probably were of an older vintage. Her identification corroborated my theory that all of the old ballads and folksongs, except for "James Bird," Jennie had learned before she was fourteen and came to Wellsville.

Said Grandma Deb to Ellen, a year or so later, "We haven't heard from Aunt Eva since Kay was up there. I wonder does she think we are asking too many questions?" My own feeling was that Aunt Eva had given me too many answers. When I had asked, cautiously, if she had known Jennie's mother, she replied, "Of course. She lived here in Wellsville."

"While Jennie was with you?"

"Yes. But she was a very peculiar woman. She lived on the other side of the tracks." Then she volunteered one other piece of information: "The reason I hired Jennie was so that her mother's second husband couldn't get her wages."

Why did she tell me what she had never told Jennie? I was too startled by her sudden candor to ask. But I came to believe that Aunt Eva had truly loved Jennie, because she gave me three great treasures: copies of the two wedding portraits and the one of Hellfire Jack with his mustang, the record-breaking Sam Tilden. I took the information — about the songs Jennie had known and about her mother — and the gift of these pictures, as evidence that Aunt Eva seemed pleased that her old hired girl was now being held in some esteem as a folksinger.

Since I wanted Grandma Deb herself to understand what was meant by the term "folksinger," I gave her a copy of *Mountain Minstrelsy of Pennsylvania* by the state historian, Colonel Henry W. Shoemaker. She, who may never have owned any book before, was ecstatic.

"God love Kay," she said. "The night I got that book, I sat up till two o'clock readin' it and singin' over to myself a lot of them pieces. I knowed them as a girl, and I knowed them again the minute I set my eyes on them, though I can't sing all of them without the book. My, that was a treat!"

Sometimes she was troubled by the words in the book. "Now that ain't the way it goes," she would say, staring at a page.

"Different people sing songs differently," I tried to tell her, but she was worried. She was sure she had picked up the song correctly when she had heard it years ago, yet here it was different—and it was printed in a book. Of course she couldn't change any of her songs to match Shoemaker's, but she did come to enjoy the knowledge that Janet and I were not the only crazy ones; there were many people still singing the old pieces and many people who thought writing them down was a good idea.

She returned again and again to her two favorite songs that she had "lost": "James Bird" and "Young Charlotte," and she relived their tragedies in her memory.

One day, I had the fun of taking Grandma Deb down the Black Horse Pike to Newtonville, New Jersey, where I had seen a sign on a little roadside shack: "Louis Dilks. Baskets of All Kinds / Made of White Oak Only." What a visit Dilks and Grandma Deb had. Her fingers, bent as they were, wandered over the baskets, remembering the skills she had learned with the Stevensons. The old man, who seemed to have very few customers, grew enthusiastic and proud as he showed his work to the old lady. I felt as if we had all skipped back sixty years.

It was as though some happy memories of a part of her early life had been restored to her. I hoped to increase that pleasure in June 1938 when the Philadelphia Folk Festival was held at Grey Tower, Beaver College. But now she balked. It had been worrisome enough when she had let Janet come to the house to listen to her sing. What would happen if she went with Kay "clear across Philadelphia"? She turned, as usual, to her granddaughter. Ellen assured her that, this time, there would be no attention directed at her, that all she would do was sit with me and listen to other folksingers. Ellen gave advice about her clothes. Ellen gave her the courage to get in the car and go with me.

The trip lies happily in my memory now. But I do have a remembrance of concealing some irritation over her worries on the way there. I did not understand that she was in pain. Ellen had had to help her get the dress over her head, so much did her left arm hurt that morning. She was also fretting that her appearance suffered because she had left at home her good gold wristwatch that Ellen and Bud had given her. She hadn't been able to fasten the catch herself; she had meant to ask me to do it, but, when I came, she got fussed and didn't want to keep me waiting, and she'd left it on the bureau.

Actually I found her appearance quite lovely. It was the first time I had seen her in a "good dress," a pretty purple and white silk. Instead of the comfy slippers, she wore stiff white oxfords, and she had all the required accessories of a lady: white gloves, white handbag, and white hat. As a special dress-up feature, she wore blue stone earrings; these made a dramatic contrast to the bits of broom straw she often wore in her earlobes while working, to keep the holes open. Her hair, thin but still three feet long, had been up in curlers all night so that it had "body." Ellen had taken out the curlers that morning, fluffed the hair around her face, and let it lie in waves under the brim of the stiff hat.

As ever, Grandma Deb's eyes dominated her face. Over the years I have sought the right word to describe her eyes, but "twinkly" is still the best I can find. She looked out at life with love and laughter. Despite the fact that Grandma Deb was totally blind in one eye — which I learned from Ellen only in 1986 — I never knew it. She had such perfect control over the eyelid and facial muscles that her personality came through unmarred.

The grand dining hall of the main college building, called "the Castle," subdued her. She was wary of this food that had been prepared by strangers. She especially warned me against the tomatoes; they weren't the "right color." We spoke to each other in whispers.

But when we sat outdoors in the grandstand and watched the folksingers and dancers, her excitement was great and her voice loud. To her, this was "better than any theater or vaudeville show which was all made up." This was reality to her, a dazzling vault backward in time to her early girlhood. She did not comprehend that this was really a public performance that the audience had paid to attend. She talked constantly and vigorously. We had to move from one part of the stands to another where there were fewer people to be annoyed. Other people exhibited quiet company manners, but Jennie Hess was fully alive again.

"Dolly Varden dresses! That's just like the one I used to have. It was a brown check with a high neck bound with a ruffle. It was trimmed with rickrack. The skirt was mostly a big flounce, like that, put on around the knees in front with a tiny ruffle standin' up and goin' up the sides. That was so the fullness and the ruffle in the back came just where you needed it so the dress wouldn't drag under and show your shape. Years ago, when I was on the farm, you didn't wear such tight dresses as now. Girls was much more modest then. But people today, they cover up what God gave them an' that's all that's necessary. You have to adapt yourself to the day. You may not approve but you dasen't fall down on the job. Mrs. Shindle, who lives next door to Madeline's house, is the same as she was fifty years ago. She's a nice woman, though."

Then the dancing began.

"They [the fiddlers] knowed their parts well. And them [the dancers] . . . I bet they been here practicin' for the last couple of days to be able to do so good. . . .

"Them dancers — you can see they're havin' good fun. You can tell that because they started to sing. There they go, hand over hand, the girls to the right and the boys to the left. And they don't none of them get mixed up. Boy, ain't that good!"

She tapped her foot in time and imitated the calls softly. Instead of the stooped, shrunken, and flabby old lady beside me, I pictured the large, lively-looking woman in the wedding photograph Aunt Eva had given me. Perhaps recalling the same period in her life, she said, "I usta love to dance when I had a free foot and a fellow to follow it. But Pop made me quit when we got married. I wish I hadn't obeyed him about that."

Afterward we visited the crafts booths. She approved the clear colors of the homemade jellies and complimented the piebakers on their flaky crusts. She spent a lot of time at the quilt display, recognizing the old patterns and congratulating the women there on the evenness of their stitches. I was beginning to be embarrassed by her remarks. She naively assumed that these were "Sunday quilts" for their best beds, rather than craft products made for competition.

I was even more embarrassed, however, by my own feelings: I thought there was too much fake "folksiness" at the folk festival. It was more a picturization of the past than a presentation of reality. Being starchly academic, I wanted "absolute authenticity." Reality was represented by this old woman beside me, but I could not explain that to her. She thought the past still existed.

Next, a spinning wheel in the Swedish-American exhibit caught Grandma Deb's attention. She stopped, wanting to show me how she had used the one at Grandmom Clemens's house in her own girlhood. The woman in the booth asked her not to touch it, barely hiding her annoyance at this familiarity with a valued relic. I attempted to move Grandma Deb on.

To my glee, we met two of Art's cousins, two very proper ladies. "Why, Mrs. Devlin!" they exclaimed. "What are you doing here?"

I puffed up. "This is where she should be! She's a better folksinger than anybody who's been out there on the stage all day."

They were surprised, if not impressed. I was very pleased that the word would get back to Gloucester. I was eager for her family, for all the friends and the neighbors who walked in and out of that friendly home, to know her real distinction. Her funny little expressions and turns of speech, her jokes, and all her songs — these made her unique. She herself, I hoped, was realizing what she was: a true folksinger. And that — as she herself would have said — "that was a mack'rel fact."

I was satisfied with our adventure, which we talked about all the way home. As we reached Art's house, she opened her handbag and took out a clean good hanky. It was the only "pay" she could give me — or so she thought. What I really still have is the memory of the graciousness of her manner, an appropriate close to our special day.

* * *

Now I wanted wider recognition for her. However, I confess that I had mixed motives. I wanted her songs to be part of the National Archive of Folk Song, housed in the Library of Congress; I wanted this validation of my own work. But I also wanted her to know the value of her songs, to know herself as a real folksinger who was helping to save the old songs she loved so much.

Over and over she had said, "I had a mother but I never knowed her. I always lived with strangers. I had to work hard — from the time I knew anything, I knew that I had to earn my way or they wouldn't keep me. An' I always wanted jus' to be Somebody."

I had come to love her so much that I too wanted her to be Somebody. But what did that mean? She had built part of her identity out of fighting major deprivations, but she had dreamt all her life of some extra achievement or recognition that would counterbalance her losses. Moreover, she was realistic; she did know that she had talents that could have won her some recognition — if she had had a chance. Now there was one way for her to achieve some of that satisfaction: by recording some of her songs. She was a true folksinger.

She could be proud of that. I began to tell her about other people singing into recording machines. I described to her how folksong collectors went about the country with machines that were like victrolas, saving these old pieces that were already being forgotten.

"Now ain't that clever!" she said.

"I wish you could hear them. One record that I heard was made down South in the mountains — by poor white people. You could hear a rooster crowing and pigs rooting around — you could hear them right in the same room with the woman doing the singing."

It was as though it was still Jennie the farm girl who responded: "That shows you what their life is like — animals loose in the house! We always kept them in the barn where they belong, when I lived on the farm."

She may have felt superior to those people — but she had no intention of allowing one of those machines in the house. She refused to be challenged by my stories and pleas. "I can't sing worth a darn any more. My voice's dried up." Such an idea was unthinkable.

Again it was her granddaughter who knew how to approach her. Ellen talked to Grandma Deb about the pleasure she had had in reliving the old times at the folk festival. Yes, she had learned that she was like "them other singers." And, yes, she would like to help Kay, but . . . her pride, her painful awareness of the deficiencies age had brought her, and her basic humility, all stood in the way of granting my wish.

"All the troubles that I've had took the singing out of me. Besides, there's a place here in my throat, like a lump, that fills up. An' my voice's cracked. You know, Granny ain't no spring chicken, dear. I jus' can't."

But finally she did agree. "I'll do it jus' for you girls."

8

"Somebody"

One more night Grandma Deb suffered through sleeping in curlers. The first thing in the morning she shuffled down the stairs, made a peach shortcake, and did what she could toward the dinner preparations. Then, she made the toilsome climb back up the stairs to remove the curlers and comb out her hair. She wore a red-check housedress that day, and again, her stiff white oxfords. She looked like what she was: a farm woman, seventy-three years old, worn, stiffened by rheumatism, but anxious to do her duty.

When the dreaded "man from Washington" came, he looked to her like a farmboy. He wore blue Levis and a blue workshirt open at the chest. He was only twenty-two, but he looked even younger. He had a thrust of dark hair that, boylike, he frequently pushed back from his forehead.

They liked each other at once; they were "Son" and "Granny," two people with a kindred love. He told her how he loved the old songs, just as she did. He told her how he had gone with his father, John A. Lomax, to collect cowboy ballads. I don't think he told her that his father was the curator and he, Alan, was already assistant curator of the Archive of American Folk Song. I doubt that he mentioned that he was already coeditor of the major work *American Ballads and Folk Songs* (1934).

Nor did he tell her that he had left college because he was driven to collect these old songs that he feared were soon going to be forgotten. He appeared relaxed and working only for the joy of sharing the old songs with her.

So she told him about herself, and her songs. Word for word, it was the same version she had given me: the account of her life as she had self-constructed it years before: "My life is a Chinese puzzle," she said. "I can never get all the parts in their right place 'n' all, like where I lived an' at what times.

"An' I never sat down to learn a piece in my life. I jus' picked them up from hearing them."

He nodded and smiled, no questions asked.

Madeline came home with a big bag of groceries and welcomed Alan in her blunt, joking way: "If you're going to hang around here, young fellow, you'd better make yourself right at home. Nobody's got time to wait on you." So he did, even meandering out into the kitchen to get himself a drink of water later in the day.

Soon they were ready to begin. He formally asked her permission to record some of her songs. After she agreed, he went out to his car and lugged in the recording machine (which looked like an old-time victrola) and his own guitar. Again he asked permission and she, now trusting this man from Washington, led him down into "Art's cellar" where he attached his wires to the radio wires down there. Then they came back up to the first floor, to the front room. He brought a straight chair from the dining room for her and, without comment, placed his little standing mike beside it. She got him a hassock and an ashtray for his cigarette. He spread open my big notebook on the floor beside him, and they were ready to begin. I was enthralled by the entire process.

But when her hand touched the mike for the first time, she drew back in fright.

"I'm like the Irishman," she warned him. "I'm no singer at all, but I'm as good a whistler as ever puckered a lip."

"That's all right with me," he drawled, in his smooth Texas voice. "Do you know 'The False Lover'?"

"'Course I do!" And so they began.

Just as she had done with me, she recited each piece first. Then she tried to sing it for him, just as she had to Janet. But the intimacy with her "girls" was not there, and doing the double task under time pressure was very disconcerting to her. Alan would be nodding and smiling, focusing on her, but occasionally jotting some notes in my big scrapbook. This wasn't having fun with her girls; this was serious business.

Sometimes, after she sang a piece, he'd ask some questions: Where had she learned it? What did it mean? She didn't realize that his machine was recording the talk as well as the tune. Never once did she notice the sound of her own voice. She could never dream — nor could I — that decades later I could sit at my desk in California and hear her say to herself, "Oh, darn, I forgot," or "I'm not high enough. I must get that higher."

At times she seemed to push the tune to fit the words; in fact, she wanted to recite only the words. "Now I have to sing it, don't I?" she asked plaintively several times. But he waited — and she tried to comply.

I am glad that I stayed in the room that day since I was able to watch a professional folklorist in the early stages of his career. His questions brought from her many insightful comments that I had not heard — because I had never dared to ask. I had gotten him there, but, as I hear now, there were times when my presence was a deterrent; she would turn to me to rescue her, especially if she thought the piece was "in that book upstairs." But otherwise she had no connection with me, or with Ellen, or with any of the people who came and went in the little house that day. Only Alan was waited on: she fixed cushions behind him when he moved to sit on the floor, leaning against the radiator. Once she rubbed his back to ease the cramping.

Unfortunately she had been correct when she said she couldn't "sing worth a darn any more." Her voice was tired, old, and weak in the upper ranges. At the time, I thought that Alan was making talk just to give her a rest after a song. But now I hear definite patterns in his questions. He wanted to know the reaction of other people in the places where she had acquired these songs, how later audiences had received her singing, and what her own values were.

After she finished her first song, "The False Lover," she chuckled a little. "About making up to the cat and how she tried to fool him, her father, you know."

When he asked, "Where did you learn that?" she stressed again that she could not give a straight account of her early life, especially during the years when she was with the Stevensons. So he switched to the topic of their music making.

"This man that you were bound to, was he a good fiddler?"

"He played violin. She played second to him. We played for dances. Jus' around in the country, wherever we was at — "

"They played the guitar?"

"No. Jus' violin. For the fun of it, as I remember."

He wanted to know about the audience reaction when she sang. For example, about "Martha Decker," he asked, "Did you ever make anybody cry when you sang that song?"

Of course she responded that people had, but she showed that she had no pride in her own skill: "Many a time. Because she was an only child. Fourteen. An' she was the last of the tribe."

He probed further: "Did she make this death because she was a wicked person?"

"No. It was the river. No. The rain, see, it came down so fast."

She answered him by quoting lines from the poem itself. She did not believe in a God who would drown a young girl, no matter if she had been wicked. To her way of thinking, that would not have been a just God.

An unshakable faith in God was integral to Grandma Deb's view of life, and she accepted without question religious expressions in people's lives and in the lives of people in her songs. The outstanding example was, of course, this "Martha Decker," which was chiefly a religious dirge, stanza after stanza after stanza. Her emotion was genuine; Martha's death was one more instance of human mortality in a part of the country where, as a child, Jennie had seen Uncle Charley Hawkins cut off his own arm and "Dad" Stevenson die of apoplexy because the doctor could not climb "the terrible hill" in time to save him.

Her greatest dilemma was in performing "The House Carpenter." She waved her hand at Alan: she needed time to get out the story and all her feelings about it. He was content to wait. So there is a long section on the recording that profusely demonstrates how deeply she could get involved in "them old pieces."

"I'm all nervous again. I'm going to get it out and then we'll hafta re-sing it. See, I haven't got it right. Stop the machine. Stop the machine . . . It don't come in right, does it?"

Then, in a few minutes she started singing:

> I've come across the deep blue sea
> All for the love of thee.

She stopped and lapsed into a summary and commentary: "Then she goes with him. They go to sea and they're only two days out before she's on the railing and she's weeping and he comes up to her and he accuses her of being homesick for her house carpenter. And she says, 'I'm not homesick for my house carpenter but I'm lonesome for my little babe.' So they sailed three days, three days she sailed, and she went back to her house carpenter. It wound up all right.

"He put her off at a port somewheres. He must've done that because she wouldn't stay with him, have anything to do with him. After she realized what steps she had taken, she was frightened, see. And there is this part he came along when she was rocking her baby — it was an old-time house with a porch. I've seen the picture, y'know, with this little story when I was a kid. I can't tell where, either.

"An' he comes along, a fine-looking chap. He rides up to her and tells her how much he loves her and how pretty she is. Asked her all about what she was doing and she told him and he asks her to go along with him, see. He tells her what he would do for her and how much money and everything and it wound up, as I said. It's kinda sad in the beginning and the ending too, y'know. She didn't really love the house carpenter very much but she loved her baby. I guess he wasn't the one. See how it is? I was only a kid — but I used to think, 'Wasn't that mean of him to take her away from that little baby?' You know, I can always think back to them little things."

It was a very long day, six hours, but she persevered. At first there were some instances where she forgot whole stanzas; sometimes she put lines in different places from the order I had in my notes; sometimes she remembered parts that she had not thought of, not in years. There was no use trying to prompt her; she was lost if she thought she was singing wrong. Sometimes she would have to clear her throat when "the place like a lump" did fill up. She asked Ellen to get her some lemon water to sip.

Letting Ellen wait on her was such a reversal of all Grandma Deb ever did that I was startled into noticing the change in her. She was sitting up as straight as she could in that uncomfortable chair, her hands idle in her lap. Her eyes seemed to be watching everything around, but they were flat and unreflecting; she simply did not see any of us in 1938 Gloucester as she went back over her dramatic old pieces.

She now had the understanding that I had wanted to give her; for that day, in that room, she knew that she was a folksinger. What she showed, especially while they were recording the old pieces, was her great respect for the songs themselves. She seldom remembered where she had learned them; she did not understand some of the vocabulary and very few of the historical or geographic references, but each song itself was an intact "story." Any discrepancies in it were due, she felt, solely to her own lack of learning or failure of memory. The fault could never be in the song.

Her subdued mood lasted through lunch, where she sat quietly beside Alan. I had never seen her like this before. Madeline had prepared a nice meal, though she attempted to be offhand about the whole proceedings. After all, she seemed to be indicating, she too knew all these pieces; her mother had taught them to her when she was a child. I felt sure, however, that her casual style masked a real pride in her mother that day.

I wasn't so sure about my own feelings toward Alan: he ate his bacon with his fingers, something I had never seen a person do before. (My theories of table etiquette were Victorian hand-me-downs.) But at dinner, when the whole family was at home, his table manners were quite proper. And he joined in the conversation far more easily than I did.

In the afternoon session, a different Grandma Deb emerged. She had given him the serious "old, old pieces" from her "young years" as a folksinger. Now she was the girl who danced, sang, and "kidded" with the hired men. She released her tremendous sense of fun. There were some pieces that she'd been singing (or reciting) for over sixty years, yet she had never stopped laughing at them, for example, "The Cruel Wife," "Johnny Sands," and "Will the Weaver." Or did those chuckles always come after she sang them because she was enough of a performer to use laughter to get laughter back from her audience?

But at times she was a little reluctant. "Now I don't know much of this," she'd object. Or, "You don't want that."

Alan would try for "just the tune" or "as much as you can remember" of these songs, such as "When I Was Young and in My Prime."

"They're only old baby rhymes. Cute to sing to the little tots, y'know. But they shouldn't be put down. They don't belong in no book, like Kay wants." She was obviously trying to censor her material so that it would be proper for the kiddies.

Even when she sang "The Frog and the Mouse" she left out one stanza. He caught her on it. She replied that it was "naughty." Yet the lines were only "The Frog and Mouse they went to bed. They pulled the covers over their head."

I managed to get a few words with him. "She knows more naughty songs than I have been able to get."

"Give me half an hour alone with her," he said. "I bet you a dollar I'll get them."

"Done," I said. "She'll never sing them to a man."

Alan replied, "You girls go on upstairs now."

So Ellen and I went up to her room, like a pair of schoolgirls. We could hear Alan, in the living room, wooing Grandma Deb with his guitar and his own singing. Then a laugh and her voice very, very low.

At the end of a half hour I returned. Grandma Deb was standing by the front door exclaiming over some baby pictures that a neighbor woman had brought in.

"Did you ever see such a family for loving babies?" I said.

"All folksingers do. Pay me." Alan Lomax was sprawled out on the floor by his machine, quite relaxed, smoking a cigarette, grinning at me.

"What? She sang them for you?"

"Come down to Washington some time, and I'll play you some versions you never got."

"How did you do it?"

"Used my guitar. Played a few tunes I thought she'd know. Then I made some little jokes about the boys who forgot to leave at ten o'clock at night and had to slide down the rainspout. Do you know what she said when you and Ellen went upstairs?"

"No, what?"

"She was laughing at you. She said, 'Don't you suppose them two learned anything in high school?'"

I was disconcerted. Ellen and I were high-school teachers. Grandma Deb had sung to a strange man what she would never sing to us. And she was right: we would have been shocked, back then.

Said Alan: "She's salty. She's more honest than you two girls. She's had more than two beaux in her life. She knows lots and is very shrewd. She's a character. Wonderful! The book should be two-thirds about her, only one-third about the songs. Keep the personal touch."

When he was packing up his equipment, he said to Ellen, "She's the youngest singer living today that I've met who didn't learn her songs from books. She's totally in the oral tradition."

Then Pop came in to meet him, and the family persuaded him to sing for Alan also. He stood stiffly, facing all of us as we sat around the dining room table. He put one hand on the corner of the buffet as if it were the bar and he was facing the saloon full of "the boys," and rendered "My Dad's Dinner Pail." Alan pronounced it "grand."

"I wouldn't have missed seeing and hearing him for worlds. I'm heartbroken that my recorder is packed up," he told Madeline who, as always, was proud of her father.

To me, Alan added, "Gramp's a rogue!"

Grandma Deb brought him a glass of milk and another helping of the peach shortcake. Then came the time to say good-bye. He made the rounds, thanking each one of us in turn, in a most mannerly fashion. Grandma Deb went out on the porch with him, and they did a Romeo and Juliet scene, he, on the steps, reaching up for her hand.

"What shall I sing to you for good-night?" she asked.

"Don't worry. I'll be back. I loved your peach shortcake. But I bet you make a wonderful apple pie."

It was a gracious farewell. I don't think either of us ever expected him to return. Grandma Deb knew that she would have had very little more to give him; I knew that he had seen the fullness of my notes and the tunes that Janet had written. And he had added thirty-seven items to the archives.

In 1941, when I sent him some other ballads I had collected in Pennsylvania, he wrote to thank me and said, "We are so busy now, in so many different directions, it is beginning to seem fantastic to record just one person."

But Jennie Devlin had had her day. Alan, a vigorous young man, was nearly exhausted after six hours of such hard concentration. Even today I can hear, on the enhanced tapes, some hints of his attempt to hasten the slow progress of the recording. But while I sat there that day, pitying his fatigue, I never realized the tremendous energy that Grandma Deb was putting forth. All that long day, her good humor, patience, gentleness, and dignity never failed. Perhaps she may actually have been less tired than he because, for that one day, she had returned to what she was in the first fourteen years of her life: a singer for applause. She was a recognized folksinger. A man had come from Washington just to hear her. At seventy-three, she *was* Somebody.

For a short period, I was Somebody too. Alan's records went back to Washington and, later, there were thirty-seven entries of songs "by Jennie Devlin, Gloucester, N.J., recorded by Alan Lomax and Kay Dealy" listed in the *Check-List of Recorded Songs in the English Language in the Archive of American Folk Song to July, 1940*. I was a bit puffed up, too, when I saw myself identified in the introduction as one of the folklorists who had made "independent expeditions in the field." But the fact was that my career as a collector had to be limited because of my lack of a "musical ear." I accepted that fact around 1940. But it had been a grand trip through nineteenth-century song.

* * *

Unfortunately, the recording was not totally successful. Besides Grandma Deb's singing problems, Alan was still using an ancient machine. Worse still, the background noises were disruptive. Instead of chickens and pigs chorusing in the background as was heard in the recording of the southern folksinger, there was the clink of silverware as the table was laid, the wail of the neighbors' baby, the banging of the screen door, and the screech of an electric saw. A radio was turned on, then off. The telephone rang, cars started up in the street outside, and a truck crashed to a standstill. Feet marched up and down the stairs in the little house, and over all was the drone of planes slowing to land at the nearby Philadelphia airport.

How far away were the sounds in the basketmaker's cabin and the farmhouses where she had learned these songs in her early years. It was totally incongruous. I can guess at what she would have said if she had ever heard this background to her songs. It would be the same thing that she told me several times in our talks: "You've got to adapt yourself to the day. You may not approve, but you dasen't fall down on the job. Things ain't like they used to be, and there ain't no use pretendin' they are."

* * *

Sometimes the times run ahead of us. For a few years, I tried to make our work into a book, but I just could not get it right. I did two complete—and totally different—versions, but I was too swallowed up by all the research I had done, and my mind was never free from the "Child-and-other complex." Not seeing any way to publish such a hodgepodge of songs, her life story, and my own independent research, I put it aside.

Unfortunately I forgot Alan Lomax's advice, which he had given me when he was packing up his equipment and we were alone for a few minutes: "Modern folksongs are as important as old ones. All folksongs should be sufficiently collected so that they may be studied, and this race to collect special gems and then tie up the records, etc., is silly. We must show social conditions, not just songs. No one in America today can answer this question: 'What is the cultural effect of our folksongs?'"

I found this question when I returned to my old notes in more recent days. Now I understand it. I see Jennie Devlin as a total person living and singing in times far different from ours. To my surprise, when I took an early draft of this book to Alan Lomax in 1987, he added, "I still remember her, too."

✳ ✳ ✳

For me there was World War II, love, marriage, children, and a career. All these years, I felt some underlying guilt about having cheated Grandma Deb. I wanted to return her songs to her in a book that would give her the same pleasure she had experienced with Shoemaker's *Mountain Minstrelsy of Pennsylvania,* but I could never do it. Yet wherever I have lived all these years, the big crumbling scrapbooks, the file folders, and the album of warped records have been there also.

Only now have I understood what Alan Lomax meant that day: "The book should be two-thirds about her, only one-third about the songs." But the songs are inseparable from her life.

I always felt guilty for I thought I had stolen her songs, but actually I had validated and preserved them. She was still singing them after I left. They were as much hers as they had ever been, and after 1938 she was able to live with the memory of having sung them to an appreciative young man who treated her like Somebody. Her songs were safe in Washington, D.C.

She told Ellen that all she wanted, after that day, was "to live to see Kay get her book." This added to my guilt, but Ellen laughed, "That's how old people tell time. They always choose some special event and say they want to live until then. You know, like a grandchild's graduation or wedding." (Yes, I do know. I set those goals now myself.) But I do wish I had been able to produce the book for her to enjoy with me.

After Johnny died in January 1948, Grandma Deb began a slow retreat from memory and reality. Gradually she ceased doing housework and spent hours just rocking on the porch, speaking less and less.

In 1952, I took my two little girls for a visit, but she, who had so loved "the kiddies," took no notice of them—nor of me. Her daughter, Madeline, another good woman, took complete care of Grandma Deb now. She was dressed, as always, in a starched and ironed housedress. Her thin white hair was combed straight back into a small knot. Her deeply wrinkled skin still had that amazing fresh-scrubbed look. Her eyes stared straight ahead, ignoring us as she had that day when she sang for Alan Lomax.

She was seated in a chair by the side of her bed. She paid no attention at all when I came in and kissed her forehead. But I thought I heard some sound, as though she were humming to herself some secret tune, but not for me and my notebooks. Our time together had run out.

Her granddaughter Ellen, however, had a miraculous farewell later that same year. In 1992 she sent me this account of the visit to Grandma Deb she and her children had made:

"On the day we arrived I had taken Hank, 5, and Hilary, 9, in to see Grandma Deb in her room. I had kissed her and they had spoken and done the same. She sat, as she had for years, quietly, patiently, not unattentive but speechless and unresponsive at any apparent level. She could, when directed, walk, open her mouth to be fed, and watch wonderingly as we passed her door. She did not rock in her rocking chair nor show any signs of discomfort.

"Some years before, I had asked my brother, who had seen her the week before our conversation, 'How's Grandma Deb, Bud?' He'd answered, 'Everything's gone but her sweetness, Sis.'

"The morning after our arrival, after the children were dressed and ready for breakfast, I said, 'Run in and kiss Grandma Deb good morning.' 'Do I have to, Mother?' This from Hilary. 'No. Not if you don't want to. But it would please Grandma.' Tears welling in the eyes, 'I don't think I can. I'll say "Hi" to her when I pass her door.'

"Hank had streaked off as soon as my suggestion was made and was standing beside Grandma Deb's rocker, patting her arm and staring into her face.

"Day after day, he would interrupt his play and tell anyone within hearing, 'I have to go see if Grandma Deb is all right.' He'd be gone five or ten minutes at a time, standing beside her, patting her arm or holding her hand. Whether he talked to her as well, we never knew, for none of us thought to check on their time together in any way.

"About six weeks after we had been home, Hank rushed into the kitchen where my mother and I were getting dinner. 'Mother! Mother!

Does Grandma Deb know "Little Birdies in a Tree?"'" 'Of course, Hank. That's where I learned it.'

"'Well, come on! Come quick!—I think she's trying to sing it to me!' And Hank dashed out of the kitchen, back to Grandma's room.

"As I dried my hands and started to follow him, my mother said, 'He's imagining that. Mama hasn't said a word in years.'

"Nonetheless, I hurried on to Grandma's room. Hank was in his usual place; this time, he was singing to Grandma, whose eyes were fixed on him. I stood behind her chair, my hands on her shoulders. With tears streaming down my face, I joined Hank's singing:

> Little birdies in a tree, in a tree, in a tree . . .
> Little birdies in a tree
> Sing a song for Ha-a-a-ank.
> Sing about the flowers . . .

"We finished the song together. Did Grandma Deb hum and join us? Did she sing with us? Forty years later, I am not sure.

"I am sure of what happened next.

"I dried my eyes, kissed Hank as I passed him, and leaned over to kiss Grandma before I went back to the kitchen.

"For the first time since we had been home, Grandma's eyes brightened as they met mine. Her thin, patient lips smiled tentatively and burgeoned with sound just behind them. A light, high, unused voice emerged:

"'He's such a ni-i-ice b—.'

"And her lips subsided and the light in her eyes faded and she was as she had long been."

Part 2

THE SONGS

"My old pieces that I know."

9

The Singer

Over a span of approximately forty years, Grandma Deb selected many songs and then passed them on to others, her audiences from her childhood to her own old age. But she had not collected songs for others; she had needed them herself. They were an integral part of her self-definition. So, since she was never without a song, we cannot truly know her without knowing her "pieces." The music is a boon to singers, but the words, plus her own comments, take us back to the woman herself.

When she was young, she sang the oldest songs. When she was old, she learned some of the youngest. This gives us a key to arranging the songs themselves in chronological order, from old English and Scottish ballads to a concert hall success of 1896. Serendipitously, we can often couple her life history with the special events that gave birth to the songs, or, at least, brought them to the localities where our folk-singer claimed them as her part of the common heritage.

As we shift from one set of songs to another, we get many glimpses of Jennie from wondering child to wise old woman. Yet she had consistency. She learned about life from the songs; she brought her own experiences to interpreting the songs.

To give one striking instance: she selected a song that had been written eleven years *after* her own birth, a song that had originated in the popular tradition, that is, one "rendered" by professional singers in theaters and concert halls, places of paid admission. There were probably hundreds of such ballads, each written to catch the interest of its moment on the stage, and each, in turn, superseded by another "sensational" piece. Yet, when Jennie Devlin heard this one particular new song, she memorized it and taught it to her children. To her it was as much a mourning piece as was "Martha Decker," the crudely written folk ballad about the drowning of a young girl in Athens, Pennsylvania, in 1842.

The self-conscious ballad that so impressed her was "The Two Orphans [Brooklyn Theater Fire]." This was an account of a tragedy that bound together the people in Brooklyn in 1876, the time of the fire, but the song itself went, by some untraceable path, out of Brooklyn and New York City. Fragments of it were retained in folk memory from Iowa to New Mexico to Texas. Where she learned it, she had no idea, but the song fit her basic qualification for acceptance in her repertoire: it was "true." It dealt with *real* people. Reality was her touchstone. Even when she recited the music-hall sentimental favorites "The Gypsy's Warning" and "The Reply," she did not weep over the untimely death of a beautiful young woman. To her the words represented a serious dialogue between a woman and her former son-in-law.

Jennie's song-world is full of strong people and violent action. When I — not suspecting that folksongs could be found in New Jersey — requested a "song for my nephew," she sang "Little Birdies" to me. But she followed it at once with "The False Lover," the story of a girl who eloped and then used strategy to drown her false lover before he could do the same to her. This girl was only the first of many resolute females that Grandma Deb sang about.

Another example was Mary, who lived "On the Banks of Sweet Dundee." Mary mourned for her plowboy sweetheart after her uncle had this low-class boy killed, but when the squire, her uncle's approved choice, tried to force himself on her, she slew both the squire and her uncle.

Mary's story is one of a group of five songs that Grandma Deb knew, all of them celebrating robust damsels who had to contend with both unsympathetic guardians and fickle lovers. In this group, the winner should be "Evalina, the Female Sailor," who cut off her hair and went to sea with her love. Whether or not he came home with her, Grandma Deb's version does not tell us, but it is good to know that she did bring back "ten thousand pounds of gold."

When young women were jilted, they bore the indignity with valor if not with common sense. In an old ballad that she knew as "Lord Arnold's Daughter," a young knight told his sweetheart that his mother was forcing him to marry the Brown Girl (for her money). The jilted blonde got on her horse, rode to the wedding uninvited, and poked fun at the ugly bride. The Brown Girl (no gentle maiden herself) killed her rival, the bridegroom killed the bride, and then he gave instructions for a three-person grave before stabbing himself.

In the 1880s, a jilted woman's revenge took a different approach. "I'll Be All Smiles Tonight" described the hauteur that the proud maiden was determined to display at the ball so that those who saw her would believe she was a heartless flirt rather than a brokenhearted woman. The times changed but a woman's pride endured.

Grandma Deb always chuckled over the broadside poem of "Western Courtship," another of her stories of a jilting. Written about the same time as "I'll Be All Smiles Tonight," this poem told an opposite lesson about women. When the frustrated male kept his word and stayed on his own side of the bed on the night before their wedding, the girl jilted him in the morning.

Frequently there are examples — gleefully reported in some of her songs — of the enduring "battle of the sexes," but in her world there was more humor than hostility, and the winners were not always the women. In truth, some of those women were shrews.

However, in her tragic songs, the suffering of the children was acute because fathers were drunk or missing. Single mothers may have been betrayed by men, but they were faithful to their children. The only exception was the mother in the ballad of "The Cruel Mother," and that was a fairy tale, not "real."

As might be expected from a singer deprived of any knowledge of her own parents, Grandma Deb had selected several songs about children who were victims of tragedy: "Martha Decker," "Feathered Warblers," "The Orphan Child," and "Poor Jim the Newsboy." But as a "baby-woman," she was always on the alert for ways to teach "the kiddies," so she had a large collection of jokes, riddles, and nursery rhymes.

The vigorous, fun-loving part of her personality was evident as she sang her dance tunes, reminiscing about the happy occasions on the farm when she frolicked with other young people. From those farm days, apparently, also came those songs that definitely have a male point of view: the "bawdy" songs. It was men who sang these songs about sex, but Jennie Hess had heard them and learned them, and she did admit to thinking them "good fun." What is important, however, is that her songs were "naughty" but not "dirty." In each of these pieces — "Western Courtship," "Your Father and Your Mother, Love," "Little Ball of Yarn," "Long Fol-de-Rol," and "Some for the Girl" — one of the partners attempts to entice the other into lovemaking, without benefit of a wedding band. But they are all merry solicitations, full of the joys of sex.

What about other aspects of her life, such as patriotism and religion? I have some newspaper poems about George Washington that she probably had read to her fellow lodge members, the Shepherds, on presidential birthdays. The old patriotic hymn "Columbia, the Gem of the Ocean" had supplied the tune of the cautionary "Have Courage, My Boy, to Say No," but, by and large, patriotism was reserved for Memorial Day and the Fourth of July.

The hymns sung in church were not hers alone, so she never sang them to me, but she did recall the old hymn tunes to which the native ballads of "James Bird" and "Martha Decker" had been set. Many of her songs have references to God and Christianity; the sentiments were those of her times, but knowing her as I did, I had no doubt of her sincerity. The earliest evidence of this was her seeking out a missionary when she was a young girl herself, so that she could learn to sing "The Converted Indian Maid."

Grandma Deb's craving for knowledge of other women's lives becomes apparent in the group of American nineteenth-century song-stories she favored. These ten "American ballads," dating in time from the composition of "James Bird" to that of "Jesse James," deal with *real* people; most of the ballads are akin to obituaries, detailing the deaths as much as the lives of individuals. The significance to us today is that the ones she remembered best were all about women: "Young Charlotte," "Martha Decker," and "Miss Riot." Lillian, in the ballad of "The Old Indian," survived but she was banished to a distant island for her attempt at interracial love. These obscure women were companions to Jennie in her harsh early life.

There was one ballad about the death of a male; that one was her favorite song, "James Bird," but even in this instance she did not know the whole song. Johnny McDermott, who spent "Eight Years in Cherry Hill," was an Irishman whose story was recited in her husband's family; he was not one of her own. She knew only parts of the other ballads about men: the ones about the dying Californian, the Boston Burglar, Jim Fisk, and Jesse James.

Not only did Jennie Hess collect the songs that gave her comfort and some acquaintance with a wider world, but in later life, as Aunt Jennie or as Grandma Deb, she also used her repertoire as a vocabulary with which to comment on the moment as well as on the human condition. Conversely, her actual comments on the songs reveal a great deal of the woman herself. Fortunately we have her remarks made to Alan Lomax in 1938; many of these remarks and his responses are presented as dialogue in the following pages. Her other comments about her pieces have been copied from my old notebooks.

It should be noted that the words of all the songs that are printed *separate* from the music in the second half of this book are from my original work; any variations that Jennie sang to Lomax and any asides she made to him are added in brackets. The words as sung to Janet

Grimler — which are printed *directly beneath* the music, as accompany-
ing lyrics — show still other changes. Thus, it is possible to study differences in the words in three renditions: those given to me, to
Grimler, and to Lomax.

The songs that Grimler did not notate were transcribed from the
Lomax/Dealy tapes in 1986 by Alan DeVries. These are "The False
Lover," "Lady of York," "Long Fol-de-Rol," "Shanghai Rooster," and
"The Little Valley."

I asked Pamela Richman to make the songs available to modern
guitar players in place of the violinists who had accompanied Jennie
Hess when she was a little busker and later when she danced with
other farm people. The chords noted in all of the songs are her
contribution.

Alan Lomax recorded Jennie Devlin's songs in 1938 on two 78 rpm
records. The Lomax/Dealy recordings are described as "Library of
Congress, Music Division, Recording Laboratory." The two records
were processed on March 7, 1941, as nos. 298-301. Enhanced tapes,
which modulate some of the background noises, were made for me
from these records. These tapes are listed in the Library of Congress as
LWO 20300, AFS 1775-1777 and 1842-1845.

Despite vagaries of tune and text, both so natural in an old folksinger, I was impressed by Jennie's mastery of different tunes, so that
she could go over and over the music with Janet. Indeed, she could
even make some corrections as she sang, under such great pressure, to
the "man from Washington." I wondered at times if it was natural
talent or the training she had had in singing to the violins. As one of
her "heirs," I am glad to hand her pieces on to other song lovers.

The False Lover

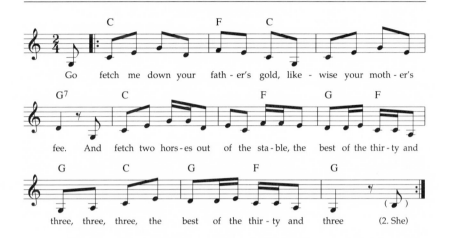

"Go fetch me down your father's gold,
Likewise your mother's fee.
And fetch two horses out of the stable,
The best of the thirty and three, three, three,
The best of the thirty and three."

She brought him down her father's gold,
Likewise her mother's fee.
She brought him two horses out of the stable,
The best of the thirty and three, three, three,
The best of the thirty and three.

She mounted upon her bonny brown,
And he the dapple gray.
They rode till they came to the merry green woods,
Three long hours before it was day, day, day,
Three long hours before it was day.

They rode till they came to the water's side
Where the lilies shone out so gay.
"For it's six kings' daughters I've drownded here,
And it's you the seventh shall be, be, be,
And it's you the seventh shall be.

"Take off your robes, your robes so fine,
And lay them down by me,
For I count your robes too rich and too costly

For to lie and to rot in the sea, sea, sea,
For to lie and to rot in the sea."

"If I'm to take off my robes so fine
And lay them down by thee,
O wheel about and turn clear round
With your eyes to the leaves of the tree, tree, tree,
With your eyes to the leaves of the tree.

"For an unrobed maid it is not fit,
For any human face for to see, see, see,
For any human face for to see."

He wheel-ed about and turned clear round
With his eyes to the leaves of the tree.
She stepped up to him so manfully
And plunged him into the sea, sea, sea,
And plunged him into the sea.

"Lie there, lie there, you false-hearted man,
Lie there, I tell unto thee.
For it's six kings' daughters you drownded here,
Just to keep you company, -ny, -ny,
Just to keep you company."

She mounted all on her bonny brown
And led the dapple gray.
She rode till she came to her father's door,
Three long hours before it was day, day, day,
Three long hours before it was day.

Then up spoke the pretty Poll-ee,
And unto Pauline did say,
"What's the matter, my pretty Pauline,
That you're out so long before day, day, day,
That you're out so long before day?"

"O, hold your tongue, my pretty par-rot
And tell no tales on me,
And gold shall be the lining of your cage,
And hang on the green willow tree, tree, tree,
And hang on the green willow tree."

Then up then spake the father dear
And unto the parrot did say,
"What's the matter, my pretty Poll-ee,

You prattle so long before day, day, day?
You prattle so long before day?"

"The cat came up to my cage door
And she tried to worry me,
And I was calling my pretty Pauline
To drive the old cat away, away, away,
To drive the old cat away."

Grandma Deb [chuckling]: "About making up to the cat and how she tried to fool him, her father, you know."

Alan Lomax: "Where did you learn that?"

Grandma Deb: "I dunno. Lots of them I could sing when I was little. I said to Kay, I've been to so many places, I couldn't tell you, the different places I've been in my young life. But whether I learned them this year or that year . . . more, I couldn't tell you. Ever since I could remember, I could sing that.

"I tell you about the violin and the second violin. I was bound out when I was somewhere between four and six years old, and, see, I was learned to do all them kind of things. And they moved around--he was a basketmaker and we wound up in Canada and all that . . ."

Her voice trailed off. Here, and in other comments she made during her day with Lomax, she seemed to be endeavoring to explain herself and her songs, hoping to give this young stranger whatever it was he needed, whatever he had come for.

Child 4: "Lady Isabel and the Elf Knight."

Lord Arnold's Daughter

Lord Arnold he rode to fair Eleanor's castle
And he knocked upon the ring.
There wasn't one so ready as fair Eleanor
To let Lord Arnold in.

"What news, what news?" fair Eleanor said.
"What news hast thou brought unto me?"
"I've come to bid thee to my wedding,
And that is sad news for thee."

"O, God forbid," fair Eleanor said,
"That such a thing should be done,
For I thought to have been the bride myself,
And thou would have been the bridegroom."

[Lord Arnold's mother forced the match because the Brown Girl was rich, but she sent Lord Arnold to tell fair Eleanor for fairness's sake. Then her mother tried to prevent her from attending the wedding, saying:]

"There never was three lovers sure
That sooner did depart."
[But Eleanor goes.]
And as she rode through every place
They took her to be some queen.

They rode till they come to Lord Arnold's castle,
And she knocked upon the ring.
There wasn't one so ready as Lord Arnold
To let fair Eleanor in.

He took her by her lily white hand,
He led her across the hall.
He sat her in the noblest chair,
Amongst the ladies all.

"Is this your bride?" fair Eleanor said.
"Methinks she looks wonderful brown.
When you might have had as fair a woman
As ever the sun shone on."

The Brown Girl had a little penknife
Which was both keen and sharp.
Betwixt the short rib and the long,
She pierced fair Eleanor's heart.

"O, God forbid," fair Eleanor said,
"That such a thing should be . . .
[She tells Lord Arnold]
For the blood is trickling to my knee."

Lord Arnold takes the Brown Girl.
He leads her across the hall.
He cut her head clear from her shoulder
And flung it against the wall.

"Go dig my grave both deep and wide
And lay fair Eleanor at my side,
And the Brown Girl at my feet."

"There never was three lovers sure
That sooner did depart."

Grandma Deb: "See how that was. Now her mother told her not to go to the wedding, but she would go anyhow. So her mother said,

> 'There never was three lovers sure
> That sooner did depart.'

"An' when fair Eleanor come there and said, 'You might have had as fair a woman as ever the sun shone on,' that meant she was light, see, and that made the Brown Girl jealous.

"Now, I can't think why it was called 'Lord Arnold's Daughter.' Maybe it could have been 'Lord Arnold's Mother' since she was the one . . ."

Alan Lomax: "But her mother told her not to go to the wedding . . ."

The chief puzzle here, obviously, is in Grandma Deb's strange title for this song, especially since there is no father mentioned in the story. Gran was puzzled by this herself. The only parallel I ever found was in one text Tristram Coffin reported as found in Iowa; in this version "Lord Thomas" is not the hero; he is the father of Eleanor.[1]

Kenneth S. Goldstein, however, suggested another hypothesis: "'Lord Arnold' is the name of the cuckolded husband in American versions of Child 81, with the ballad denouement involving the Lord cutting off his wife's head."[2] Since the two ballads share this gory ending, the names of the noble axe-wielders might have become confused in the memories of American folksingers. However, neither of these putative parallels can account for the word "Daughter" in Grandma Deb's song title. Other than this peculiarity, the ballad seems like other versions reported by collectors all over America.[3]

My personal amusement on finding this gory item in *Warner's Series: Forty-four Readings and Recitations* was great, since these selections were intended for school performances and the publishers boasted that they formed "a class of readings that can be approved by a refined taste and a cultivated judgement."[4]

Child 73: "Lord Thomas and Fair Annet."

1. Coffin, *British Traditional Ballad*, 68–70.
2. This information was transmitted to me verbally by Goldstein. This is also the case in all other instances of quotations or information from Goldstein, unless noted otherwise.
3. Leach, *Ballad Book*, 242–44.
4. Rice, *Warner's Series*, 8:1890.

Lady of York

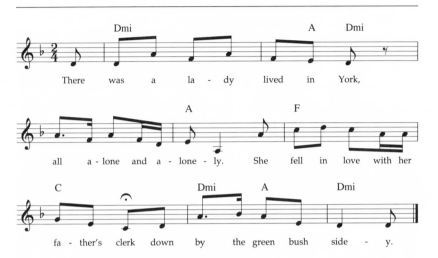

There was a lady lived in York,
All alone and a-lonely.
She fell in love with her father's clerk,
Down by the green bush side-y.

She had a garter long and straight,
All alone and a-lonely.
She tied them by their little hands and feet,
Down by the green bush side-y.

She had a penknife keen and sharp.
All alone and a-lonely.
She pierced them through their tender little hearts,
Down by the green bush side-y.

She buried them under the marble stone,
All alone and a-lonely,
And then she turned for to go home,
Down by the green bush side-y.

She's a-walking through her father's hall,
All alone and a-lonely,
And there she saw two little babes
Playing trip-trip and ball,
Down by the green bush side-y.

"O, babes, O, babes, if you were mine,
All alone and a-lonely,
I would dress you up in silks so fine,
Down by the green bush side-y."

"O, mother, dear mother, we once were thine,
All alone and a-lonely,
But you dressed us not in silks so fine,
Down by the green bush side-y.

"You had a garter long and straight,
All alone and a-lonely,
You had a pen-knife keen and sharp,
Down by the green bush side-y.

"You buried us under the marble stone,
All alone and a-lonely.
And then you turned for to go home,
Down by the green bush side-y.

"O, mother, dear mother, heaven is high,
All alone and a-lonely,
But that's the place you cannot fly,
Down by the green bush side-y.

"O, mother, dear mother, hell is low,
All alone and a-lonely,
And there's the place where you must go,
Down by the green bush side-y."

Alan Lomax: "Where is York?"
Grandma Deb: "Some county. Kay will tell you."
Alan Lomax: "A very sad song. Did that happen when you were a girl?"
Grandma Deb: "Well, I learned it that way. When I sang it, it always made me feel — any of these pieces — made me feel pensive. You know what I mean? Like 'Martha Decker' did. See, in olden times, son, when anything happened seriously like that, why there'd be a cabinet[1] from it. Lots of them pieces I could sing when I was little, better than I can sing them now."

This is a "revenant" ballad, that is, the characters come back to life. It is the only supernatural story that Jennie Devlin learned. She accepted the horror of babies returning from the grave to demand revenge; when children were wronged, justice had to be meted out in this world or the next.

What is noteworthy in her lengthy yet effective rendition is her omission of the stanzas in which the lady gives birth to the twins. Had Jennie repressed these stanzas? I think she might never have heard them. She might have been sheltered from such knowledge, as other children were. What was it that was being hidden from innocent girls? The fact that women can have babies even when they don't have husbands? Or that mothers can murder their own children?

Child 20: "The Cruel Mother" or "Down by the Greenwood Side."

1. "Cabinet" is the word on the tape. I have no clue about its meaning.

The House Carpenter

"Well met, well met, O my own true love,
Well met, well met, O," cries she.
"I've come across the deep blue sea,
And it's all for o'er the love of thee."

"If I am to give up my house carpenter,
And also my little baby,
What have you got to support me upon,
On the banks of the old Tennessee?"

"I have six ships a-sailing the sea,
And one hundred and ten
Of your own countrymen
For to be at your command."

[So she goes with him][1]

She picks up her dear little baby,
And kisses it one, two, and three,
Saying "Stay at home with your daddy,
While I go sailing on the sea."

The idea that a mother would abandon her child was shocking to Jennie, who had been a motherless child, but it was equally so to Almeda Riddle, a twentieth-century folksinger, who recalls how she herself reacted when her father sang "The House Carpenter's Wife": "I thought that was a terrible thing, this mother leaving that baby. That was the thing that struck me the worse, you know, the mother deserting the child. I wasn't too concerned with the husband at that time. I don't know, maybe I subconsciously felt he got what he deserved — he couldn't hold his wife. But the child, I thought that was terrible. . . . And when she drowned, I remember getting great satisfaction out of the thought that she got her just desserts. Even a child can have thoughts like that."[2]

Jennie Devlin's version lacks any retributory conclusion. She insists that her story is complete: the penitent parent did get back to her child. Was this the exact way she had learned it as a child, was the ending she gave us due to memory loss in old age, or was there was some psychological significance behind Jennie's omission? She insisted that the mother and child had to come together again.

Our singer herself added to the mystery, for she said: "There was two or three 'House Carpenters.'" I originally conjectured that Jennie must have seen broadsides of the older English variants of "James Harris" or "The Daemon Lover," but Kenneth S. Goldstein has located at least three different ballads with the title "The House Carpenter," not just three different versions of the same words and music. So we may take Jennie's words at face value.

Goldstein has also noted that the history of this ballad has been traced by David Harker, who found that it had been registered by Laurence Price in the 1680s.[3]

Child 243: "Daemon Lover," "James Harris."

1. After making this comment, she recited the following stanza.
2. Abrahams, *A Singer and Her Songs*, 9–10.
3. See Harker, "The Price You Pay."

Georgie

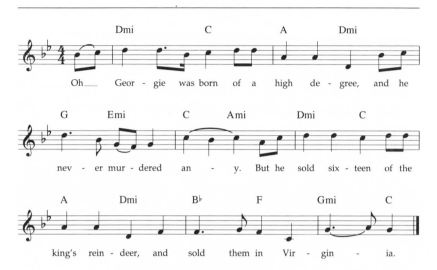

O Georgie was born of a high degree,
And he never murdered any.
But he stole sixteen of the king's reindeers
And sold them in Virginia.
[And stole them in Geneva]

O Georgie was hung with a silken cord,
Such cords they were not many,
For he who came from a high degree,
And was loved by royal Anna.

Grandma Deb: "He was one of them English bluebloods. She drove off in her carriage . . . she goes somewhere to get him a reprieve or whatever you call it. But she never did. All she ever got was this silken cord."

Alan Lomax: "Who was royal Anna, do you know?"

Grandma Deb: "She was his sweetheart. She was rich, I guess. She stuck up for him."

For no reason that I know, Grandma Deb substituted "Geneva" for "Virginia" on the day she sang this for Alan Lomax. Since neither place is the home of reindeer, it seems likely these animals were the king's "reign" or "royal" deer. My original guess seems confirmed by the lines in *Rise Up Singing*, the 1988 anthology of American folk music: "He stole sixteen of the king's royal deer / And he sold them in Bohenny."[1]

Child 209: "Geordie."

1. Blood-Patterson, ed., *Rise Up Singing*, 18.

Charlie

Charlie loves good cakes and ale,
Charlie loves good candy.
Charlie loves to kiss the girls,
When they're clean and handy.

Grandma Deb used to sing this to the kiddies, as she remembered: "I knew that tune, too. But not any words no more than these." However, she never sang it for me or for Janet Grimler.

This looks like a nursery rhyme, but in fact it has connections both with English royalty and with American play-party games. Carl Sandburg writes that "the indications are that the Charley of this song may be the Prince Charlie [sic] of Jacobite ballads; he figures in songs of the Scotch Highlanders who were harassed during Prince Charlie's time, left their homes to take up life in the Alleghenies and to spread westward."[1]

That this secret toast to "Prince Charlie" had been turned into a nursery rhyme was certainly apparent in the lines I myself chanted as a child: "Over the river, and over the sea, / And over the water to Charlie." I never knew who Charlie was, but I thought he must be an especially nice little boy.

1. Sandburg, *American Songbag*, 161.

On the Banks of Sweet Dundee

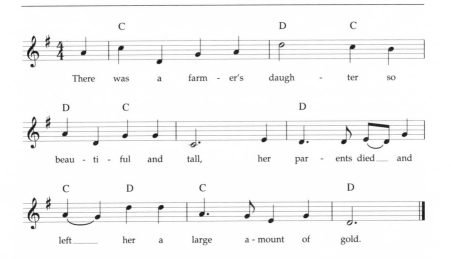

There was a farm - er's daugh - ter so
beau - ti - ful and tall, her par - ents died___ and
left___ her a large a - mount of gold.

There was a farmer's daughter,
So beautiful and tall,
Her parents died and left her
A large amount of gold.

She liv-ed with her uncle,
The cause of all his woe,
And now I must tell you,
[And now I'll tell you]
She proved his overthrow.

Her uncle had a plowboy
Which Mary loved so well,
And in her uncle's garden [garding],
The tales of love would tell.

Her uncle rose one morning,
All for to go away.
He knock-ed at the maiden's door,
And unto her did say —

"Arise, my pretty fair maid,
And a lady you shall be.
The squire is waiting
On the banks of sweet Dundee."

"I care not for your squire [squa-ar],
Your duke nor your lord, likewise.
My Willie's eyes appear to me
Like the diamonds in the skies."

"Begone, you unruly female,
You ne'er shall happy be,
For I'll bribe a press gang
And slay him or tie him to a tree.
[For it is my intentions for to tie him to a tree
Or bribe a press gang to slay him,]
On the banks of sweet Dundee."

The press gang came unruly
When he was all alone.
So manfully fought for liberty
Although 'twas ten to one.

His blood did flow in torrents,
"Pray kill me now," said he,
"For I die for the love of Mary,
On the banks of sweet Dundee."

As Mary was walking out one day,
Lamenting for her love,
The squire he came upon her,
All rivalled for to prove.
[A rival for to prove.]

He put his arms around her
And thought to throw her down,
When a pistol and a sword she spied
Beneath his morning gown.

The sword she picked out
And the pistol she used quite free.
She fired and killed the squire
On the banks of sweet Dundee.

Her uncle, hearing the noise,
He hastened to the ground,
Saying, "Since you've killed the squire,
In chains you shall be bound."

"Stand back, stand back, dear uncle.
Abounded I'll not be."
Her sword she drew, and her uncle slew,
On the banks of sweet Dundee.

A doctor being sent for,
A man of noted skill,
Also a lawyer,
To write him down his will.

He willed his gold to Mary,
She fought so manfully.
He closed his eyes, no more to rise,
On the banks of sweet Dundee.

Alan Lomax: "Why do you think he left her his gold when she'd just shot him?"

Grandma Deb: "I think . . . she must have been his brother's child. Or his sister's."

Alan Lomax: "But she had killed him."

Grandma Deb: "Well, he knew he was wrong, see? He killed her lover."

Alan Lomax: "Oh, the lover had been killed?"

Grandma Deb: "Yes, the plowboy. He was her lover. He was her sweetheart. And her uncle caught them in the garden. That's what made him angry. And the uncle didn't want her to marry him. He gets up this morning, knocks on her door, and talks to her. Tells her that he wants her to marry the squire. But she don't care for no squire nor nobody else. 'My Willie's eyes appear to me like the diamonds in the skies.'"

Alan Lomax: "So now the uncle's dying."

Grandma Deb: "And he's sorry. He knew, after all, that he'd been married himself an' . . . so he knew he was wrong and he left her his money."

Kidson has the text that I found is closest to Jennie Devlin's; he offers parallels with a British ballad of 1723 and a broadside of 1740.[1] The song was circulated throughout America, in songbooks such as *DeMarsan's American Songs and America*, and *DeMarsan's American Songs and Ballads, Patriotic, Popular, Etc. of 1860*. The Devlin version is one of five in the *Check-List*. Titles sometimes vary by omission of "On" or "Sweet."

Laws M 25.

1. Kidson, *Traditional Tunes*, 54.

The Banks of Claudy

'Twas in the month of May,
Down by young Florrie's garden,
Fair Betsy she did stray.

I own she did not know me,
I being in disguise,
"My pretty fair maid,
Why are you out so late?
What is that noise at yonder gate?"

[She's weeping. He tells her that Johnny is dead.]
And when she heard those dreadful news,
She fell into despair,
And wringing of her hands
And tearing of her hair.

Saying, "Since Johnny has gone and left me,
No other man I'll take.
All in some lonesome valley,
I will wander for his sake."

His heart is filled with joy
He could no longer stand.
He took her in his arms,
And said, "Nancy, I am that man.

"I am that false young man
Who you thought was slain.
Now since we've met on Claudy's banks,
We'll never part again."

Alan Lomax did not record Grandma Deb's version, but the *Check-List* names several other singers; there are some variations in the title. There is a version in the *Harvard College Collection of Broadsides Printed in the Nineteenth Century*. However, there have been different opinions about the song's roots. Scarborough said it is "a folk song familiar in Great Britain which has been parodied on the minstrel stage and circulated rather widely."[1] Belden considered it "an Irish adaptation";[2] and a good claim for an Irish origin was given by Kidson, who traced it to Bunting's *Ancient Music of Ireland* of 1848: "Bunting noted that [the song] came from a harper named Higgins in 1792."[3] D. K. Wilgus shared with me some of his own research on the influence of the Irish *aisling* form on English songwriters.[4]

There is a problem with this song: not only did Lomax not record it at all, Grimler took only the music. When I could not make the first lines sing together, I consulted W. D. Snodgrass, poet, musician, and friend. He demonstrated that the tune and words would fit if I used the first stanza from Kidson:

'Twas on one summer morning, all in the month of May,
Down in one flowery garden, fair Betsy did stray.
I overheard a damsel in sorrow to complain
All for her absent lover who plows the raging main.

"Betsy" was the name Grandma Deb used in the first stanza; she did not comment on the fact that the returned lover called his sweetheart "Nancy." If I had called her attention to this discrepancy she would have simply said, "That's just the way I remember it."

Laws N 40.

1. Scarborough, *Song Catcher*, 266.
2. Belden, *Ballads and Songs*, 154.
3. Kidson, *Traditional Tunes*, 89.
4. See Wilgus, "The *Aisling* and the Cowboy."

Tarry Trousers

As I walk - ed out one___ bright sum - mer

eve - ning, all for to take the air so___

clear, I ov - er - heard a moth - er, she was

talk - ing to___ her daugh - ter dear. "O, daugh - ter, dear

daugh - ter, I think you'd bet - ter mar - ry, not

live a sin - gle life an - y more." "Now,

moth - er, dear moth - er, I think I'd bet - ter

tar - ry, and wait for my charm - ing sail - or boy."

As I walk-ed out one bright summer's evening,
All for to take the air so clear,
I overheard a mother,
She was talking to her daughter dear.

"O, daughter, dear daughter,
I think you'd better marry,
Not live a single life any more."
"Now, mother, dear mother,
I think I'd better tarry,
And wait for my charming sailor boy."

"O, sailor boys you know are apt to wander.
In some far distant lands they will go.
And will leave you broken-hearted.
[All for to leave you broken-hearted.]
O, Nancy, dear, do hear to me."

"I suppose you had rather
I'd wedded to some farmer
Which I never could enjoy my own heart's delight.
But I'm for the boy that wears the starry trousers
Which 'pear to me like diamonds so bright."

[He comes back.]
She lays her head on her true lover's shoulder,
Tears down her cheeks like fountains did flow.
Crying, "Willie, dear Willie, why did you deceive me?
Why break the promise made a month ago?"

Grandma Deb: "She'd fallen for him, see. The mother had been trying to stop her. Now why? I often ask myself, 'What went wrong?' She wouldn't take the one her mother wanted. She waited for her sailor boy, 'that wears the starry trousers / which 'pear to me like diamonds so bright.' But then the last line says he made a promise 'just a month ago.'

"What made her cry on his shoulder? I'd try to figure out what went with it, but I couldn't get it. Now why?"

This was an English folksong. Alan Lomax marked it in my notebook as "Night Song," but I never found it under this title. I found two examples in English folksong collections,[1] and Kenneth S. Goldstein says he has found it "frequently in Canadian Maritime tradition, especially in Newfoundland." I found only one American version, and that is in Sharp's book from the southern Appalachians.[2] However, this source may explain the hero's desertion since it includes a stanza that is missing between Grandma Deb's fourth and fifth stanzas:

> "The boat's now a-sailing, the anchor's a-weighing,
> Time, time, heart and hand.
> So long as it be, I can no longer tarry,
> My darling little girl, don't you grieve after me."

1. Vaughan Williams, *Folk-Songs from the Eastern Counties.*
2. Sharp, *Folk Songs of England*, 2:6.

Evalina, the Female Sailor

Ev - a - li - na sat on the ver - an - da,_____ Look - ing
out on the sea____ so cold._____ There she
saw____ her charm - ing young sail - or,_____ Her
sail - or so true and so bold._____ "I'll
cut off my beau - ti - ful locks, love. I'll
put on a jack - et of blue._____ I'll
sail____ a - cross the wide o - cean____ a -
long with my sail - or so true."_____

> Evalina sat on the veranda,
> Looking out on the sea so cold.
> There she saw her charming young sailor,
> Her sailor so brave and so bold.

> "I'll cut off my beautiful locks, love.
> I'll put on a jacket of blue.
> I'll sail across the wide ocean.
> Along with my sailor so true."

> Three long years she served him faithfully,
> The girl in the jacket of blue.
> She returned to her father and mother,
> With ten thousand pounds in gold.

Grandma Deb: "It's a waltz tune. It doesn't say what happened to him, but I guess it turned out all right . . .

"There's another 'Evalina,' but it's dirty:

> Evalina and I one night went walking in June,
> We walked all along by the light of the moon.

"Then there's some part like 'Evalina, she cried . . . and as she laughed. . . .' She got this baby by him, but I don't remember more about that 'Evalina.'"[1]

This is probably a British folksong. The *Check-List* mentions two called "Evaline," but I find no real mate for this song, and Alan Lomax did not record it. Of course there is a long tradition of the girl who disguises herself as a boy for love's sake and goes off to sea. Belden links all such songs with the Warrior Maiden archetype, with its limitless permutations and combinations.[2] The disguised maiden could also have been an Irish heroine, a descendant of the pseudo-aisling type, as described by Wilgus.[3]

What is this song, really, with its capitalistic conclusion? It certainly looks American in the beginning, with the girl on the veranda, chatting with her sweetheart. But in the end she brings home British coin of the realm, not the sweetheart. How many stories were stitched together here?

1. According to Cray, *Erotic Muse*, 125, there is a "Sweet Evalina" in Randolph's "Unprintable" manuscript, 290–12.
2. Belden, *Ballads and Songs*, 171.
3. Wilgus, "The *Aisling* and the Cowboy," 292.

My Father Was a Spanish Merchant

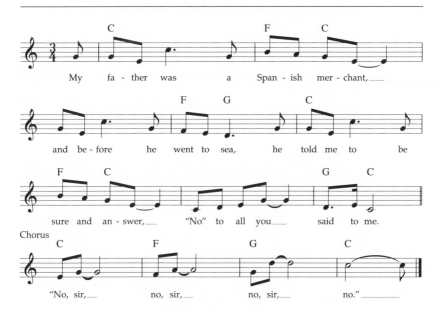

My father was a Spanish merchant,
And before he went to sea,
He told me to be sure and answer,
'No,' to all you said to me."

CHORUS:
"No, Sir. No, Sir. No, Sir. No."

"If when walking in the garden,
Plucking flowers all wet with dew,
Tell me, would you be offended,
If I walked and talked with you?"

CHORUS

"If, when walking in the garden,
I should ask you to be mine,
And should tell you that I loved you,
Would you then my heart decline?"

CHORUS

Randolph notes that this is a "Courting Song, goes back to 17th century."[1] Usual titles for this are "No, John, No" or (as in the refrain here) "No, Sir, No."

This song was popular on the concert stage, from Vauxhall Gardens to the American concert stage and to amateur singing groups. I well remember my father, a baritone soloist, singing it in the early 1920s in Philadelphia. Folksong collectors found this "jaunty little piece"[2] all over the United States, from New England, to Iowa, to Texas. In 1988, it was still in print, an entertaining memory from years ago.[3] Yet the song also has a shady past. According to Kenneth S. Goldstein, "Cecil Sharp, who collected it both in England and the United States, knew it as a bawdy song which he found necessary to bowdlerize before he would publish it."

1. Randolph, *Ozark Folksongs*, 3:184–85.
2. Korson, *Pennsylvania Songs*, 50–51.
3. Blood-Patterson, ed., *Rise Up Singing*, 126.

The Butcher's Boy

In Jersey City where I did dwell,
The Butcher's Boy I loved so well.
He courted me both night and day.
He courted my young heart away.

I used to wear my aprons low.
He followed me through frost and snow.
But now I wear them to my chin.
He oft passes by, but never calls in.

Grandma Deb: "You know, that means she's goin' to have a baby. She don't have no waist no more. There's something, too, about diggin' her grave because he's broken her heart."

Few of the "Butcher's Boy" songs contain Jennie Devlin's terse description about pregnancy: "I used to wear my aprons low . . . but now I wear them to my chin." Belden calls this the "apron-high motif,"[1] but even his examples subordinate the facts about the unwanted pregnancy in order to emphasize the treachery of the male. Why did Jennie Devlin not use the more common motif of the rich girl who steals the weak-kneed boy from the poor girl? Perhaps this is the way the song was passed on to her, but there is always the possibility that her own observations—and Aunt Eva's warnings about the seduction and abandonment of poor girls by rich boys—may have conditioned her memory. Would that real butcher's boy, who wanted to court her when she was a girl in Wellsville, have been as cowardly as this if he had made her pregnant? Grandma Deb's version was a strong warning against losing your character.

Laws P 24.

1. Belden, *Ballads and Songs*, 201–7.

The Old Oaken Chest

Grandma Deb: "That's another sad one. Yes, I usta know it. She was jus' married and they was playin' hide and seek. . . . But they never found her. Years 'n' years later, somebody opened up this old chest and there were her bones . . . and her wedding dress."

This is Jennie's recollection of a British broadside ballad that was made into an early nineteenth-century American song. It appeared in the *National Temperance Songster of 1855* and other songbooks. Helen K. Johnson, who gives it as "The Mistletoe Bough," traced it back to one "Thomas Haynes Bayly, founded on a story by Samuel Rogers, about an Italian girl of illustrious parentage who was wedded to a noble youth."[1] Once more a European aristocrat was turned into a middle-class American character.[2]

Laws P 21.

1. Johnson, *Our Familiar Songs*, 299–300.
2. "The Old Oaken Chest" also appeared in the following songsters: *Beadle's Songs of the Olden Time* (New York, 1863); *Delaney's Song Book No. 7* (New York, n.d.); *Wehman's Song Book No. 3* (New York, n.d.); *DeMarsan's Singer's Journal No. 16* (New York, n.d).

Mary of the Wild Moor

"Oh, father, dear father, come down.
Come down and open the door.
For the child in my arms it will perish and die,
By the wind that blows o'er the wild moor."

Grandma Deb: "This fellow that she went away with was untrue to her. And her father must've been deaf. I seen a picture of this once and it showed her an' she was wrapped in a plaid shawl. She kep' the baby warm in this shawl, see, though she froze herself."

When the music was being notated, the tune to this very popular song was so familiar to all of us[1] that Janet Grimler didn't bother to take it down — and now I don't remember it. Nor did I take the words, because I wouldn't let Grandma Deb sing it relying on Shoemaker's book.[2] Yet she did know how to sing it; she knew most of the words.[3] I should have allowed her a little time to read and recall it.

Laws P 21.

1. Leach, *Ballad Book*, 733.
2. Shoemaker, *Mountain Minstrelsy of Pennsylvania*, 98.
3. Some songsters that printed the words were: *DeMarsan's Singer's Journal No. 1* (New York, n.d.); *Wehman's Song Book No. 28* (New York, n.d.); *Delaney's Song Book No. 2* (New York, n.d.); *Beadle's Dime Song Book* (New York, 1859); *Beadle's Pocket Songster No. 4* (New York, 1866).

Bless the Boat That [First] Brought Me Over

I have no record that "Bless the Boat" ever became part of American song lore, especially since neither Johnny nor Jennie Devlin ever sang it, to my knowledge. But the song was certainly part of the Anglo-Irish tradition and was known to some immigrants who successfully made the trip to America. The expression "Bless the boat that brought me over" was in frequent use among all the Devlin family.

D. K. Wilgus collected several versions of the original comic song. They all tell of the Irishman who goes to seek a better life in England or Scotland, but his adventures, especially seasickness, are so unpleasant that he is happy to return to Ireland.[1]

1. Wilgus, interview, UCLA, April 13, 1989.

The True Paddy's Son

Eighteen, be gobs, I was diggin' up the land,
With my brogues upon my feet,
And the spade unto my hand.
I off with my brogues,
And shook hands with my spade,
And I'm off to the war
Like a dashing young blade.

CHORUS:
Mush-a-too uden do,
Sing wack fol-la-lay,
Mush-a hi eiten toddy,
Mush-a-too uden do.

The first thing they gave me was an old blue coat
With twenty-four Irish buckles
To buckle up my throat.
The next thing they gave me,
And says I, "What is that?"
And, be gobs, it is a feather
For to cock up in my hat.

CHORUS

The next thing they gave me was an old white horse,
All saddled and all bridled
With my two legs across.
I off with the saddle
And shook hands with the bridle,
And the monkey jumped the straddle
And I rode him to the devil.

CHORUS

Nine years and it's over
And thank God it wasn't ten!
We'll all go back to Ireland
Diggin' praties again.
To hell with the country
And the devil with the king,
We'll all go back to Ireland
Diggin' praties again.

CHORUS

Grandma Deb: "People'll think I've gone nuts for sure! I can't say all them bad words!" She meant "hell" and "devil" in the last stanza. But of course she did say them, after the ladylike protest.

Shoemaker, like Grandma Deb, called this "The True Paddy's Son,"[1] and both were correct, although many American versions give "Song." In the Child Manuscript Collection at Harvard, it was "Son," referring to the "wild Irishman" who fought for England but was very, very glad to get back to Ireland.[2]

Mellinger Henry, in a letter to me in 1938, recommended the song under the title "Here's to All My Cocks and Hens," which was an English folksong.[3] Cecil Sharp called it specifically "an Irish song of the Napoleonic wars."[4]

Typical of the taming down of the song is the title of one American version, "The Boy on the Land." G. Malcolm Laws, Jr., lists it as "True Paddy's Song," with the alternate title of "The Kerry Recruit."[5] In Laws's song the country boy is afraid of shooting for fear that he himself will get shot. How unlike our wild Irishman, who took off the saddle and rode "to the devil." It is the vehemence in the last stanza that sets Jennie Devlin's song apart from any others I have found. I suspect she learned it from her Irish in-laws.

"Praties" are potatoes, and a "brogue" is a rude kind of homemade shoe, generally made of untanned hide, worn by Irish peasants.

Laws J 8.

1. Shoemaker, *Mountain Minstrelsy of Pennsylvania*, 225.
2. Child Manuscript Collection, Harvard College Library.
3. See Williams, *Folk Songs of the Upper Thames*, 284.
4. Sharp, *English Folk Songs*, 228.
5. Laws, *American Balladry*, 132.

Rock the Cradle, John

O, rock the cradle, John,
O, rock the cradle, John.
There's many a man
Rocks another man's child
When he thinks he's rocking his own.

This was a recitation. Alan Lomax recorded it the day he came to meet Grandma Deb. I found no other in the *Check-List*. "Rocke the Cradle, John" was licensed by Laurence Price in 1631, thus giving it a legal English origin. What Grandma Deb recited was only a fragment; the words of the entire poem are in *Delaney's Song Book No. 11.*[1] However, the American chorus has a significantly different ending:

Rock the cradle, John,
Rock the cradle, John.
An old man married
Had better be buried
Than rocking the cradle alone.

1. A copy of the recitation with the citation was sent to me by a librarian, New York Public Library, August 3, 1938.

Rocking the Baby to Sleep

One night af - ter rock - ing the ba - by to sleep, I took a short walk down the street. And there to my sur - prise I saw with my eyes, my wife and a sol - dier six feet. Hee - lee - ha, le ho, lee, hush - a - bye ba - by, toss - ing the ba - by ev - er so high. Hee - lee - ha, le ho, lee, hush - a - bye ba - by, toss - ing the ba - by ev - er so high.

(Spoken:) O, show me the man
Who never has had
O, the dear little baby boy.

(Sung:) One night after rocking the baby to sleep,
I took a short walk down the street.
And there, to my surprise,
I saw with my eyes,
My wife and a soldier six feet.

CHORUS:
Hee-lee-ha, le ho, lee,
Hush-a-bye, baby,
Tossing the ba-a-by ever so high.
Hee-lee-ha, le ho, lee,
(Or: "Hee-lee, hay lee, ho-lee")
Hush-a-bye, baby,
Tossing the ba-by ever so high.

When first I saw them,
I really grew wild.
When I passed them, I gave them the smile.
Says I, "You've been hugging and kissing in fun,
While I have been rocking your baby to sleep."
["The while I've been rocking your baby to sleep."]

CHORUS

Grandma Deb: "The chorus is a 'grand right and left.'"

This was an Irish comic song made into a dance tune. Grandma Deb sang this for Alan Lomax immediately after reciting "Rock the Cradle, John." At that time, Lomax wrote in my notebook: "A popular song to be found in songsters. 'Rocking the Baby to Sleep.'" Then in 1960, he published the cowboy song "Run Along, You Little Dogies," with an unexpected chorus:

Hush-le-ci-ola, little baby, lie easy
Who's your real father may never be known.
O it's weeping, wailing, rocking the cradle.
And tending a baby that's none of your own.

Lomax believed that this totally divergent chorus might have crept in from an Irish song, "The Old Man's Lament," which had circulated widely on broadsides.[1]

Other American collectors have titles such as "Rock All the Babies to Sleep" or "Rock the Dear Baby to Sleep," but they are without music.[2] Perhaps all of these are variants of one basic text that changed its wording as it changed locale.

Another fascinating part of the history of this folksong is its hint of a connection between dance and play-party tradition. Grandma Deb's own directions show that she and her friends sang and danced to it. She never used the term "play-party," but a clue to this treatment was offered by Bertrand Bronson: "Watch for repetition of 'nonsense words' in a ballad as being an indication of 'play-party tradition.'"[3] Randolph includes an Ozark version of "Rock All Our Babies to Sleep" as a "play-party" song.[4] This would explain the rambunctious direction in Grandma Deb's memory to "toss the baby ever so high."

1. Lomax, *Folk Songs of North America*, 372–75.
2. Leach and Glassie list both titles among folksongs still current in 1973 (*Guide for Collectors*, 13).
3. Bronson, *The Ballad as Song*, 45.
4. Randolph, *Ozark Folksongs*, 3:117–19.

Will the Weaver

"Moth - er, moth - er, I am mar - ried, O, that long - er I had tar - ried. For my wife she does de - clare, that the bree - ches she will wear."

"Mother, mother, I am married,
O, that longer I had tarried
For my wife she does declare
That the breeches she will wear."

"Son, O, son, what is the matter?
Does the daughter scold or flatter
[Does the daughter fawn or flatter]
Or is she a-gad around?
[Or is she a-gadding round]
Tell, O, tell, my darling son."

"She is like a roving riot.
She is bad as any pirate,
At the tavern with her crew,
Willy and the Big John, too."

"Go home and give your darling wife her due,
[Go give your darling wife her due]
And let me hear no more from you."
Home he went like wandered rages
And he rapped on the door like thunder.

"Who is there?" the weaver cried.
"It is my husband. You must hide."

[So he goes up the chimney. The husband builds a roaring fire. The smoke came pouring out . . . When the weaver gets home, his wife asks him why he's so black . . .]

> "I met with robbers in the woods,
> They blacked my eyes and stole my goods."

Grandma Deb: "It's awful cute towards the end. Her husband builds a roaring fire . . . [chuckles] and then the smoke comes out!"

This comic folksong is of British origin. That twentieth-century singers were far from grasping all the fun of the old English story was demonstrated when Grandma Deb's neighbor, Mrs. Shindle, explained to me that "a chimney sweep is some kind of a bird."

Shoemaker's Pennsylvania version was much closer to Grandma Deb's than any other I found, but, like all the others, it lacked those two last lines that Grandma Deb thought were the funniest part of the whole story. She never failed to chuckle over the fact that Will escaped from the cuckolded husband only to face the justifiable ire of his own wife.

Laws Q 9.

1. Laws, *American Balladry,* 277.

Billy Boy

O, where have you been, Bil - ly Boy, Bil - ly Boy? O,
where have you been, charm - ing Bil - ly?__ I've__ been to see my wife, She's the
joy of my life, She's a young thing and can't leave her mom - my.__

"O, where have you been, Billy Boy, Billy Boy?
O, where have you been, charming Billy?"
"I've been to see my wife,
She's the joy of my life,
But she's a young thing and can't leave her mommy."

"Can she make a cherry pie, Billy Boy, Billy Boy?
Can she make a cherry pie, charming Billy?"
"Yes, she can bake a cherry pie,
Quick as cat can wink an eye,
But she's a young thing and can't leave her mommy."

"Can she make a feather bed, Billy Boy, Billy Boy?
Can she make a feather bed, charming Billy?"
"She can make a feather bed
Quick as cat can shake her head,
But she's a young thing and can't leave her mommy."

"Can she make your wedding shirt, Billy Boy, Billy Boy?
Can she make your wedding shirt, charming Billy?"
"She can make a wedding shirt,
She can do it in a jerk,
But she's a young thing and can't leave her mommy."

"How old is she, Billy Boy, Billy Boy?
How old is she, charming Billy?"
"Twice six, twice seven,
Twice twenty and eleven,
But she's a young thing and can't leave her mommy."

The whole family loved this song. Grandpa Devlin sang it along with Grandma Deb, and I could hear snatches of the others singing it in other parts of the house the night she gave the song to me.

This is an old English nursery song.[1] It was very popular all over America. There are nineteen singers listed in the *Check-List*.[2] Randolph has seven versions from the Ozarks, but Brown tops all others by reporting forty-seven different texts collected in North Carolina.[3]

1. Randolph, *Ozark Folksongs*, 1:391–93.
2. Scarborough has three pages of tunes in the Appendix to *A Song Catcher in the Southern Mountains*.
3. Brown, *Frank C. Brown Collection*, 3:155–69.

The Scolding Wife

Too lean, too raw, too roast,
I always am complaining.
I do find fault with everything,
Although it's my own providing.

These four lines were frequently quoted by Grandma Deb, who disapproved of chronic fault-finders. I found no other American imports, but there
were some worthy ancestors in Great Britain. The entire song was treated in
D'Urfey's Pills, including a short humorous song by Robert Burns, written for
Johnson's *Scots Musical Museum.* Burns titled it "The Joyful Widower" and
adapted it to the air of "Maggie Lauder."[1] Burns's third stanza is very similar to
the one that Grandma Deb quoted. This stanza also appeared as a complete
poem without a tune, in a broadside called "The Scold,"[2] and as "The Scolding
Wife," with music, in 1869.[3]

1. D'Urfey, Thomas, ed., *Wit and Mirth: or Pills to Purge Melancholy* (usually referred to as
   D'Urfey's Pills).
2. No. 33 in a series, *The Charms of Melody, or Siren Melody,* published in Dublin, n.d.
3. *A Pedlar's Pack of Ballads and Songs* (Edinburgh: William Patter, 1869).

The Cruel Wife

There was an old woman in Slab City
A woman as I've heard tell,
She loved her husband dearly
But another man twice as well.

She went into the doctor's
To see if she could find
O, something or other
That would make the old man blind.

He said, "You take three marrow bones,
And make him take them all.
I bet you a yearling heifer
That he can't see you at all."

[And that's what she did.]

She got three marrow bones.
She made him take them all.

"O, dear," said he, "you're such a darling wife,
But I can't see you at all."

Said he, "Now I would drown myself,
If I only knew the way."
"O, dear," said she, "I'll lead you there,
For fear you'll go astray."

She took him by the hand
And led him to the shore,
"O, dear," said he, "You're such a darling wife,
You'll have to push me o'er."

She stepped three paces back
That she might take a spring.
He stepped aside so gently
That headlong she went in.

And when the old woman came up,
She hollered as loud as she could bawl.
"O, dear," said he, "You're such a darling wife,
I can't see you at all."

The old man was so tenderhearted,
For fear that she might swim,
He up with a great big hickory pole
And he pushed her farther in.

And now my poem's ended,
I'll not sing any more,
But wasn't she a great big fool,
She didn't swim ashore?

Grandma Deb could never sing the stanza beginning "The old man was so tenderhearted" without having to stop to laugh. She'd laugh again when she finished the song. "She didn't swim ashore, see, because he had this long pole!"

Lomax listed this song as "Wife of Kelso" in the *Check-List*, and so Laws lists it in his study of the American loci, when he cites a singer in "New Jersey."[1] Scarborough was the only other person I have found who called it "A Cruel Wife."[2] There are broadsides (especially some in the Child Collection, vol. 2) from Ireland and England, but in America, like many other imports, it was transformed into a play-party song.[3]

Laws Q 2.

1. Laws, *American Balladry*, 274. The singer, of course, was Jennie Devlin.
2. Scarborough, *Song Catcher*, 239.
3. Brown, *Frank C. Brown Collection*, 2:450.

Johnny Sands

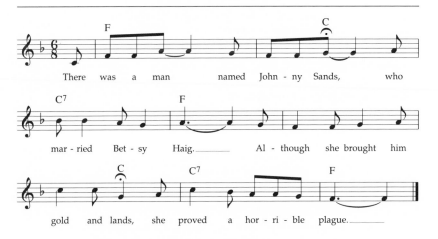

There was a man named Johnny Sands,
Who married Betty Haig.
Although she brought him gold and lands,
She proved a horrible plague.

O, my, she was a scolding wife,
Full of her capers, whims.
He said that he was tired of life,
[Says he that he was tired of life]
And she was tired of him.

"I'll drown myself. If I the courage lack,
And try to save my life,
Pray tie my hands behind my back."
"I will," replied his wife.

She tied them fast, as you may think,
And when securely done,
"Now stand," says she, "upon the brink,
And I'll prepare to run."

So down the hill his loving bride
Now ran with all her force
To push him in.
He stepped aside,
And she fell in, of course.

> O, splashing, dashing, like a fish,
> "O, save me, Johnny Sands."
> "I can't, my dear, if I but would
> For you have tied my hands."

Grandma Deb: "This is a parody of 'The Cruel Wife.'"

Alan Lomax: "Did you recite that when you were a girl?"

Grandma Deb: "Well, like I say—yes. I had some lodges in my later years—you know, when you go to different lodges, you are called on. So during the meeting, sometimes they are arguing, and I'll think, 'I'll just sing 'em that and that'll fix their feet.'

"You know, you have to give them something educational an' interesting. I don't sing them any more. I just recite them, as I said."

This is an American folk ballad.[1] Sheet music was published by Oliver Ditson in 1842, with John Sinclair given as the composer.[2] It was enormously successful. It appeared as a broadside in 1855,[3] and also in at least twenty different songsters. Kittredge noted that "though founded on a folk tale, it is literary and hardly older than the '40s of the nineteenth century, and its extraordinary currency is due to its having been sung by the Hutchinsons, the Continental Vocalists, and other singing troupes of that time."[4]

Grandma Deb insisted that "Johnny Sands" was a parody of "The Cruel Wife." The two sets of words she sang and the two different tunes, which I have reproduced here, prove that she did know two quite separate versions, and that the one she called "the parody" was, indeed, younger than "The Cruel Wife." Belden, Brewster, Brown, Eddy, Pound, Randolph, and Warner do not distinguish the pair sharply. Laws makes the correct separation, and his citations prove which one was the British and which the popular American version.[5]

Jennie probably learned "The Cruel Wife" during her early years with the Stevensons and only encountered "Johnny Sands" later in the replays she heard of music hall favorites.

Laws Q 3.

1. Harvard College Library broadside #25254.10.5. Also listed as one of the "50 Old American Songs (1759–1858) in the Harris Collection," Brown University Library.
2. Sheet music in Library of Congress, which I found in 1937–38.
3. My old note reads: "By J. A. Johnson, song publisher of Philadelphia and by J. Andrews, New York, circa 1855."
4. *Journal of American Folklore* 25:12.
5. There are twenty songbooks and songsters pertaining to these two songs listed in the *Journal of American Folklore* 35:385. Laws, *American Balladry*, 274.

The Frog and the Mouse

Mr. Frog he lived in a well, lo, linktum laddy-o.
Mr. Frog he lived in a well, lo, linktum-lo.
Mr. Frog he lived in a well,
Missus Mouse, she lived in a mill,
Lo, lo, lo, lo, lo, linktum laddy-o-day.

Mr. Frog a-wooing came, lo, linktum laddy-o.
Mr. Frog a-wooing came, lo, linktum-lo.
Mr. Frog a-wooing came,
He took Miss Mouse upon his knee,
Lo, lo, lo, lo, lo, linktum laddy-o-day.

"I will have you, if you'll have me, lo, linktum laddy-o.
["If I'll have you, will you have me?"]
I will have you, if you'll have me, lo, linktum-lo.
I will have you, if you'll have me."
But trip and bit was all he got.
Lo, lo, lo, lo, lo, linktum laddy-o-day.

Mr. Rat came home at noon, lo, linktum laddy-o.
Mr. Rat came home at noon, lo, linktum-lo.
Mr. Rat came home at noon,

"Who's been here since I've been gone?"
Lo, lo, lo, lo, lo, linktum laddy-o-day.

"There's been a worthy gentleman, lo, linktum laddy-o.
There's been a worthy gentleman, lo, linktum laddy-o.
There's been a worthy gentleman,
If I'll have him, he will have me."
Lo, lo, lo, lo, lo, linktum laddy-o-day.

Mr. Rat he 'greed to that, lo, linktum laddy-o.
Mr. Rat he 'greed to that, lo, linktum-lo.
Mr. Rat he 'greed to that,
And Parson Bet he tied the knot.
Lo, lo, lo, lo, lo, linktum laddy-o-day.

The mouse and frog they went to bed, lo, linktum laddy-o.
The mouse and frog they went to bed, lo, linktum-lo.
The mouse and frog they went to bed.
They pulled the covers over their head.
Lo, lo, lo, lo, lo, linktum laddy-o-day.

Just then the cat came out on the wall, lo, linktum laddy-o.
Just then the cat came out on the wall, lo, linktum-lo.
Just then the cat came out on the wall,
And scat! the kittens will have you all.
["And scat! you hussy, I'll have you all."]
Lo, lo, lo, lo, lo, linktum laddy-o-day.

Variant lines in this song are as they were recorded by Lomax.

Grandma Deb: "Now if that ain't jus' a kid's piece to sing to the babies when you put them to sleep. If that ain't jus' silly!

"There was another song, 'Frog Went Courtin', '" but that's a diff'rent song, diff'rent tune, y'know. I don't remember much of that."

A nursery song, this is given as number 175 in the Opies' *Dictionary of Nursery Rhymes*. Grandma Deb identified two different songs with two different tunes: hers and the much more popular song "The Frog's Courting" or "Frog He Would A-Wooing Go." Hers is the only song called "The Frog and the Mouse" in the *Check-List*, but there are thirty-one examples of "The Frog's Courting." I have found only one old source where both songs were included: *A Little Book of Songs and Ballads, Gathered from Ancient Musick Books, MS, and Printed by E. F. Rimbault*, published by Smith in London in 1851. Here were listed "The Marriage of the Frogge and the Mouse," on page 87, and "The Frog's Wedding," on page 89. In 1973, Leach and Glassie's *Guide for Collectors* encouraged folksong collectors to look for both "The Frog and the Mouse" and "Mr. Frog Went A-Courtin'."

Strim-stram Pally

> Strim-stram Pally.
> Double-alley, pally, ting, tang.
> Timricktum-pally-minne-kimeo.
> Kimey karey, gilty, karey.
> Kimey-karey-kimey.
> Strim-stram-pally,
> Double-alley pally, ting, tam.
> Timricktum-pally, minne, kimeo.

Grandma Deb felt compelled to recite this set of nonsense lines with all possible speed immediately after she sang "The Frog and the Mouse."

Alan Lomax: "What is that?"

Grandma Deb: "I don't know *what* that is. I used to sing that to the kids when they was little. I don't know if that goes with 'The Frog and the Mouse' or not. It is a sort of parody of it, only it's too long to say every time. An' there's no tune to it."

That said, she raced through it again.

Lomax listed this as "Sing Song Kitty Won'tcha Kimeo." There are several other sets of nonsense verse similar to this in the *Check-List*, apparently all sung as separate pieces. But Grandma Deb could not separate her song and its "crazy" words.

"Kimeo-karo" lines, as would be expected, have many, many variations in the nonsense syllables, including sounds and rhythms. They seemed to me like a genre of their own, without any context or connection to a "story"; I wondered why Grandma Deb felt so obligated to race through her lines each time she sang "The Frog and the Mouse." However, in the old Ridgway Branch of the Philadelphia Library Company, in my original research in 1937–38, I did find the one piece of evidence that firmly grounds the song and the nonsense stanza together in a way very similar to the Jennie Devlin combination. This is a poem in *The Popular National Songster: Lucy Neal and Dan Tucker's Delight*, dated 1845:

> There was a frog liv'd in a well,
> With a rigdame bulle metter kimo,
> And mistress mouse, she kept the mill,
> With a rigdame bulle metter kimo.
> Kimo kairo delto kairo kimo kairo kimo,
> Strim stram pomme diddle larre bone,
> Rigdame rigdame bulle mette kimo.

When I Was a Little Boy

When I was a little boy,
My value for to show,
I laid my head in my sister's lap,
I tripped over Peakeley
And never touched the ground.
I met a great giant also there.
I taught him how to sing and whistle
To wrastle, hop, and to jump.
I beat him out of all his games
And killed him when I'se done.
The people then rewarded me
For the deed that I had done.
They gave me gold and silver
A-bout two hundred ton.
I made me a little bit of a box,
About four acres square,
And into that little box
I placed my gold and silver also there.
I started for Turkey shore,
I traveled like an ox,
And in my britches' pocket
I slipped this little box.
And when I got to Turkey,
They turned me out a door,
They wouldn't trust me with a dram
Because I was so poor.
So I bought me a little dog,
I think its color was brown.
His legs they were four rod long,
His ears were three feet wide,
And all around the world in half an hour,
Upon him I could ride.
I bought me a little ox,
I think his color was red.
His horns would reach from pole to pole,
His head up to the skies,
And a hummingbird took him in her bill
And to her nest did fly;

And every time he'd beller,
You'd hear him ten miles around
Which caused the Columbia walls
For to tumble down.
I bought me a little hen
A-comin' from the fair.
I set her on a mussel shell;
She hatched me a hare.
The hare became a milk-white horse
And fifty cows besides.
And ye can tell a bigger jeest,
I'm sure you'll tell a lie.

Alan Lomax: "What's that?"
Grandma Deb: "It's just a funny old piece."
Alan Lomax: "What does 'jeest' mean?"
Grandma Deb: "I don't know. I wish I knew."
Alan Lomax: "What is 'Peakeley'?"
Grandma Deb: "I don't know. I don't know what 'Peakeley' is, and I don't know what 'jeest' means."
Alan Lomax: "I wonder what 'Columbia' means."
Grandma Deb: "I don't know that, either. It's a story. It's a lie, you know. One of these silly things. No, that didn't have no tune. Ain't it crazy? Little boys always loved that one."

"When I Was a Little Boy" is a swapping song based on an old English folk poem.[1] It can be found, with tune, in the *Penguin Book of English Folk Songs*, but there is one very important difference between this (or indeed any other version that I found) and Grandma Deb's poem: her "little boy" is not frightened by a giant; he himself has strength and daring. He does a great deed in conquering and then killing the giant so that "The people then rewarded me / For the deed that I had done." In this way "When I Was a Little Boy" is a magic piece for children. And, indeed, it is listed as number seventy-one in the Opies' *Dictionary of Nursery Rhymes*.

The song in the *Penguin Book of English Folk Songs* that Vaughan Williams said was collected in Shetland in 1947 does explain the terms that Grandma Deb (and I) did not know: "Peakeley" was "Kingston Hill," and "Columbia walls" was a substitute for the steeple of the church of St. Paul in London that had come tumbling down. This confusion, however, helped give the poem an American locale since "Columbia" was a commonly used name for America. A "big jeest" was a big lie.[2]

1. Vaughan Williams and Lloyd, eds., *Penguin Book of English Folk Songs*, 101.
2. Kenneth S. Goldstein calls it a "lying song," which he has also found in Newfoundland and Labrador.

James Bird

(Spoken): Sons of freedom, listen to me,
And sad news I'll tell to thee
Sad were the scenes of parting,
Mothers wrang their hands and cried.
Maidens wept their loves in secret,
Sisters tried their griefs to hide.

Mary tried to say, "Farewell James,"
Waved her hands but nothing spoke.
One sweet kiss he snatched from Mary,
Pressed his mother's hand once more.

"Good-bye, Bird, may Heaven protect you,"
And the last scenes of parting broke.

. . .

Where is Bird? The battle rages,
Is he in the strife or no?"
Now the cannons roar tremendous.
Dare he meet the hosti foe?

(Sung): "Leave the deck," exclaimed brave Perry,
"No," cries Bird, "I will not go.
Here on the deck I took my stations.
Ne'er will Bird his colors fly.
I'll stand by you, gallyant captain,
Till we conquer or I die."

Thus they fought, both faint and bleeding
Till the Stars and Stripes arose.
Victory having crowned their efforts,
All triumphans to repose.
[What's "triumphans"?]

But did Bird receive a pension?
Was he to his friends restored?
No, nay, never, to his bosom
Clasped the girl his heart adored.

"Read this letter, Brother, Sister.
'Tis the last you'll hear from me.
'Tis sad news I write to thee.
I must suffer for deserting
On the brink of Niagry."

See him kneeling on his coffin.
Sure his death can do no good.
Hark, oh, my God, they have shot him!
See his bosom stream with blood.

Grandma Deb: "Bird got mixed during the fighting and got on the wrong boat. He was with Captain Perry, and he was supposed to be with Captain Thomas. Now these two captains were enemies, so afterwards, Captain Thomas said Bird was a deserter, just to get even with Captain Perry. He ordered Bird to be shot. Captain Perry heard about it and rode relays of horses to get there in time. He rode one white horse to death. But Captain Thomas knowed he might try to save Bird so he set his watch ahead and shot Bird five minutes early. Captain Perry didn't make it.

"There was water already in the grave, and Bird thought that was 'a hard thing' as he stood at the edge, waiting to be shot and put into it.

"Those first lines at the beginning [marked "Spoken"] were the first cracks in my memory till Kay brought me that book. Then I remembered it all. My, I was glad to have it again.[1]

"Moody and Sankey was a hymn book, years and years and years ago. Tune of 'James Bird' was in that book." [I recognized it as "Come Thou Fount of Every Blessing."]

This is an American ballad with a known author. Charles Miner, an editor for the *Wilkes-Barre Gleaner*, wrote the poem on April 28, 1815, after reading Bird's farewell letter to his parents informing them that he was going to be shot as a deserter. Bird gave absolutely no explanation. His letter was more of a religious exhortation, promising to meet them in heaven. There was an official addendum: "Sentence was carried out on November 11, 1814."

Bird had gained great glory in his hometown because men who had served with him in the Battle of Lake Erie returned with tales that Bird had personally helped Perry win his victory over the British. How could somebody who had been such a hero then be a deserter? Obviously he could not.

Miner's poem soon became a ballad, sung to four different tunes. Its popularity was highest during the Civil War, but by 1935, when Bird's bones were transferred from the Erie Museum to a family plot in a cemetery outside of Wilkes-Barre, no references were made to the ballad during the graveside service. However, the tombstone repeats one of the most popular beliefs about Bird: that he had not deserted but had only set forth to help his country in the Battle of New Orleans.[2]

Laws 5.

1. In the last line of stanza three, Jennie sang "hosti" for "hostile." "Brink of Niagry," at the end of stanza seven, was "the brig Niagara" in the original.
2. This summary is based on my research conducted in 1937-38, utilizing federal and Pennsylvania state records, extensive correspondence with historical societies in New York and Pennsylvania, plus reminiscences by Bird family members, some of the militiamen, and Charles Miner. Copies of Bird's last letters to his family were furnished to me by the Wyoming Historical Society in Wilkes-Barre, Pennsylvania. Additions to the Bird legend are in Thompson, *Body, Boots, and Britches,* 206, 344.

Young Charlotte

Young Charlotte lived on a mountain side,
In a wild and lonely spot;
No dwelling there for three miles round
Except the father's cot.
Her father kept a social board,
And she was very fair,
He loved for to see his daughter dressed,
For he loved his daughter well.

The tune and the first eight lines are exactly as Grandma Deb sang them to me, and then later to Alan Lomax. The rest of the song, she assured us, was exactly like the version in "her book," Shoemaker's *Mountain Minstrelsy of Pennsylvania.*

Alan Lomax: "Do you know 'Young Charlotte'?"

Grandma Deb: "I know it well. If I could go over it a couple of times, out of my book upstairs, y'know, I could sing all that song. I know that much."

Alan Lomax: "How long have you known this song?"

Grandma Deb: "Oh, for years. Whether it was this year or that year, I jus' couldn't tell you. Mrs. Shindle — next door — she has a box of old-time pieces. She has it in that box.

"But it's the story. You know, 'her father loved his daughter well.' She was all he had. It was a shame, wasn't it?"

This is another American ballad by a named author, Seba Smith (1843). Other titles for it are "The Frozen Girl" and "Sweet Charlotte." Grandma Deb's comment "It was a shame, wasn't it?" refers to the drama in the song: Young Charlotte, wearing a light shawl, insisted on driving to a dance in an open sleigh. When the sleigh arrived at the party, she was frozen to death.

Laws G 17.

Martha Decker

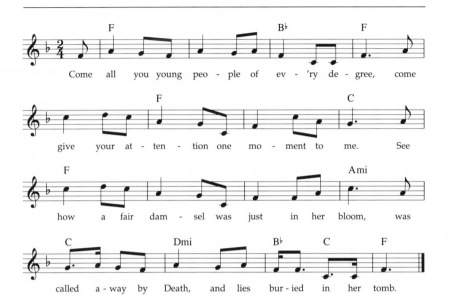

Come all you young people
Of every degree,
Come, give your attention
One moment to me.

See how a fair damsel
Was just in her bloom,
Was called away by Death,
And lies buried in her tomb.

She was scarcely thirteen,
Most obedient and kind,
Possessed of a ladylike
Temper and mind.

The youngest of all,
Being handsome and bright,
Her mother being dead,
She was her father's delight.

She started one Monday,
With a niece still more young,
To go to her sister's
Beyond the Chemung.

To pay a short visit
And then go and see
The sister, the mother
Of her compa-ny.

They placed them on horseback
And then they did seem
Not to be afraid
Of the mud and the stream.

A friend going with them,
And he did remain
Until the other shore
In safety they'd gained.

She ended her visit
And started to gain
The next place appointed
In spite of the rain.

The river had risen
Both riley and high,
But little did she think
That so soon she must die.

Her horse being antic
A blunder did make.
A girth from the saddle
Did instantly break.

And plunged this fair damsel
Beneath the swift waves
And none there were able
Her life for to save.

The people ran down
[The neighbors ran down]
To the shore and did cry,
"God help her and save her,
I fear she must die."

No boats being ready,
No hands there to save,
Poor Marthy goes down
To a watery grave.

And when she arose
There were some were so near
As her lamentations
Distinctly to hear.

Crying, "Mercy, oh dear,
Is there none here can save
Or must I go down
To a watery grave?"

Her horse running home
Soon alarmed all her friends.
They ran to the river
While wringing their hands.

Crying, "Oh, my dear sister,
Are you in this stream,
And can we do nothing
Your life to redeem?"

She sank never alive more to rise
Until Jesus comes down
In a cloud from the skies
And awakes all the nations
That sleep in the ground
And then her dust will arise
And be found.

The people collected,
A hundred or more,
They raked the deep eddy,
They searched well the shore.

No trace of poor Marthy
Could find anywhere,
And still they continued
To search with great care.

And loud peals of cannon
Ascend to the skies.
They're trying her slumbering
Body to rise.

The fish cleaves the river
And seems in a fright.
The birds have all flown
And refuse to light.

The river is covered
With boats and with men.
They're trying her slumbering
Body to regain.

But all was in vain
Till four days had expired
When three of the people
Were virtually mired.

Espied her caught fast
On a mill dam below,
And quickly the news
To her friends it did go.

A servant from Jesus
Came down in great haste
And rescued her body
From that awful place.

She was soon conveyed
To her sister's from where
She started on Monday
To go with such care.

Oh, see her dear father
And hear his deep sighs,
As going to the carriage,
He sees where she lies.

He raises his hands
Up to heaven in tears,
Crying, "Martha, my child,
But I can't make you hear.

"Are you my dear Martha,
So altered I see,
That I've fondled, I've dandled,
I've rocked on my knee?

"Well pleased with your prattle,
And rolled in my arms?
Now you must be food
For the poor hungry worms."

In Factoryville churchyard
Her body now lies,
I hope her dear soul
Is with God in the skies.

Forever to sing:
"Sweet redemption from sin,
Through the blood of Christ
Jesus made holy and clean."

Alan Lomax: "Tell me, what do you know about the song, about Martha Decker?"

Grandma Deb: "Oh, that *is* old. I was only a little girl when I come upon this rock. In the narrows of the Chemung River, y'know. It was long and narrow, going into Athens, Pennsylvania, and the stone had on it how she . . . she . . . her life and her accident, how she met it, written on that stone. And we used to stop—you know how people are—and read the stone over 'n' over.

"And when she was drownded, this song, the song came right away about it. Like several of my pieces that I know are real true songs, and they were put out jus' the same time [as the event] in olden times. But now they're put in the paper and they're forgotten tomorrow."

Alan Lomax: "And you don't know anything more about Martha Decker?"

Grandma Deb: "No, only about this rock. It had come down the mountain and it landed just at the edge of the river and the sand 'n' stone was all around it so the river never washed it away. In the summer you could ford the river barefooted, but in the spring and fall it was very high."

Alan Lomax: "Well, when you sang that song, did people weep and . . ."

Grandma Deb: "Always had the blues? Yes. It was always a pitiful scene."

Alan Lomax: "Did you ever make anybody cry when you sang that song?"

Grandma Deb: "Many a time. Because she was only a child. Fourteen. An' she was the last of the tribe."

Alan Lomax: "Supposed to be a very beautiful girl?"

Grandma Deb: "Yes. And her description on that stone was where I got that idea. And, of course, in the song: she was 'beautiful and bright / Her mother being dead / she was her father's delight.' She was the last one, the baby of the family."

Alan Lomax: "Did she make this death because she had been a wicked person?"

Grandma Deb: "No. It was the river. No. The rain, see, it came down so fast and raised the river and the horse, the horse slipped. But Kay looked and she said the stone's been removed. She found all the rest, but I jus' can't tell you where that stone was."

In the tenth stanza, "riley" means muddy. "Sweet redemption," mentioned in the last stanza, is also the name of the hymn tune to which the ballad was sung.

"Martha Decker" is a local funeral ballad. It is listed in the *Check-List* as "Mother Dicker," and by Belden as "Martha Dexter."[1] There are obvious influences of broadside ballads here; for example, the line "a fair damsel was just in her bloom" is much like the song (found in American songsters) "Caroline of Edinburgh Town."

But the real parallel for this long-winded, earnest dirge is with the whole tradition of mourning ballads, some of which were sung as a corpse was being carried to the grave, according to my informants.

In 1937 I set out to learn about Martha Decker, using the clue in the ballad, "Factoryville churchyard," and Grandma Deb's description of the Chemung River, near Athens, Pennsylvania, where, she believed, she had seen a rock marking the place of the drowning.

With helpful suggestions from a policeman in Elmira, New York, and the owner of a gas station on the highway to Waverley, I found that "Factoryville" had been the name of East Waverley (now Wilawanna) and that it was really closer to Elmira than to Athens. Then I was able, quite literally, to run our poor ballad-heroine to ground, in the East Waverley churchyard where an old stone, sidling into the earth, read:

MARTHA
daughter of Henry & Eliz.
DECKER
died
August 1, 1842;
aged 13 years
8 mo. and 24 d's

Kneeling at her grave, I took a picture, remembering little Jennie's emotions when she had first learned the ballad.

The next morning I canvassed people living near the graveyard. One man said he'd just heard the story of Martha Decker the week before — "but it wasn't no poem." I was directed to another house, and there I found the only evidence that little Martha had not been forgotten as soon as she was buried. I was shown an old notebook with a newspaper copy of the ballad pasted in, but there was no date and no name of the newspaper. A few members of the Kirkpatrick family who were there that morning said they only slightly remembered the poem, and, of course, nobody knew a tune. But they gave me permission to copy the handwritten last stanza that had obviously been added by somebody — perhaps the same person who had clipped and pasted the ballad — who was unable to resist a little additional proselytizing.

Although she's now dead, may she ne'er be forgot.
Her youthful companions be solemn in thought.
To Factoryville churchyard in sadness repair,
For it will not be long before they must lie there.

Next I was directed to the home of the oldest woman in the area; she was ninety-two, so she must have been born in 1845, three years after Martha died, but she insisted that she had known Martha, "a good little girl," who had taken her to school every day before she was "drownded." She announced that the song was by "some Rogers" and she was firm about my having made a mistake in taking down the year of death from Martha's tombstone.

It seemed to me then that the ballad was lost, apart from its place in Grandma Deb's memory, but later I learned that it had traveled a little before it gave up the ghost. It had been recorded in 1910 in Missouri, as "Martha Dexter," and was printed by Belden in his first edition of *Ballads and Songs Collected by the Missouri Folk-Lore Society* (1940).[2] This itinerant ballad had two significant changes: almost all of the religious allusions had been deleted, including the entire last stanza, and a "literary" second stanza had been inserted:

> She was as the flowers that bloom in the morn,
> Her parents' fond hope now blasted and gone;
> The sweet stem is shaken, for death hath its bound;
> The flower is forsaken and lies underground.

Both of these added last stanzas lessen the impact of the agony that people in Athens/Waverley had suffered and were still remembering when Jennie Hess came to live in the vicinity.

Laws G 34.

1. Belden's 1955 edition of *Ballads and Songs* carried a note about my search for "Martha Decker" (521–22), Lomax having told Belden about my research.
2. Laws never saw Belden's note and concluded that the status of "Martha Dexter" was "doubtful, with insufficient annotation and not reported from traditional singing since 1920" (*Native American Balladry*, 271). Neither did he suspect that "Mother Dicker," as the title was rendered in the *Check-List*, was a typographical error for the title of this ballad, which Alan Lomax recorded in 1938.

Miss Riot

A   Verses 1, 5, 6, 10

Come all you peo - ple, young and old, a sto - ry is so bold,_____ con - cern - ing of a la - dy. Miss Ri - ot was her name.____ She was poi - soned by her own true love, and he hung for the same.____ Young

B   Verses 2, 3, 4, 7, 8, 9, 11

Ma - ry she was beau - ti - ful, not of a high de - gree.___ Young Hen - er - y Green was weal - thy, as plain - ly you shall see.___ He said, "My dear - est Ma - ry, if you will be my wife,____ I will guard you as a pa - rent all through this gloom - y life."___

Come all you people,
Young and old,
A story is so bold,
Concerning of a lady.
Miss Riot was her name.
She was poisoned by
Her own true love,
And he hung for the same.

Young Mary she was beautiful,
Not of a high degree.
Young Hen-er-y Green was wealthy,
As plainly you shall see.

He said, "My dearest Mary,
If you will be my wife,
I will guard you as a parent
All through this gloomy life."

She said, "My dearest Hen-er-y,
I fear it will not do,
For you have rich relations.
I've none so rich as you.

"And when your mother hears of it,
She will bar me from the door.
I'd rather you'd marry some richer girl
Who has wealth laid up in store."

He said, "My dearest Mary,
Why do you torment me so?
For I swear by all that's sacred [sa-ca-red],
And ever to prove true.

"And if you longer do refuse,
I swear I'll end my life,
For I don't want to live no more
If you can't be my wife."

So then, believing all he said,
She then became his wife,
But little did she think, poor girl,
Or e'er did she expect,
That he would take the life of one
Whom he'd sworn to protect.

They hadn't been married scarce a week
When she was taken ill.
Great doctors they were sent for,
And none of them could say,
It was also ascertained by them,
She must go to her grave.

Her brother, hearing of the news,
His sister he came to see.
"Oh, sister dear, you're dying,
The doctors tell to me.

"Oh, sister dear, you're dying,
Your life is at an end.
Now haven't you been poisoned
By the one you thought your friend?"

"Now since I'm on my dying bed
And know that I must die,
Now since I'm going to my God,
The truth I'll not deny.

"For I know that he has poisoned me.
Now, brother, for him send,
For I love him just as dearly
As when he was my friend."

Young Henry getting the tidings,
His wife he came to see.
"Oh, Henry, dearest Henry,
Are you so deceived in me?"

She gave three shrieks for Hen-er-y
And fell into a swoon.
He gazed on her indiff'rently
And in silence left the room.

An inquest on her body
Held according to the law,
Young Henry apprehending,
Confined in Troy jail.

Awaiting for his sentence,
For the court would not give bail.
And when receiving his sentence
And sent back to his room,
All for to be hanged,
It was his awful doom.

It was a very sad ending
Of his most wretched life,
A-murdering of his dearest dear,
His own, beloved wife.

Alan Lomax: "Where did you learn this?"
Grandma Deb: "It was in Troy, New York. That's one of the places Steven-
sons took me — the basketmakers. They'd go to these places, playing — I can't
remember — but they'd always take me along. Hair clear down to my knees.
Flaxen hair, tow head, no expression to it.
  "And she would teach me lots of these little things. An' that's where I'd
learn my little steps 'n' all. And I'd sing 'em at these places."
Alan Lomax: "Did you ever hear why he poisoned her?"
Grandma Deb: "No, I never did know why. I jus' can't say."
Alan Lomax: "How long have you known the song?"
Grandma Deb, "Oh, for years. Like I said."

Laws gives this as a murder ballad of 1845 native to America.[1] Apparently
"Riot" should have been "Wyatt." The more common title was "Henry
Green." No other title like Jennie Devlin's was found; probably hers resulted
from an error in oral transmission over the years. The ballad, containing a
mystery about motive as well as details of the crime, horrified good people and
kept interest alive.[2] Indeed, Carl Carmer included it in *Songs of the Rivers of
America* in 1942, ninety-seven years after poor Mary Ann Wyatt Green had
drunk her arsenic tea.
  The ballad itself contains the basic details, but the summation appears on
the joint gravestones of the husband and his murdered bride in Berlin village,
Rensselaer County, New York:

Henry C. Green
Born Dec. 30, 1822; Died Sept. 10, 1845.
Prepare to Meet Thy God.

Mary A. W. Green
Died Feb. 17, 1845 in the 23rd Year of her age.
This monument is erected by the citizens of Berlin in memory of Mary Ann
Wyatt, wife of Henry G. Green, who was married Feb. 9, 1845; and on the
14th day of the same month was poisoned by her husband with arsenic,
without any real or pretended cause.
Beautiful, intelligent and virtuous, she was wept over by the community,
and the violated law justly exacted the life of her murderer as a penalty for
this crime.[3]

An official account of the incident appeared in *History of the Police Department of Troy, N.Y., from 1786 to 1902:*

> In the month of November, 1844, Green, who was a merchant, lost his stock as the result of a fire. Soon after a company of temperance performers gave an exhibition in Berlin. Mary Ann Wyatt, a young girl of 18, was in the company. Her beauty made a deep impression upon Green who attended the exhibition. He at once enlisted with the company, met Miss Wyatt, and became engaged to her. He married her in great haste, a week previous to the date set for the ceremony, and soon after meeting her.
>
> A week after her marriage, Green began to administer arsenic to his wife, which he mixed with beverages she drank. During her illness and while he was left to watch her, he continued to give his wife poisoned drinks. Death resulted subsequently. Green was then brought to trial.
>
> The jury brought in a verdict of "guilty" after which Judge Amasa J. Parker addressed the prisoner at some length, saying among other things that the crime of which he had been found guilty exceeded in enormity any of which he had ever heard.
>
> Green was hanged on the tenth day of September, 1845. Previous to his execution, and after he had been taken to jail from the court room, where he had heard the verdict, Green fainted. The Hon. Martin Townsend was at that time district attorney.[4]

Over the years, as might be expected, new elements were added to the legend. For example, in 1917, Professor Mary Augusta Scott, of Smith College, sent a letter to the *New York Evening Post* in which she concluded, "Green gave himself up to justice, it was related, because his victim haunted him."[5]

In 1937, L. C. Jones published a facsimile of a broadside version of the ballad and gave a motive to explain Henry's conduct: he had been jilted. Instantly, determined to show he wasn't hurt, Henry rushed to join the Scovell Temperance Show when it came to Berlin, Rensselaer County. He swept poor Mary Ann off her feet. But the former sweetheart grew jealous; she wanted him back, and Henry assiduously set about making himself a widower.[6]

Another dimension was added by an informant a few years later:

> Although the hanging on September 10th was a "private" one, to which only fifty carefully elected spectators were admitted, for twenty-four hours before the execution crowds flocked from afar until two or three thousand were jammed into the interesting proximity of the jail. At 3:40 P.M. the murderer-bridegroom mounted the scaffold to join the fifty fortunates in singing "Rock of Ages"; thereafter his power to entertain was limited to a confession, published five days after the execution, and to a printed broadside ballad in 24 stanzas, probably sold before Green was hanged.[7]

Actually there were at least two other ballads, similar in text, from about the same time period. Mary Augusta Scott reported on one that had been sent to her in 1908, called "The Benner Song." When she queried the Troy Public Library, a librarian sent her the two tombstone inscriptions, so Scott tried to match them to the poem she had. Some sample lines will suffice to show the power of sincerity in Grandma's song in comparison with these "elegant verses." Now Mary Ann Green is "Delia," and her murdering spouse, "Benner." Here are some of the key sections:

> O breathe a dirge o'er Delia's tomb,
> For her no more the violets bloom,
> For her the lily mourns . . .

> She from the hand of him she loves,
> And by his artful flattery moved,
> Received the fatal cup.

> By him assured 'twould cure her cold,
> With cheerful courage she then took hold,
> And drank the poison up.
> But soon, alas, her snowy neck,
> And dimpled chin, and rosy cheek,
> With crimson-spotten o'er.

> . . .

> Instead of wedding suits appear
> A winding sheet and sable bier
> Borne slowly to the tomb. . . .

Scott's article, with the entire "Benner Song," was reprinted in the *Troy Times* of May 22, 1917, and was immediately answered by the librarian of the Troy Public Library, who stressed all the differences in ages and circumstances between the Greens and the Benners. But, at the same time, the librarian reported that there was still a third ballad on file, and she asked for readers' help in completing it. Apparently she got no answers, since there was nothing else in the library file when I came along. This is version three:

> She stood upon the temperance stage
> 'Mid scenes of rare display,
> A graceful, brilliant youthful maid,
> The gayest of the gay.
> Her dark eyes shed a living light
> The radiance all her own,
> Her lips a rose leave and her voice
> A sweet, low dulcet tone.

> . . . she called him to her side,
> "Ah, Henry, have I 'ere deceived?"
> "No," coldly he replied.
> A poisoned chalice he obtained
> And to her lips he gave;
> She drank it all, the fatal dregs
> Were deadly as the grave.

Laws F 14.

1. Laws, *Native American Balladry*, 198.
2. Leach, *Ballad Book*, 792–93.
3. This was copied for me by Fanny C. Howe, librarian, Troy Public Library, September 8, 1937.
4. Frederic T. Cardoze, *History of the Police Department of Troy, N.Y., from 1786 to 1902*, 77. A copy of this account was supplied to me by the editor of the *Troy Record*, July 27, 1938.
5. Scott's letter was reprinted in the *Troy Times*, May 22, 1917. A copy was supplied to me by Fanny C. Howe in 1937.
6. Jones, "Folksongs of Mary Wyatt and Henry Green," 14–18. Includes facsimile of a broadside version.
7. Thompson, *Body, Boots, and Britches*, 441–43.

The Dying Californian

This was a fragment of a "ballad-like piece."[1] Grandma Deb said, "I know that tune, but not no words any more." The folksong, which first appeared in 1859, described the fate of a loving man who had set out to get riches for his family. Belden explains the sufferings of the gold-seekers: "The passage to California by water, whether around the Horn or across the Isthmus, was fraught with danger, especially of disease."[2] This piece, then, could be taken as an answer to the questions in "The Orphan Child" about the fate of the missing father.

1. Laws, *Native American Balladry*, 277.
2. Belden, *Ballads and Songs*, 350–51.

The Old Indian

1. Come all ye peo-ple far and near, a la-men-ta-tion you shall hear, con-cern-ing of a la-dy gay, as with an old In-di-an she ran a-way. 2. It was her com-plex-ion was so great, she then re-solved to be his mate. She says, "I'll go a-long with you and nev-er love no oth-er man."

Come all ye people far and near,
A lamentation you shall hear,
Concerning of a lady gay,
As with an old Indian she ran away.

It was her complexion was so great.
She then resolved to be his mate.
She says, "I'll go along with you
And never love no other man."

They mounted their horses; they rode along,
They rode till they come to the Indian-town.
And at the hut they did call in
To rest herself along with him.

And when her brother found they'd gone,
Straightway after them he came.
And brought with him two hundred men
Resolved to bring them back again.

They mounted their horses; they rode along,
They rode till they came to the Indian-town.
And at the hut he did drive up,
Saying, "Lillian, what does this mean?

"Oh, sister dear, can this be true,
One of our father's family.
As with the old Indian you've run your race,
Our father's family to disgrace?"

"Yes, brother dear, I know 'tis true,
One of our father's family.
So, brother dear, I pray me kill,
For I shall love the old Indian still."

They beat the old Indian severely,
Until this lady she fainted away,
A-thinking of what she had done
As with the old Indian she had run.

To Fisher's Isle she was sent,
And straightway to jail he went,
Resolved to keep them far apart,
But still the old Indian he kept her heart.

This is a mourning ballad. The *Check-List* has only this entry, and I never found any clue to the history of the event or to the song itself, although I questioned local historians and other folklorists. Mrs. Bentley (Aunt Eva) told me that she also had known the song but that Jennie was already singing it when she came to work for her, in 1879. Mrs. Bentley had no information at all about the origin of the story.

This piece is especially interesting as evidence of the contemporary attitudes toward miscegenation. The Indian was not mobbed (as a black man probably would have been), but he was jailed and the white woman was banished for putting this stain on the family's honor. However, note that, at the beginning, the audience was called upon to hear "a lamentation," and the conclusion was sympathetic toward the faithful Lillian.

Eight Years in Cherry Hill

Come all ye Philadelphy citizens,
And listen unto me.
A letter I received from a prisoner
A-stating that he was ill.

It's about one Johnny McDermott
That I'm about to sing,
He being intoxicated
One morning in the spring.

Broke into the house of Johnny McPhillin
And [was] a-taken to jail.
Sentenced to eight years in Cherry Hill,
Sentenced to hard labor in the walls of Cherry Hill.

And now you've heard my sentence,
And don't you think it hard?
Taken before them judges,
They gave me eight years in Cherry Hill.

On that great day of judgment,
When them judges go before their God,
They will visit a harder place
Than the high walls of Cherry Hill.

Now all you kind-hearted parents
And listen unto me.
Keep your children off the streets
And from bad company.
For it was dancing schools
And night walking
That brought me to Cherry Hill.

The words of this local ballad were pieced together by members of the Devlin/Eaves family, especially by Grandpa Deb, who had been born in the Irish area of South Philadelphia. I never had the luck to find anyone else who knew it, not even the warden of "Cherry Hill," the nickname of the Eastern State Penitentiary in Philadelphia, whom I queried in 1938.

According to Kenneth S. Goldstein, a song entitled "Ten Years in Cherry Hill" appeared in *Delaney's Song Book No. 4*. Since this particular series was published by Delaney between 1870 and 1890, it seems a reasonable guess that the song predated Grandma Deb's arrival in Philadelphia.

For me, the most significant aspect of finding this ballad was the demonstration that songs were composed in urban as well as rural areas. Some of each became folksongs, that is, they "went into tradition."

Another point of fascination for me was seeing how folksingers would combine their own realistic lines with some that had become stock pieces perpetuated by the "ballad press" (in song books and songsters). Compare the last lines of "Cherry Hill" with the last two stanzas of "Rinordine":

> Come, all you fair maids,
> A warning take by me,
> Quit night walking
> And shun bad company.

> For if you don't, you will surely rue
> Until the day you die
> And beware of meeting Rinordine
> All on the mountain high.[1]

In our Philadelphia ballad, the dangers of meeting an unhealthy spirit on "mountains high" were exchanged for the evils of "dancing schools." And the "Come all ye" in "Rinordine" is addressed to fair maids instead of potential burglars, but the tone of the warning and the specifics against "night walking" in both songs were conventional references to street walkers and the men who followed them.

1. Belden, *Ballads and Songs*, 286–88.

The Boston Burglar

"The Boston Burglar" was a fragment of a British broadside. Grandma Deb said of this, "I can sing it for you if the tune comes." But the tune never came, which is a pity because, judging from the eleven stanzas printed by Eddy, it seems likely that "Eight Years in Cherry Hill" owed much to this better-known ballad. Again there was warning about walking the streets at night, lest the innocent young man end up in a penitentiary.[1]

Laws L 16A and L 16B.

1. Eddy, *Ballads and Songs from Ohio*, 205–6.

Jim Fisk

"Did you know the song 'Jim Fisk'?" I asked.

"He never went back on the poor," Grandma Deb instantly replied.

She knew, as did most people, that Fisk had sent a trainload of food to Chicago after the Great Fire of 1871. The irony is that Jim Fisk was no hero; he was an unscrupulous man who made a fortune as a member of the corrupt Tweed Ring in New York. He was murdered in 1872 and by 1874 there was sheet music, "Jim Fisk," or "He Never Went Back on the Poor." This made him an American folk hero.

Laws has a fragment of this song.[1] Belden cites this as "built upon an older homiletic, 'Remember the Poor,' of which there are several copies in the Harvard Library."[2]

Laws F 18.

1. Laws, *Native American Balladry*, 200–201.
2. Belden, *Ballads and Songs*, 415.

Jesse James

This is a fragment of a ballad native to America.[1] The *Check-List* has eleven recordings, including one sung by Woody Guthrie. Belden identified Jesse James as "probably the most famous son of Missouri — after Mark Twain."[2] The song was composed immediately after James was shot in 1882.[3] Grandma Deb thought that Jesse, like Jim Fisk, was a "friend of the poor," but she could only recite the popular lines about "The dirty little coward that shot Mr. Howard / And laid poor Jesse in his grave." Like many of us, she was chiefly impressed by the detail that Jesse had been straightening a picture when he was shot in the back, certainly not an appropriate end for an American Robin Hood.

Laws E 1.

1. Laws, *Native American Balladry*, 176.
2. Belden, *Ballads and Songs*, 401. Detailed references are in Brown, *Frank C. Brown Collection*, 2:558–59.
3. Lomax, *Folk Songs of North America*, 351.

Western Courtship

Away in the West,
If my memory serves well,
There lived a young couple,
Called Robin and Nell,

Who sparked a long time,
Till one day Robin said,
"We have sparked long enough,
Now let us get wed."

At once Nell consented
And Robin began
To furnish the house
Like a sensible man.

The day was appointed
And the ring Robin got.
He sought out the preacher
To tie up the knot.

After asking the place,
And also the night,
"I'll be there," said the preacher,
"All things being right."

Well, soon the night came,
When Nell was to change
Her sweet maiden name.

Together they went
To their dear little home
To wait there until
The good preacher should come.

They waited and waited
And no preacher came near
Of course the young couple
Thought it was queer.

It now being very late,
A knock came at the door.
That it was the preacher
They thought pretty sure.

But on opening the door,
A note they obtained
That said that night
The preacher was detained.

But it stated also that
If they would stay,
He would come very early
The following day.

When Robin read this
He was sorely perplexed.
With Nell at his side,
He could not be vexed.

"Well, Nell," said Robin.
"What are we to do?
We've only one bed.
How I wish we had two!"

"Oh, I can fix that,"
Nell quickly replies.
"Put a chair in the center
For the bed's quite wide."

And to show she meant
Just what she had said,
Got hold of a chair
And placed it in bed.

"No, Robin," said Nellie,
"You lie over there,
And I'll lie here
But don't move the chair."

"Well," Robin replied,
For Nell's plan was so good,
He could not object.
And I wonder who could?

It now being very late,
They began to undress
But the feeling of Robin
I'll never express.

They got into bed
With the greatest of care
And Robin laid down
With his face toward the chair.

So he might gaze
Through the legs of the chair
On Nellie's sweet lips
And her beautiful hair.

"O, how tempting," thought he,
"Is a woman like Nell.
I don't wonder now
That poor Adam fell."

He peeped and he sighed,
And he sighed and he peeped,
And he felt that no mortal
Was ever so tried.

Oh, how his heart beat
As the sweet Nellie breathed,
As he saw the clothes move
And her sweet bosom heaved.

And as she had told him
To not move the chair,
At length he turned over
In utter despair.

The night he thought long
But when day broke,
Dear Nellie played on him
A most serious joke.

Not speaking a word,
From the bed she arose,
At once proceeded
To pack up her clothes.

When Robin saw this,
He jumped out of bed,
And asked, "What is wrong?"
To which our Nellie said,

"I'm going to go home,"
And threw back her hair.
"For I'd never marry a man,
Who wouldn't move the chair!"

Robin saw he had missed it,
But what could he say?
"Come back, my Nellie!"
But she hurried away.

Grandma Deb: "This poem, which is not a song, just a story, was printed on one side of a penny sheet sold at the fair in Elmira, New York. That's how I got it."

Grandma Deb had no trouble remembering this lengthy poem when she recited it for me. The story bears a resemblance to the old English folksong "Get Up and Bar the Door," a contest of wills between a man and a woman. However, in our story, the woman wants the man to dominate her. Her sexual expectations were certainly not ladylike. The whole tone is similar to that of some of Grandma Deb's "naughty" songs, but she thought it was proper enough so that she could bring this broadside to Philadelphia with her.

Kenneth S. Goldstein commented on the thematic relationship between this and "Katie Morey" (Laws N 24) and "The Baffled Knight" (Child 112): "All three pieces are about a young man who won't take advantage of a situation when it is forced upon him, and he is thus the humorous, sorry, and pitiful butt of this erotic story."

Your Father and Your Mother, Love

(He) "Oh, your father and your mother, love,
In yonder room they lie.
They're embracing one another, love,
So why can't you and I?"

(She) "They're embracing, they're embracing, love,
Without a fear or doubt,
So roll me in your arms all night,
And I'll blow the candle out."

A bawdy song, its more common title is "Blow the Candle Out."[1] Grandma Deb's title, "Your Father and Your Mother, Love," was apt since, from a song with four stanzas, she remembered only the one that could be totally disconnected from the story and applied as needed by any pair of lovers. She sang these lines as a dialogue, citing the parents' activity as tacit permission for the girl to do likewise. These eight lines, by themselves, might be all the encouragement that a farm boy would need to tease a farm girl at a dance.

Laws 17.

1. Laws, *American Balladry*, 257.

Little Ball of Yarn

It was in the month of May
For the lambs did skip and play
And the birds they were singing to their charms.
It was there I spied a maid
And unto her I said,
"May I wind up your little ball of yarn?"

CHORUS:
The blackbird and the thrush,
They were looking down on us
As I wound up the little ball of yarn.

"Oh, no, kind sir," said she,
"You're a stranger unto me,
And I fear you have got some other charms.
You had better go to those
Who have money and fine clothes,
For to wind up their little ball of yarn."

CHORUS

I put my arms around her waist,
And I gently laid her down,
Intending not to do her harm.
And there to her surprise,
I rode between her thighs,
As I wound up the little ball of yarn.

CHORUS

Grandma Deb to Alan Lomax: "Then there's something 'bout pretty young maids that go willing in the shade should beware of strangers."

Grandma Deb [some months later]: "'Kay, you're bad! Puttin' such stuff in a book!"

Lomax did not record the Devlin version of this bawdy song, although I don't know why. Surprisingly there is one version listed in the *Check-List* — and that is by the same "modest" singer who had thought it was not proper to sing "Down by the Greenwood Side" in front of a little girl.

Once again we see Grandma Deb's personal and quite serious treatment of one of her pieces. She did not consider it "bawdy." It was "only a dance tune," she told us. She did not condemn the girl although it is evident that "the pretty young maid" went willingly into the stranger's arms.

"The Little Ball of Yarn" well illustrates Jennie Devlin's attitude toward sex: she felt it was good clean fun. In all of the versions of this song in Ed Cray's second edition of *The Erotic Muse,* there are nasty consequences: the man gets venereal disease (described with coarse detail) and, nine months later, he is arrested for fathering an illegitimate child. Even Grandma Deb's charming image of "the blackbird and the thrush / They were looking down on us / As I wound up her little ball of yarn" is mutilated in another version: "And a jaybird and a thrush raised hell in the brush / While I wound up her little ball of yarn."[1]

1. Cray, *Erotic Muse*, 89–95.

Long Fol-de-Rol

Oh, mother dear, you know I'm not to blame.
For you have often minded the same —
Left your relations, your parents and all
An' followed my ol' daddy for his long fol-de-rol.

He took you to dances, to theaters and to balls
And night-times he pleased you
With his long fol-de-rol.

Grandma Deb: "I won't sing that. That's bad. I only sang it one night when we was cuttin' up. We was carrying on here, the girls 'n' me." (Fortunately, the version given here was already in my notebook before Alan Lomax came.)

Grandma Deb described it as "only a dance tune." Lomax did persuade her to sing all the words to him, but it was not listed in the *Check-List*. Note that in speaking to her mother, the girl stresses the power of the sex drive, which she knows her mother understands. In fact, she seems to be demanding co-conspirator status with her mother (an interpretation suggested by Lomax).

Mrs. Russell Had a Bustle

Mrs. Russell
Had a bustle.
Mr. Bush
Gave it a push.
Mr. Pretty
Gave it some titty.
Sent it back
To New York City.

I have never found anything about this comic poem, but I do not agree
with Grandma Deb that it was only "crazy stuff for kids." She must have
known that "to give titty" was to breast-feed a baby. I keep thinking about the
famous beauty, Lillian Russell, renowned for her bust as well as her bustle.

Some for the Girl

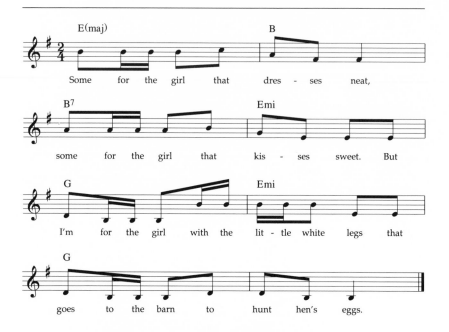

Some for the girl that dresses neat,
Some for the girl that kisses sweet.
But I'm for the girl with the little white legs
That goes to the barn to hunt hens' eggs.

Some for the girl that dresses neat,
Some for the girl that kisses sweet,
But I'm for the girl with the lily-white thighs
With a hole in her belly like a dead hog's eye.

This is the bawdy song that Grandma Deb sang for Alan Lomax when Ellen and I were out of the room. It is the only one of her "naughty" songs that escaped from the "Delta" collection of "indecent material" in the Library of Congress; surprisingly, it made its way into the *Check-List*.

Shanghai Rooster

1. I've a farm out in the west, of the farms it is the best. I've a cross-eyed mule with freckles and red hair. I've an old Texas steer with a wart on his left ear, but now he's gone to climb the Golden Stair.

2. But my poor old Shanghai rooster who battle he befell with a brammy who fought him long and brave. And his wife is in the barnyard sitting on a lump of coal, she is weeping for her Shanghai rooster's tail

never crow again, or flirt with some old hen, he's a masher and his middle name is Jay. At the hour of half past eight, he is at the garden gate, singing "cock-a-doodle-do," goodbye, Jay.

3. He will

Or he's

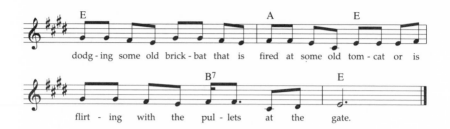

dodg - ing some old brick - bat that is fired at some old tom - cat or is

flirt - ing with the pul - lets at the gate.

I've a farm out in the West
Of the farms it is the best.
I've a cross-eyed mule
With freckles and red hair.
I've an old Texas steer
With a wart on his left ear
But now he's gone to climb the Golden Stair.

But my poor old Shanghai rooster
Who battle he befell
With a brammy who fought him long and brave.
And his wife is in the barnyard
Sitting on a lump of coal.
She is weeping for her Shanghai rooster's tail.

He will never crow again.
Or flirt with some old hen,
He's a masher and his middle name is Jay.
At the hour of half past eight
He is at the garden gate
Singing "cock-a-doodle-do." Good-bye Jay.

Or he's dodging some old brickbat
That is fired at some old tomcat
Or is flirting with the pullets at the gate.

Grandma Deb: "Jus' a crazy song."

"Shanghai Rooster" is a comic song with sexual tones. I found no mate, but I did identify Grandma Deb's tune with the music of Carl Sandburg's song in "She Promised She'd Meet Me."[1]

1. Sandburg, *American Songbag*, 207.

Three Little Girls A-Sliding Went

Three little girls a-sliding went
All on a summer day.
The ice fell out
And they fell in.
The rest they ran away.

Now had these children been at home
Or sliding on bare ground.
Ten thousand pounds to one penny
They wouldn't all been drowned.

Grandma Deb: "'All on a summer day,' too, mind! No ice then! An' they couldn't have been 'sliding on bare ground!' Impossibilities, y'know."

The long history of this nonsense poem/play-party song appears in the *Oxford Dictionary of Nursery Rhymes.* In America the song was often more than "a crazy joke to amuse the kiddies," as Grandma Deb described it. In the Ozarks, it was popular as a play-party song, with a tune like "Sir Roger de Coverley," and the game itself was similar to a Virginia reel.[1]

1. Randolph, *Ozark Folksongs,* 3:394.

Pop Goes the Weasel

All around the vinegar jug
The monkey chased the weasel.
The monkey kissed the cobbler's wife,
And Pop goes the weasel.

Here, a traditional British game has been made into an American play-party dance. One imported British broadside gives several stanzas showing the popularity of this cheerful song, one version implying that even "Albert and the Queen" also danced "Pop Goes the Weasel."[1]

Randolph defines "weasel" as a metal tool used by hatmakers in England; when it was pawned it was "popped."[2] But in America, a weasel is an animal not wanted in anybody's house, so it would be fine to have him chased out by a monkey. In a figurative sense a weasel is a treacherous or sneaky person, one who would tattle on anybody, and so he deserves to be "popped." There are many versions of this song: the only unchangeable part is the vigorous punch line at the end.

1. *Harvard College Broadsides.*
2. Randolph, *Ozark Folksongs,* 3:368–69.

Old Maid's Song

There's many a bachelor born to wed,
Pre-haps there's one for me.
If so what a nice little wife I'll make,
And happy my lord shall be. [She drops hanky here]

CHORUS:
But if for me, such a lot is cast,
Such happiness in store,
I'm willing to wait, I'm willing to wait,
Just one little short year or two more.

Whene'er I go out upon the street,
I'm always sure to meet,
They either step on my dress behind
Or tread on my tender feet.

CHORUS

The *Check-List* gives this as "There's Many a Bachelor Born to Wed." Another title in the *Check-List* may also be for the same song, since its title incorporates Jennie's direction: "Drop the Hanky, a Play Party Song."

Why Don't the Boys Propose?

Why don't the boys propose, Mother,
Why don't the boys propose?
Here I am nearly twenty-one,
Why don't the boys propose?

When I was originally doing the research on these songs, a friend of mine lent me a family treasure, a songster owned by her grandmother, with the date of 1890. Beside this poem it contained "Johnny Sands," "Bobbin' Around," and "Mary of the Wild Moor." I reluctantly returned the songster, although this was the only sighting I had of these four lines. Now my friend and the songster are long gone. Kenneth S. Goldstein, however, found these same lines for me in *Beadle's Dime Song Book No. 6* (N.Y., 1860).

Bobbin' Around

Josh and I___ went to church
I left Josh right in the lurch } as we went bob - bin' 'round.

Josh and I went to church
As we went bobbin' round.
I left Josh right in the lurch,
As we went bobbin' round.

Grandma Deb: "They're only old baby rhymes. Cute to sing to the kiddies."

This is a dance tune.[1] As could well be expected, this jolly song appeared, in many verses, in print many times, such as in *The Bobbing Around Songster* printed in Philadelphia in 1851. Sheet music with "words and music by W. J. Florence" was printed in 1855. Sometimes billed as "Yankee Song," it was a great comic favorite of the 1850s.[2]

1. For full text, tune, and detailed explanations, see *Songs of Yesterday*, ed. Jordan and Kessler, 221–24.
2. Kenneth S. Goldstein has found the words in several songsters, among them: *Wehman's Song Collection No. 9* (N.Y., n.d.); *Beadle's Dime Song Book No. 6* (N.Y., 1860); *Delaney's Song Book No. 16* (N.Y., n.d.); and *DeMarsan's Singer's Journal No. 23* (N.Y., n.d.).

Captain Jinks

I'm Captain Jinks of the Horse Marines,
My horse I feed on corn and beans.
Of course, it's quite above my means,
But I'm a captain in the Army.

This dance tune has often been described as a Civil War song. It appeared in many songsters, such as *The Captain Jinks of the Horse Marines Songster of 1868.*[1] Sigmund Spaeth called it "a musical comedy song made famous by the 'great' William Lingard, about 1869."[2] Collectors described it as a folksong, as a minstrel song, or as a popular street song; it was very popular as a play-party song.[3] To Grandma Deb, it was a "dancing song." The stanza that she remembered is number two in Spaeth's set of verses. Spaeth added an interesting footnote: "Captain Jinks of the Horse Marines" was also the title of the play in which Ethel Barrymore made her stage debut in 1901.

1. Some of the other songsters in the Goldstein collection are *Beadle's Dime Song Book No. 23* (N.Y., 1860); *Beadle's Half-Dime Singer's Library No. 2* (1878); *Delaney's Song Book No. 10* (N.Y., n.d.); and *DeMarsan's Singer's Journal No. 1* (N.Y., n.d.).
2. Spaeth, *Weep Some More,* 47.
3. Randolph, *Ozark Folksongs,* 3:354–56.

New Shoes

Do you see them? Do you see them? Do you see my new shoes? With a hole in, with a hole in, with a hole in the toe? With a hole in the toe, with a hole in the toe. Do you see my new shoes, with a hole in the toe?

Do you see them?
Do you see them?
Do you see my new shoes?
With a hole in,
With a hole in,
With a hole in the toe?

With a hole in the toe,
With a hole in the toe.
Do you see my new shoes,
With a hole in the toe?

Grandma Deb: "A schottische. Part of a square dance. The violin played and we all sang and danced. Silly, when you think of it. 'Course they wouldn't be new shoes if they had a hole, would they?"

Lomax marked this dance tune as "Do You See Them?" but there are no other *Check-List* titles that I can match with it. There are, however, five tunes listed as "Schottische," which was Grandma Deb's descriptive term for the tune.

Jim-a-long, Joe

Hey git along, Jim-a-long, Josie.
Hey git along, Jim-a-long, Joe.
I went downtown to see my Rosie.
Hey git along, Jim-a-long, Joe.

"Jim-a-long, Joe" is a minstrel song/play-party dance. In *Traditional American Folk Songs*, Warner identifies this as "written by Edward Harper who sang it in his drama, *The Free Nigger of New York* about 1838."[1] There is also a broadside in the Brown University Library with the same date; Foster Damon, custodian of the Harris Collection, called this "another sweeping success in the burnt-cork tradition." Sheet music was published by Firth and Hall in 1840. Sigmund Spaeth found it as a "plantation song" in Burleigh's *Negro Minstrel Melodies*.[2]

There was a rich tradition of black folksongs available to creators of the minstrel show,[3] and there was a flourishing pseudo-Negro tradition created by white imitators. An example of the latter is *Lucy Neale's Nigga Warbler Songster*, in which there is a version of "Jim A-long Josey" in fourteen stanzas, proclaiming that the black narrator wins every dance contest, in the American "tall tales" tradition.[4]

However, "Jim-a-long Joe" had another life as a play-party tune, as reported in various articles in the *Journal of American Folklore* from 1911 on.[5] "Jim along" meant "come along" or "get along." Sweethearts liked the game played to this music, but the watching elders frowned on it, since it meant that the boy won the privilege of an embrace if he caught a girl trying to run across a circle of dancers, from one side to the other.[6]

1. Warner, *Traditional American Folk Songs*, 408–9.
2. Spaeth, *Weep Some More*, 103–4.
3. Scarborough, *On the Trail of Negro Folk-Songs*, 105.
4. This songster is in the collection of the library of the Pennsylvania Historical Society.
5. Randolph, *Ozark Folksongs*, 3:385.
6. Mahan and Grahame, "Play-Party Games," *Palimpsest* 10.

When I Was Young

When I was young and in my prime I court-ed the girls____ all the time. I'd take them out each day for a ride and al - ways had one by my side. Hi - de - hi, hoop - de - do, How I love to sing to you for I can sing with joy and glee, though I'm not as young as I used to be.

> When I was young and in my prime
> I courted the girls all the time.
> I'd take them out each day for a ride
> And always had one by my side.
>
> CHORUS:
> Hi-de-hi, hoop-de-do,
> How I love to sing to you.
> For I can sing with joy and glee,
> Though I'm not as young as I used to be.

I originally found the Jennie Devlin version of this minstrel song/dance tune in number 74 of the *Delaney Song Book* series, and Kenneth S. Goldstein adds another place: *Beadle's Dime Song Book No. 5* (N.Y., 1870). Its minstrel parallel is shown by a "dialect" piece in number 24 of *DeMarsan's Song Books,* which offers the philosophy of one "Ebenezer Clam," who encourages "white folk" to be like him. "Now what's the use to fret or sigh or lying idly down to die?" he asks.

"White" versions differ drastically. Frequently the old man still thinks he is vigorous enough to court the girls as he used to do. But other versions are more honest: "I'm Not As Young As I Used to Be."[1] Grandma Deb's song, typically, admits the facts but stresses that joy and glee are still possible. What gives her song its vitality is the nonsense line, "Hi-de-hi, hoop-de-do," of the chorus, the marker for a dance piece.

1. Randolph, *Ozark Folksongs*, 3:181–84. "I'm 72 Today" and "Uncle Joe" are fragments similar to ours, but not identical; they are not dance tunes.

Shoo Fly

1. Oh,   Le - na, wash the   dish - es, Oh,   Di - nah, sweep the   room. Oh,
2.   Mis - ter Stone's a - com - ing, he's   com - ing here   to - night, so

Han - nah, set   the   chairs   back,   all a - round   the   room   2. For
dance a - round the cor–ner girls and   try   to   be   po - lite. ____

Shoo fly,   don't   both - er   me,   shoo fly,   don't   both - er   me.

Shoo fly,   don't   both - er   me for   I be - long to Com - pa - ny G. My

mas - ter rides in the   af - ter - noon, I   fol - low with a   hick - 'ry broom. The

po - ny rared and   then he kicked, and threw ole mas - ter   in the ditch.

Jim - my crack corn, don't   care,   Jim - my crack corn, don't   care.

Jim - my crack corn, don't care, for mas - ter's gone a - way.

Oh, Lena, wash the dishes,
Oh, Dinah, sweep the room.
Oh, Hannah set the chairs back,
All around the room.
For Mr. Stone's a-coming,
He's coming here tonight,
So dance around the corner, girls,
And try to be polite.

CHORUS:
Shoo fly, don't bother me.
Shoo fly, don't bother me.
Shoo fly, don't bother me.
For I belong to Company G.

My master rides in the afternoon.
I follow with a hickory broom.
The pony reared and then he kicked
And threw ole master in the ditch.

Jimmy crack corn, don't care.
Oh, Jimmy crack corn, don't care,
Oh, Jimmy crack corn, don't care,
For Master's gone away.

CHORUS

Grandma Deb: "When you wanted to teach the kiddies how to do something, they'd put it in a song, like this. 'Lena, wash the dishes' and 'Dinah, sweep the room,' that's clear. But puttin' the chairs away from the table . . . you had to set them back against the wall. I dunno why, but that's what was done."

What about this housekeeping opening, which has nothing to do with the rest of Gran's song? I can only conjecture that it had floated in from some other (and quite different) song before it was taught to Jennie Hess.

After this unrelated stanza comes a chorus of "Shoo, Fly," an enormously popular minstrel comic selection and a song much more than just "a crazy piece to sing to the kiddies," as Grandma Deb considered it. In the Ozarks, it was popular as a play-party song, with a tune like "Sir Roger de Coverley," and the game itself was similar to a Virginia reel.[1]

We have another major difficulty here. Our version of the song itself seems to have been composed of two well-known songs rolled into one, "The Blue-Tail Fly," and "Shoo, Fly, Don't Bother Me!" I have never found this combination anywhere. Attention was mostly paid to "Shoo, Fly!" and there were many parodies. One I particularly enjoy showed the vogue: it was called "Shoo, Fly on the Brain!" The words were:

> As through the streets you pass along,
> You hear one universal song:
> One that haunts you to dinner or to tea—
> Shoo, fly! don't bodder me.[2]

I surmise that Grandma Deb heard two songs and put them together because of the word "fly." "Shoo Fly" might seem to be connected with "The Blue-Tail Fly." Both, of course, were minstrel songs, and good dance tunes. In their second titles, though, the difference shows. "Shoo Fly" is also known as "Shoo Fly, Don't Bother Me." "The Blue-Tail Fly" appeared in *The Ethiopian Glee Book* in 1844. It was known as "Jimmie Crack Corn."

Laws 243

1. Lomax, *Folk Songs of North America*, 506.
2. Marks, *They All Sang*, 257, gives 1869 as a date for "Shoo, Fly," but Spaeth, in *Read 'Em and Weep* (63), called it "the most popular nonsense song of the Civil War."

Katie Lee and Willie Gray

Two brown heads with tossing curls,
Red lips shutting over pearls;
Bare feet white and wet with dew,
Two eyes black and two eyes blue,
Little girl and boy were they,
Katie Lee and Willie Gray.

They had cheeks like roses red.
He was taller than 'most a head;
She, with arms like wreaths of snow,
Swung her basket to and fro,
As she loitered, half in play,
Chatting there to Willie Gray.

"Pretty Katie," Willie said,
And there came a dash of red
Through the brownness of his cheek.
"Boys are strong and girls are weak,
And I'll carry, so I will,
Katie's basket up the hill."

Katie answered, with a laugh,
"You shall only carry half."
And then, tossing back her curls,
"Boys are weak as well as girls."
Do you think that Katie guessed
Half the wisdom she expressed?

Men are only boys grown tall.
Hearts don't change much, after all.
And when, long years from that day,
Katie Lee and Willie Gray
Stood again beside the brook,
Bending like a shepherd's crook—

"Pretty Katie," Willie said,
And again the dash of red
Crossed the brownness of his cheek,
"I am strong and you are weak.
Life is but a slippery steep
Hung with shadows cold and deep.

"Will you trust me, Katie dear?
Walk beside me without fear?
May I carry, if I will,
All the burdens up the hill?"
And she answered, with a laugh,
"No, but you may carry half."

Close beside the little brook,
Bending like a shepherd's crook,
Washing with its silvery hands
Late and early at the sands,
Is a cottage where today
Katie lives with Willie Gray.

On a porch she sits, and lo!
Swings a basket, to and fro,
Vastly different from the one
That she swung in years a-gone.
This is long and deep and wide,
And has rockers at its side.

This also was a piece in the repertoire of the Hutchinson Family. *Beadle's Dime Song Book No. 14* (N.Y., 1864) and *Beadle's Half-Dime Singer's Library No. 9* (N.Y., 1878) both have it in full, but its continuing popularity was proven when I found it in volume 33 of *Werner's Readings and Recitations* (1892).

Calomel

"O send for the doctor and be quick."
The doctor came with much good will
And freely gave his calomel.

. . .

"Give this to him three times a day,
For I must be upon my way."

This was composed by J. J. Hutchinson; I made a pencil copy of the words and music, dated 1843, in the Music Room of the New York Public Library.

Laws considered it a "ballad-like piece, excluded from consideration" because it belonged in the category of "satirical and fanciful pieces having little basis in reality."[1] Spaeth reprinted it in *Weep Some More*, in 1927.

1. Laws, *North American Balladry*, 277.

Down in a Diving Bell

Down in a diving bell
At the bottom of the sea,
There is the prettiest place
The fishes for to see.

Down in a diving bell
At the bottom of the sea,
Pretty little mermaids, sweet little mermaids,
Oft came courting me.

Once I caught a mermaid
To kiss her was my wish,
But like an eel, she slipped away.
You can't hold on to fish.

Her mother brought her back to me
And whispered in my ear
That if I liked her, then,
[If I liked her daughter, then,]
We might get married in a year.

The church that we were married in
Was on an oyster shell.
The parson wore a bathing gown,
The codfish rang the bell.

And now that we are married
And live happy in the shade,
There's nobody anywhere so happy
As I and my pretty mermaid.

From this song Grandma Deb took her favorite lines for describing the impossible: "But like an eel, she slipped away. You can't hold on to fish!"

The mermaid, that object of ancient folkloric fascination, met a modern mechanical wonder — the diving bell — and the result was this song, which, as another old folksinger told me circa 1938, was written "about some time before the Civil War." The diving bell, used to prepare riverbeds to support the weight of bridges, was also put to a jolly use, lowering spectators to the ocean floor at amusement parks. I remember that there was one on the great Steel Pier in Atlantic City when I was a child.

Sheet music to which our version corresponds was copyrighted by Alfred Lee, "published by J. L. C. & Co.," but without a date.[1] Scarborough recorded a version "as sung by the truly admirable W. F. Sinclair, the greatest Serio-Comic Singer in the U.S.," but she also gives no date.[2] I found it in my early research in *DeMarsan's Singer's Journal No. 43* (N.Y., n.d.). Kenneth S. Goldstein has supplied one specific date: 1871, the year when *Starr's Songbook No. 3,* which included these words, was published by Beadle in New York.

1. I consulted this sheet music in the Music Room, New York Public Library.
2. Scarborough, *On the Trail of Negro Folk-Songs,* 311.

Pretty Pond Lilies

I'm waiting in the lane for you, darling,
Ling'ring as the hours roll by,
Attracted by the rippling of the water,
In the pond where the pond lilies lie.

Pretty pond lilies, I pluck them for you,
Fresh from the water, sparkling with dew.
Take them from me as a token so true,
Pretty pond lilies I've brought unto you.

CHORUS:
Ho ho ho-on-e ho.
Hoo he ho, hoo he ho. Ho he ho.

Grandma Deb said to Janet Grimler in 1938, "Pretty, ain't it!"

Grimler could not fit words to what she considered the second version of the tune, as she explained in the note she left me (see p. 90). Larry Czoka, who prepared the music for this book, has suggested that the chorus might well have been a yodel. Lomax did not record the song at all.

Marks, in his recollections, *They All Sang*, lists this among the "1,545 Songs Outstanding in My Memory," as an old favorite. He writes, "It was composed and sung by Bobby Newcomb, a singer-producer," but he gives no date; this was the usual careless method of this old song salesman/publisher.[1] Kenneth S. Goldstein located it in *Delaney's Song Book No. 17* (N.Y.), but here too it was without a date.

1. Marks, *They All Sang*, 254.

Little Birdies

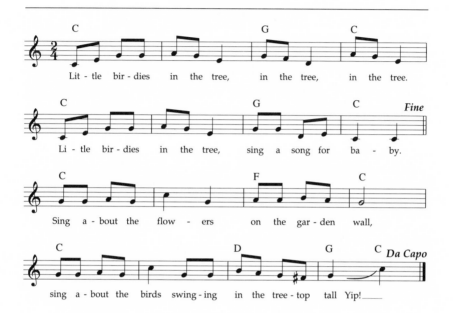

Lit - tle bir - dies in the tree, in the tree, in the tree.

Li - tle bir - dies in the tree, sing a song for ba - by.

Sing a - bout the flow - ers on the gar - den wall,

sing a - bout the birds swing - ing in the tree - top tall Yip!

CHORUS:
Little birdies in the tree, in the tree, in the tree,
Little birdies in the tree,
Sing a song for Baby.

Sing about the flowers on the garden wall,
Sing about the birds swinging in the treetop tall, Yip!

CHORUS

Sing about the farmers, planting corn and beans,
Sing about the steamship, I know what it means, Yip!

CHORUS

Grandma Deb to Kay: "You change the 'baby' to the name of the kid, y'know, like Ellen or Bobbie."

This is a children's song. It is also known as "Little Birdies in the Tree." There are eleven entries for this in the *Check-List*. As "Sing a Song to Me," it appeared in *The Arbor Day Manual*, edited by Charles Skinner (Syracuse, 1896).

The Gypsy's Warning

Do not trust him, gen - tle la - dy,___ though his voice be low and sweet. Heed not him who kneels be - fore you,___ gent - ly plead - ing at thy feet. Now thy life is in its morn - ing,___ cloud not thus thy hap - py lot. Lis - ten to the gyp - sy's warn - ing,___ gen - tle la - dy, trust him not.

"Do not trust him, gentle lady,
Though his voice be low and sweet.
Heed not him who kneels before you,
Gently pleading at thy feet.
Now thy life is in its morning,
Cloud not thus thy happy lot.
Listen to the Gypsy's warning,
Gentle lady, trust him not.

"Do not turn so coldly from me,
I would only guard thy youth
From his stern and withering power
I would only tell the truth.

I would shield thee from all danger,
Save thee from the tempter's snare —
Lady, shun the dark-eyed stranger.
I have warned thee. Now, beware.

"Lady, once there lived a maiden,
Pure and bright, and like thee, fair.
But he wooed and wooed, and won her,
Filled her gentle heart with care.
Then he heeded not her weeping,
Nor cared he her life to save.
Soon she perished. Now she's sleeping
In the cold and silent grave.

"Keep thy gold, I do not wish it.
Lady, I have prayed for this.
For the hour when I might foil him,
Rob him of expected bliss.
Gentle lady, do not wonder
At my words so strange and wild.
Lady, in that green grave yonder
Lies the Gypsy's only child."

Laws termed this "ballad-like, melodramatic and sentimental, of professional origin."[1] Written and composed by Henry A. Gourd, it was published in Brooklyn in 1864, and its popularity was instantaneous. In 1919 a singer in Pennsylvania recalled: "It was popular fifty years ago,"[2] and this statement was borne out by the research of John Harrington Cox in 1925.[3] Alternate titles are "Lady, Shun the Dark-Eyed Stranger" and "Do Not Trust Him, Gentle Lady."[4] The latter was the title used when Alexander Graham Bell, demonstrating his new invention in 1878, had "Do Not Trust Him, Gentle Lady" sung into the transmitter, thus making it the first song ever heard on the telephone.[5]

1. Laws, *Native American Balladry*, 277.
2. Shoemaker, *Mountain Minstrelsy of Pennsylvania*, 93.
3. Cox, *Folk Songs of the South*.
4. Kenneth S. Goldstein's additions are: *Beadle's Half-Dime Singers' Library No. 13* (N.Y., 1878); *Gipsy's Warning Songster* (N.Y.: R. M. DeWitt, 1867); *Delaney's Song Book No. 3* (N.Y., n.d.); *DeMarsan's Singer's Journal No. 2* (N.Y. n.d.).
5. Randolph, *Ozark Folksongs*, 4:219–22.

Reply to the Gypsy's Warning

La - dy, do not heed her warn - ing.___ Trust me,
thou shalt find me true. Con - stant as the light of
morn - ing___ I will ev - er be to you. La - dy,
I will not de - ceive thee,___ fill thy guile - less heart with
woe. Trust me, la - dy, and be - lieve me,___ sor - row
thou shalt ne - ver know.

"Lady, do not heed her warning.
Trust me, thou shalt find me true.
Constant as the light of morning
I will ever be to you.
Lady, I will not deceive thee,
Fill thy guileless heart with woe.
Trust me, lady, and believe me,
Sorrow thou shalt never know.

"Lady, every joy would perish,
Pleasures all would wither fast,
If no heart could love and cherish
In this world of storm and blast.

E'en the stars that gleam above thee
Shine the brightest in the night;
So would he who fondly loves thee
In the darkness, be thy light.

"Down beside the flowing river,
Where the dark green willow weeps,
Where the leafy branches quiver,
There a gentle maiden sleeps.
In the morn a lonely stranger
Comes and lingers many hours.
Lady, he's no heartless stranger,
For he strews her grave with flowers.

"Lady, heed thee not her warning
Lay thy soft white hand in mine.
For I seek no fairer laurel
Than the constant love of thine.
When the silver moonlight brightens,
Thou shalt slumber in my breast.
Tender words thy soul shall lighten,
Lull thy spirit into rest."

Grandma Deb to Kay: "This goes to show you, there's more'n one side, sometimes."

She had sung "The Gypsy's Warning" to Janet Grimler without a note in hand, but when Alan Lomax came, Grandma Deb insisted on using a newspaper clipping to sing "The Reply" into his microphone.

Using the same tune as "The Gypsy's Warning," "The Reply" (sometimes called "The Answer") also directly addresses the same speechless bride-to-be: "Lady, do not heed her warning."[1]

I found "The Warning" and "The Reply" properly partnered in a *Delaney Songster* of the 1890s, and Kenneth S. Goldstein has some other songster citations: *Beadle's Half-Dime Singers' Library No. 13* (N.Y., 1878); *Delaney's Song Book No. 5* (N.Y., n.d.); *DeMarsan's Singer's Journal No. 2* (N.Y., n.d.).

1. "The Reply" is discussed in Belden, *Ballads and Songs*, 35; Brewster, *Ballads and Songs of Indiana*, 273; Shoemaker, *Mountain Minstrelsy of Pennsylvania*, 94.

Baby's Got a Tooth

George dear, George dear,
Can't you guess the truth?
George dear, George dear,
Bless the little youth.
Do get up and light the fire,
Turn the gas a little higher,
Go and tell your Aunt Maria,
Baby's got a tooth!

Grandma Deb recited this fragment, but she seemed unimpressed by it so I didn't press her for the tune. "Oh, yes," she said, "everybody knows that. I can sing it for you if the tune comes."

I located this in *The Minstrel*, "Edited by Samuel Hosfeld, Music Director of Carncross Minstrels, printed in Philadelphia, 1883. Words by Charley Reed, arr. by H. Wannemacher." No tune was given, as was usual in minstrel songbooks. Two other songsters that contain the words are *Beadle's Half-Dime Singer's Library No. 10* (N.Y., 1878), and *Delaney's Song Book No. 10* (N.Y., n.d.). The song with music can be found in Carmer's *Songs of the Rivers of America*.

Look Me in the Eye, Johnny

"Look me in the eye, Johnny,
Look me in the eye.
What keeps you out so late?
And here I have to sit alone
To think and watch and wait.

"You say you want to take a smoke
And, therefore, must roam.
Now you have my full consent
To smoke your pipe at home.

"And then I've heard it hinted
And I cannot help but think
You spend your time and money, too,
With those who love to drink.

"I think it is preposterous,
You know it isn't right
To keep me up until you come
At one o'clock at night."

"I look you in the eye, Sally,
I look you in the eye.
Your very bold assertion
I certainly do deny,

"Fact is, I had intended
Coming from the store
But it got dark as Egypt
And the rain began to pour.

"So I thought I'd stop with
Cousin Molly Rose a little while.
You know you always said she
Had a prepossessing smile.

"I tell you we had quite a time
With cider, cake, and song.
But little did I think, my dear,
I'd stayed half so long.

"I look you in the eye, Sally,
And tell me it was wrong?
For I had no intentions, dear,
With staying half so long."

"I look you in the eye, Johnny.
You always call me 'dear.'
Why you won't stay at home
I think is very queer.

"If Cousin Molly wants a beau,
She need not well disguise.
If she can't get one without,
Just let her advertise.

"I've come to this conclusion,
Not to stand it any more.
And if you're not in by ten,
I'll bolt and bar the door.

"You know you can't deceive my eyes,
You cannot cheat my nose,
Or talk of liquor that you get
At Cousin Molly Rose."

"I look you in the eye, Sally.
A woman loses her ammunition
When she scolds a man.
The use of kind persuasive words
Is far the wiser plan.

"Now that I should perchance
Return a little late,
Don't let your tongue unwind itself
At such a rapid rate.

"But meet me with a pleasant smile
And bid me welcome home
And you will find, to your surprise,
I'm not inclined to roam.

"Now look me in the eyes, Sally,
And hear what I propose.
We'll go together, after this,
To visit Molly Rose."

This recitation was from an unknown source, probably a newspaper column. Grandma Deb gave this without the slightest memory slip and with more dramatic intonation than she used in her "old pieces." This demonstration of how to make a marriage work would have been a favorite for her to read at her lodge. I believe this was one of the last pieces she ever memorized.

The Converted Indian Maid

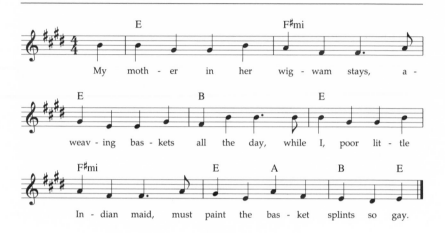

My mother in her wigwam stays,
A-weaving baskets all the day,
While I, poor little Indian maid,
Must paint the basket splints so gay.

My brother in his bark canoe
Has gaily o'er the water flew.
He shoots the wild duck on the brake
And catches white fish in the lake.

My father o'er the mountains dread,
He shoots the wild deer in the head.
He brings them home for mother to stew
In the big pot, for me and you.

The white man coming from the East,
He taught us heathens how to read.
Now I can read and I can sew,
My Savior's name I also know.

I can read and I can spell,
My Savior's name I love so well.
I can read and I can sew,
My Savior's name I also know.

Grandma Deb: "A woman missionary sang this, and I liked it so much I asked her to teach it to me, when I was a girl on the farm. There was an old Indian grave on the farm, too, but I guess that's gone, too, now."

"The Converted Indian Maid" is an American missionary song. I have no information other than that Mrs. Bentley ("Aunt Eva") recognized it and told me that Jennie had known it before she came to Wellsville in 1879.

Have Courage, My Boy, to Say "No"

You're starting today on life's journey,
Along on the highways of life.
You'll meet with a thousand temptations,
Each city is evil and bright.

CHORUS:
Have courage, my boy, to say "No."
Have courage, my boy, to say "No."
But if you are tempted to enter,
Think twice, even thrice, e'er you go.

The gambling halls are before you.
See the lights, how they dance to and fro.
But if you are tempted to enter,
Think twice, even thrice, e'er you go.

CHORUS

The bright ruby wine may be offered.
No matter how tempting it be,
From poison stings like an adder,
My boy, have the courage to flee.

CHORUS

This world is a stage of excitement.
There's danger wherever you go.
But if you are tempted to enter,
Have courage, my boy, to say "No."

CHORUS

Grandma Deb: "I don't know where I heard it. I guess I did learn this at the Salvation Army. Maybe in Wellsville. Good, ain't it!"

This temperance song is given in Sankey and Moody's *Sacred Songs*, "Words by Ira D. Sankey and H. R. Palmer; tune by Palmer. Copyright 1887."[1] However, the tune in the Sankey hymnal is quite different from the one Grandma Deb used. She sang the words of this song to the tune of "Columbia, The Gem of the Ocean." When her words are bent to fit the patriotic hymn, there is a very satisfactory emphasis to the ending.

1. Sankey and Moody, *Sacred Songs*.

Feathered Warblers

In that old gray village churchyard,
I can see a grassy mound.
Underneath my mother's sleeping
In the cold and silent ground.

CHORUS:
Brightest flowers cluster round her.
Feathered warblers sing their song.
Oh, my heart's so sad and lonely,
Since my mother's dead and gone.

I was young, but I remember
That sad day when Mother died.
I sat there a-watching, waiting,
Then she called me to her side.

Whispering, "I'll not see the morning,
For the angels bid me come.
Trust in God; we'll meet in Heaven,
When our earthly cares are done."

CHORUS

I have sat many lonely hours,
Looking at the skies above me,
Wondering if it'll be long
Before the angel voices call me
To the place where Mother's gone.

CHORUS

Lomax notation gives this as "In That Old Gray Village Churchyard," but I never found it under any title.

My Mother's Prayer

I never shall forget the day
I heard my dear old mother say,
"You're leaving now my tender care,
Remember, child, your mother's prayer."

Whene'er I think of her so dear,
I feel her angel spirit near.
A voice comes floating through the air,
Reminding me of Mother's prayer.

For Grandma Deb there was a certain linkage between "Feathered War-blers" and "My Mother's Prayer" that I never have fathomed. Although she sang the verses and the chorus of "Feathered Warblers" to Janet Grimler, she always insisted on following that by reciting the words to "My Mother's Prayer." She seemed to feel that items dealing with a dead mother should be kept together.

I did locate "My Mother's Pray'r," by J. W. Van De Venter and W. Weeden.[1] However, I cannot see any connection between this and "Feathered Warblers." "My Mother's Prayer" is a hymn of an adult's repentance, not the lament of a motherless child. Apparently Grandma Deb did not know the tune, which seems strange to me as I myself can still sing it. It was very meaningful to my mother; she sang it, along with "Where Is My Wandering Boy Tonight?," after my brother left home to seek his fortune in Florida in the 1920s.

1. Bilhan, *Soul-Winning Songs*, n.p.

The Drunkard's Lament

Don't go out to-night my dar - ling, Do not leave me here a-
lone.___ Stay at home with me, my dar - ling, For I'm so
lone - ly when you're gone.___ Oh, my God, he's gone and
left me, With a curse up - on his lips.___ No one
knows how I have suf - fered from the curs - ed cup he drinks.

"Don't go out tonight, my darling,
Do not leave me here alone.
Stay at home with me, my darling,
For I'm so lonely when you are gone."

Oh, my God, he's gone and left me,
With a curse upon his lips.
No one knows how I have suffered
From the cursed cup he drinks.

Hark! I hear the heavy footsteps,
Hear the rap upon the door,
They have brought me home my husband,
There he lies upon the floor.

No caress of mine can wake him.
All he craves is rum, more rum.
All my fondest hopes have perished,
All have faded, one by one.

Grandma Deb: "I know what this's all about--a husband who drinks."

This is a temperance song. In the torrent of nineteenth-century songs on the great evil of drink, it appears that two titles got mixed. What Grandma Deb called "The Drunkard's Lament" was identified in the Kentucky highlands as "The Drunkard's Wife."[1] The real twin is the song in which the drunkard dies, realizing that he has lost home and family; this is correctly titled "The Drunkard's Lament." Further complication arises from the existence of another "Drunkard's Wife," as published by DeMarsan in Philadelphia between 1871 and 1874, and in undated sheet music by Loder.[2] In that version, the drunkard reforms in time, and we leave him happily cured, in his wife's arms.

It was the wife's lament, not the husband's, that Jennie, wife of Hellfire Jack Devlin, learned.

1. Fuson, *Ballads of the Kentucky Highlands.*
2. I consulted these in the Music Room, New York Public Library, c. 1938.

The Orphan Child

They said I was but four years old
When Father went away.
Yet I have never seen his face
Since that sad parting day.

He's gone to dig the precious gold
Beneath California skies.
Dear Aunty shows me on the map
Where that far country lies.

I begged him, "Father do not go,
For since my mother died,
I love no one so well as you,"
And clung to his side.

The tears went trickling down my cheeks
Until my eyes were dim.
Some were in sorrow of the dead
And some with love of him.

He knelt and prayed to God above
His little daughter spare,
"Until we both shall meet again
And keep her in Thy care."

And so I've done these four long years
Within my lonely home,
Till every shadow wears his shape.
Why don't my father come?

"Father, dear Father, are you sick
Upon the strangers' shore?
Grandmother says it must be so.
Oh, write to us once more!

"And let your little daughter come
To soothe your restless head [bed]
Or press the cordial to your lips
Or hold your aching head."

I muse and listen all alone
While the stormy winds are high.
I think I hear his tender tone.
I call but no reply.

By my mother's tomb I love to sit
Where the weeping willows wave.
[Where the green branches wave.]
Oh, who would help an orphan child
To find her father's grave?

See "The Dying Californian" for an account of the conditions endured by men trying to get to the gold fields in the 1840s.

Poor Jim the Newsboy

1. {
Poor Jim the news - boy, one cold win - ter day,
Fa - ther was wait - ing, his poor heart did sink,

work had been poor, he had made lit - tle pay.
when he came home took his earn - ings for drink.

Ti - red and hun - gry and chilled with the cold,
Then when he asked for a mere mite to eat,

count - ed the pa - pers that day he had sold.
threw him a - gain out in the street.

Chorus

Thou - sands to wan - der in the street,

beg - ging for bread to eat.

Mon - ey to gam - ble to drink and to cheat;

on - ly a grave for wan - der - ing feet.

Poor Jim the newsboy, one cold winter day,
Work had been poor, he had made little pay.
Tired and hungry and chilled with the cold,
Counted the papers that day he had sold.

Father was waiting. His poor heart did sink,
When he came home, took his earnings for drink.
Then, when he asked for a mere crust to eat,
Threw him again out in the street.

CHORUS:
Thousands to wander in the street,
Begging for bread to eat.
Money to gamble, to drink, and to cheat;
Only a grave for poor wandering feet.

Slowly he walked to the corner saloon,
Said to the man in the drinkers' room,
"Please don't sell my father more drink,
Then with the money, he'll buy bread, I think.

"All of the money for papers I've sold,
Father has took; I'm hungry and cold."
Only a curse, and his poor tired feet,
Wandered again out in the street.

CHORUS

Down in a basement, behind the dark stairs,
Jim crawled for shelter to whisper his prayers.
Prayed as he once prayed at his dear mother's knee,
"God bless dear Father, and poor little Jim."

Angels were coming; his eyes had grown dim.
Said after prayers as he'd learned to repeat,
"God pity Jim, out in the street."

God heard the words that his lips tried to speak,
God saw the teardrops that froze on his cheek,
Made the last snowdrops his last winding sheet,
Took little Jim up from the street.

CHORUS

Alan Lomax: "I'll bet people cried when you sang 'Poor Jim.' Did they?"
Grandma Deb: "Yes, they often did. 'God took poor Jim up from the street.'
That was sad."

"Poor Jim the Newsboy" is a temperance ballad. This is the only one with this title listed in the *Check-List*. Songs about children who had been orphaned by the deaths of alcoholic fathers or starving mothers were common.[1] This was reality. Ten-year-olds were treated by law as adults and allowed to die in the streets.[2]

1. *Delaney's Song Book No. 41* (N.Y., n.d.).
2. "Orphan Trains," *Smithsonian*, August 1986, 95–103.

The Little Pallet of Straw

I'm lying alone in this garret,
While the sleet and the snow's falling down.
Yet God knows I'm hungry and helpless.
I wish that my Jessie would come.

For Jessie went out early this morning,
And she kissed me good-bye as she said,
"I soon shall return, dearest mother,
Whether I get pennies or bread."

But the storm's growing on, and I'm weaker.
I fear I shall see Jessie no more.
For when she returns she will find me
Lying dead on the pallet of straw.

Would to God that my child had a father,
Or someone to watch her with care,
Or someone to guide and protect her,
And then I would die without fear.

Grandma Deb: "That poem impressed me awful at the time . . . the poor
soul. I found it somewheres and memorized it. When Madeline first heard it,
she cried and cried."

When I was examining the songster collection in the Library of Congress, I
found that this song had been very popular. I noted especially its appearance
in Dumont's *Pallet of Straw* and *HMS Pinafore* songsters and *Delaney's Song Book*
(which has a probable date of 1894). In *When the Moonbeams Gently Fall Songster,*
the words are ascribed to Edward Wise; they were sung to the same tune as
"Over the Hills to the Poor House."

To Jennie Devlin there was nothing melodramatic about this song; it was a
true lament of a dying woman leaving a fatherless child. The mother does not
fear the wrath of the Eternal but only the earthly safety of her child. Once again
there is the theme of the motherless child.

What made the sufferings of the poor bearable was the surety of a happy
home in the hereafter. This is shown in many of Grandma Deb's pieces. The
last words of "Young Charlotte" were "I'm growing warmer now." To
Grandma Deb this meant that the frozen girl had entered heaven, there to
meet with Martha Decker, Mary Ann Wyatt, Poor Jim, and this single mother.

Irish Song

Oh, go to old Ireland
And there you will know,
How many it takes
To milk an old ewe. ["That's a sheep."]
It's two to her head,
And two to her hams,
And two little paddies
To beat up the lambs.

CHORUS:
Ho, ho. Ho, laddie, ho. ["Turn the corners here."]

Go into the houses
To dirty your knees.
Go into the bedroom
You're covered with fleas.
The fleas are big enough
For to crack corn,
And never run down
Your old countryman born.

CHORUS

Apples and buttermilk
Seven years old,
Skippers and fleas,
They've grown very bold.
The skippers and fleas
Are alive on the floor,
And the maggots are making
The buttermilk roar.

CHORUS

Pull down your cap, Paddy,
And hang down your head.
Think of your country
And wish you were dead.
Your father's a cuckold,
Your mother's a witch,
And you're a Scotch-Irishman
Son of a bitch.

CHORUS

Grandma Deb to Kay Dealy: "A dance-jig. Like a Virginia reel."
Grandma Deb to Alan Lomax (when he was recording it): "Oh, those words are too bad." Then she broke into an embarrassed laugh, and sang them.

This was sung to the tune of "The Irish Washerwoman" and given that title by Lomax. There are nine titles like this in the *Check-List*.

Grandma Deb's joy in the song was due to its exaggeration and its "craziness." She never thought of it as mocking the Irish, but rather as laughing at farm life. Most of all, she enjoyed it as a fast dance tune—in fact, the "naughty" last stanza (which I never found elsewhere) may well have been added by a high-spirited dancer.

The Irish Ain't Much

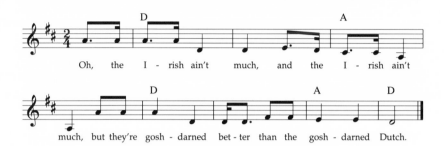

Oh, the Irish ain't much,
And the Irish ain't much.
But they're gosh-darned better
Than the gosh-darned Dutch.

Be aisy, Mary-Ann,
Be aisy, Mary-Ann.
You never seen a Dutchman
Could lick an Irishman.

Grandma Deb: "I was jus' Dutch, y'know. But Pop, he was Irish. So who wins?"

I found no exact match for this music-hall comic song, but there are two parallels in *Delaney* songbooks: in book 1, the song is titled "I Don't Like the Irish, But I'd Like to Hear Somebody Say as Much," with words and music by John H. Flynn, 1901; in book 37, "It Takes the Irish to Beat the Dutch," words by Ed Madden, music by Theodore F. Morse, 1903.

Second-Handed Clothes

Oh, they sent for me to the old countree
And now they got me here
And the business they have got me in
Is second-handed clothes.

The driver's got a big, red nose
And the jackass's got a big leg
But they just suit the business
In second-handed clothes.

A comic song, this was probably part of a music-hall skit making fun of immigrants, yet it is not a dialect piece.

I Bought My Coat of a Tailor

I bought my coat of a tailor
Who lived upon the street.
I bought my shoes of a shoemaker
To cover my naked feet.

My britches they are ragged,
And hardly fit to wear,
And every time I do stoop down
My knee it does go bare.

Grandma Deb: "There used to be a tune to it."

This is a nursery song. Grandma Deb never remembered the tune, and for her purposes it was not necessary because it was one of her "kiddie pieces." To her this was one more opportunity to laugh at human conceit. Imagine somebody spending money on a coat and not for the more essential nethergarments!

I Schust Came Over from Schermany

I schust came over from Schermany
This country for to see.
My broder vat keeps one beer saloon,
He writes one letter to me.
He says, "Pack up your trunks shure quick
And lave the Faderland,"
And if the steamboat should sink,
It makes me nothings out.

CHORUS:
I'm Hanna Johann from Schermany,
I lives on sauerkraut.
And if the people calls me green,
It makes me nothings out-out-out,
It makes me nothings out-out-out
It makes me nothings out.

And on the schip I meets vun gal
Carlvoly was her name.
Her mouth vas big and her hair vas red,
And she valked a leetle lame.
Her mouth vas like one small barn door
She had rheumatiks mit de gout.
But I don't care, for her heart vas gut,
And that makes me nothings out.

CHORUS

I popped the question right away,
You should have seen her smile.
The tears rolled down her Grecian nose.
She kissed me all der while.
I was the happiest mine self,
I could sing and laugh and shout.
"Oh, Carlvine, if I should die,
'Twould make me nothings out."

CHORUS

Grandma Deb: "I never can get that poor German off the boat! And what did he do with her on land?"

This is another comic song. It was probably part of a music-hall skit making fun of German immigrants, but in a good-humored way.

My Grandmother's Old Armchair

My grandmother, she,
At the age of eighty-three,
One day was taken ill and died.
After she was dead,
Of course the will was read,
By the lawyer as we all stood by his side.

How they tittered,
How they laughed,
How my brothers and my sister laughed,
When they heard the lawyer declare,
Granny'd only left to me
Her old armchair.

One day the chair fell down
And to my surprise I found,
The seat had fallen out upon the floor.
And there to my surprise,
I saw before my eyes,
Three hundred pounds in notes or more.

How they cursed,
How they swore,
How my brothers and my sister swore,
When they heard what Granny'd left me
In her old armchair.

Grandma Deb: "Everybody knows 'Grandfather's Clock.' Y'know: 'It stopped short / Never to run again / When the old man died.' And this is the song that goes with it."

There is a good version of this music-hall song in Warner's *Traditional American Folk Songs*.[1] According to Scarborough—who recorded a version much like this, and the same tune to it also—this was an "amusing old song of British origin" that she had copied from a manuscript ballad book.[2] Her theory about its provenance was correct: according to Goldstein's research, the original song was by John Read, an English songwriter. This accounts for the fact that the Grandmother left pounds, not dollars, in the chair.

There is an undated *Grandmother's Chair Songster* as volume seven of the *Dumont Series of Songsters*. Although Edwin Barry's *Grandmother's Chair Songster* was published by A. J. Fisher in 1879, Anne Warner has the original copyright as 1880. The song was "popular in the Ozarks in the '80s."[3]

"My Grandmother's Old Armchair" illustrates Grandma Deb's selectivity in choosing songs to dictate to me. Knowing that this song's companion piece, the better-known "Grandfather's Clock," also copyrighted by John Reed, was now a popular favorite (children all loved to sing the "tick, tock" refrain), she hadn't bothered to recite or sing it to me. But she believed that the twin piece had been forgotten, so she brought it out of her memory for my collection. This is another example of her liking to pair songs: "The Cruel Wife" and "Johnny Sands"; "The Gypsy's Warning" and "The Reply"; and now these two. She considered her collection unique and so described it emphatically: "These are my pieces that I know."

1. Warner, *Traditional American Folk Songs*, 246–47.
2. Scarborough, *Song Catcher*, 373.
3. Randolph, *Ozark Folksongs*, 3:224-27.

My Dad's Dinner Pail

1st verse only

1. Pre - serve that old ket - tle___ so black - ened and worn, it be -
longed to my fa - ther be - fore I was born. It
hung in the cor - ner be - yond on a nail, 'twas the
em - blem of la - bor,___ 'twas my Dad's din - ner pail. 2. It___

All other verses

glist - ened like sil - ver so spark - ling and bright, Dad was
fond of the tri - fle that held his wee bite. In
sum - mer or win - ter, in rain, snow, or hail, I have
car - ried that ket - tle,___ my Dad's din - ner pail.

Preserve that old kettle so blackened and worn,
It belonged to my father before I was born.
It hung in the corner beyond on the nail,
'Twas the emblem of labor,
'Twas my dad's dinner pail.

It glistened like silver, so sparkling and bright,
Dad was fond of the trifle that held his wee bite.
In summer or winter, rain, snow, or hail,
I have carried that kettle, my dad's dinner pail.

When the days they were stormy, my father'd stop home.
He would polish that kettle as clean as a stone.
He would joke with my mother, and at me he would rail,
If I'd just lay a finger on my dad's dinner pail.

When the bells ring for noontime, my father'd come down.
He'd eat with the workmen about on the ground.
He would share with the laborers and say he'd go bail,
For you can't reach the bottom of my dad's dinner pail.

There's a place for the coffee and also the bread,
Corn beef and cabbage, and oft, it was said,
"Go fill it with porter, with beer, or with ale,"
As the drink would taste sweeter from my dad's dinner pail.

Grandma Deb: "This was Pop's song. He'd always sing it when he'd been drinkin' and was three sheets to the wind and the fourth one dragging."

Although Alan Lomax did not record this music-hall comic song from either Grandpa or Grandma Deb, Janet Grimler had already preserved it for us. The words were written by Edward Harrigan; music by Dave Braham; copyright 1883, William A. Pond and Company, publishers.[1] "My Dad's Dinner Pail" was a popular Harrigan and Hart number that celebrated the working man. It was included (among many places) in *Delaney's Song Book No. 21*, but in that printing there are many words in the so-called "Irish dialect," such as "wid" for "with," "beyant" for "beyond," and "clane" for "clean." Even in his cups, Johnny Devlin never used dialect. He was a genuine — not a stage — Irishman.

1. Goldstein's collection includes this song as found in *Wehman's Song Book No. 19* (N.Y., n.d.) and *Delaney's Song Book No. 12* (N.Y., n.d.).

I Wish I'd Been Born a Boy

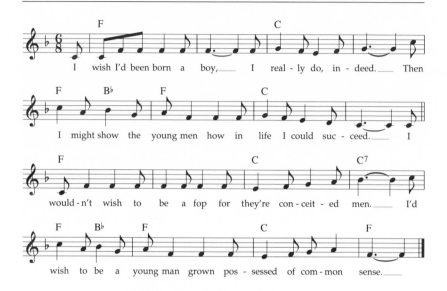

I wish I'd been born a boy,
I really do, indeed.
Then I might show the young men
How in life I could succeed.

I wouldn't wish to be a fop,
For they're conceited men.
I'd wish to be a young man grown
Possessed of common sense.

I wouldn't cheat my washer woman,
My board I'd always pay. . .

The second line in the second stanza obviously ends with a forced rhyme. The original was "for they've conceit immense." Ellen Eaves Henneke is adamant about the use of "men" here because Grandma Deb always winked at the word, at least when she sang it to other women, poking fun at the "airs" men gave themselves. This is all that Grandma Deb could recall of a very long song.

In *DeMarsan's Singer's Journal No. 16*, this is introduced "as sung with great success by Miss Alice Siedler."

Putting on Style

Eighteen eighty-six,
January first,
I thought I'd write a poem
If I did a Hearst.
Sitting by the window,
Something made me smile,
It was a young gentleman
Putting on style.

CHORUS:
Putting on agony,
Putting on style.
What's so many people
A-doing all the while? (Repeat)

Young men in carriages
Going like mad,
With a pair of horses
He borrowed of his dad.
Cracks his whip so lively,
Makes his lady smile.
It doesn't mean anything.
He's putting on style.

CHORUS

Young men from grog shops,
Smoking dirty pipes,
Looking just as green
As a pumpkin partly ripe.
He drinks and chews tobacco,
He gambles a while.
It doesn't mean anything.
He's putting on style.

CHORUS

Young men from colleges
Make a great display.
Using such jaw-breakers
In all they have to say.
Can't be found in Webster,
Nor within a mile.
It doesn't mean anything.
They're putting on style.

CHORUS

Young ladies go to church
Just to see the boys.
Laugh and giggle all the while
At every little noise.
Turns her head this way,
Then to that a while.
It doesn't mean anything.
She's putting on style.

CHORUS

Preacher's in the pulpit,
Shouts with all his might,
"Glory, Hallelujah!"
The people's in a fright.
They think the Deuce is coming,
Down in double file,
But it doesn't mean anything.
He's putting on style.

CHORUS

Grandma Deb: "'A Hearst'? I don't know what that is, but the song's good, ain't it!"

This poem was such a favorite in Jennie's family that the chorus line was frequently used in everyday situations, such as the time I walked in wearing a new dress and was greeted with "Look at Kay! Jus' putting on style!"

This satire on hypocrisy starts with a reference to William Randolph Hearst, the king of "yellow journalism." His editorials and slanted news stories were attacks on "hypocrites," especially politicians.

Cazden gives a listing of text/tune sources for this song.[1] My own favorite discovery was the use of the song, with very similar words, in *The Arkansas Woodchopper's World's Greatest Collection of Cowboy Songs with Yodel Arrangements.*[2] This opened to me the possibility that there may have been yodeling choruses in some of her other songs, such as "Pond Lilies"; none of us thought to ask the question of Grandma Deb.

An explanation of the phrase "putting on style" is offered in the anthology of American folksong *Rise Up Singing*: "The 1880s, when this song was first sung, was an era of tight corsets for the ladies, and the phrase was current: 'Let's take the agony out of putting on the style.'"[3]

1. Cazden, *Folk Songs of the Catskills*, 78–81.
2. This volume was published in Chicago by M. M. Cole in 1931.
3. Blood-Patterson, ed., *Rise Up Singing*, 4.

The Two Orphans [Brooklyn Theater Fire]

One evening bright stars they were shining,
And the moonbeams shone clear o'er our land.
Our city was in peace and quietness,
While the hour of midnight were at hand.

CHORUS:
Oh, I ne'er can forget those "Two Orphans,"
Bad luck seemed for to be in their way.
It seems they were brought to our city
The lives of our dear ones to take.

The doors they were opened at seven
And the curtains were rolled up by eight.
Those that had seats they were happy,
And those outside mad they were late.

The play had gone on very smoothly
Till the sparks from our scenes did fly.
Then men, women, and children,
"Oh, God! spare our lives," they did cry.

Then hark! Don't you hear the cry, "Fire!"
How dismal those bells they do sound.
Our Brooklyn Theater was burning
And burning fast to the ground.

Next morning, among the black ruins,
Oh, God, what a sight met our eyes.
The dead they were lying in all shapes,
And some we could not recognize.

Poor mothers were wailing and weeping
For sons that were out all the night.
Oh, God, may their souls rest in Heaven,
Among the peaceful and bright.

What means this great gathering of people
Upon such a cold dreary day?
What means this great long line of hearses
With tops plumed in feathery array?

Far out in the country, at Greenwood,
Where the winds make the low willow sigh,
It is there where the funeral is going,
The unknown dead for to lie.

CHORUS

Alan Lomax: "How long have you known this song?"

Grandma Deb: "A good while. I haven't heard any new songs of late. Only what the radio sings and all that crap. But my pieces--what I have learned long ago . . . But everybody knows this one."

Alan Lomax: "Is that a true song?"

Grandma Deb: "It *is* a true song."

Alan Lomax: "Do you remember when that happened?"

Grandma Deb: "Yes, I do . . . but when was it? I don't remember when — ?"

This is a minstrel ballad/songster. *Two Orphans* actually was the title of a melodrama written in France. It was only mildly successful there and in London, but when it was brought to America in 1874, it attracted "the masses," that is, working people, who became absorbed in the story of two destitute sisters, one of whom was blind. The play was so successful that the starring actress bought the rights and played in it for almost twenty years.[1]

That success does not seem to have been hampered by the great fire that broke out during a performance in the Brooklyn Theater one night in 1876, with a loss of 295 lives. (Jennie was eleven years old at the time.) The ballad was composed under the title of "Two Orphans,"[2] although it does not refer to the play but to the real-life tragedy in the theater. In the *Check-List* there are recordings under both titles.

1. Geller, *Grandfather's Follies.*
2. *Beadle's Half-Dime Singers' Library No. 19* (N.Y., 1878).

I'll Be All Smiles Tonight

I'll deck my brow with roses
For the loved one will be there,
And the gems that others gave me
Shall shine within my hair.
And even those who knew me
Will think my heart grown light.
Though my heart may break tomorrow,
I'll be all smiles tonight.

CHORUS:
I'll be all smiles tonight.
Though my heart may break tomorrow,
I'll be all smiles tonight.

And when the dance commences,
Oh, how I will rejoice.
I'll sing the songs he taught me
Without a faltering voice.
And even those who knew me
Will think my love has grown light.
Though my heart may break tomorrow,
I'll be all smiles tonight.

And when the door he enters,
With his bride upon his arm,
I will stand and gaze upon him
As though he were a charm,
And when he smiles upon her
As once he smiled on me,
He'll know not what I suffer.
He'll see no change in me.

And when the dance is over,
And all have gone to rest,
I will think of him, dearest mother,
The one that I love best.
He once did love and believe me
But now he's cold and strange.
He sought not to deceive me,
False friends have wrought the change.

CHORUS

Grandma Deb: "She wouldn't let him know, see, how much it'd hurt her. She jus' kept it to herself."

Sheet music of this song gives it as "Waltz Song. Words and music by T. B. Ransom. Harms and Co., Publishers, N.Y., 1879."[1] Ford reprinted the song,[2] and Marks lists it among his "great favorites" of the eighties and nineties.[3]

Grandma Deb was positive that she did not remember any tune; she did, however, recite all the words with relish. This is another of her pieces about the courage of a jilted girl.

1. I consulted a copy in 1938 in the Music Room, New York Public Library.
2. Ford, *Traditional Music of America*, n.p.
3. Marks, *They All Sang*, 239.

The Man on the Flying Trapeze

Perhaps she's on the railway
With the swells so fair.
Perhaps she's up in a balloon
Flying through the air.
Perhaps she's dead, perhaps alive,
Perhaps she's gone to sea.
Perhaps she's gone with Brigham Young
A Mormon for to be.

I hope she'll have a lot
Of squalling brats to keep.
I hope they cry and kick all night
And never let her sleep.
I hope her chimneys they will smoke
And her lodgers never pay
And German bands and organ-grinders
Annoy her every day.

Grandma Deb: "These are extry stanzas—after the girl has run away with this trapeze fellow."

Although there were parodies of many popular songs, Grandma Deb differentiated between parodies, which only utilized a well-known tune, and extra verses that add to the original story as these do.

This was a music-hall song. There was an actual "man on the flying trapeze." His name was Leotard; he had invented his own "flying trapeze" and was brought from France to perform in a large music hall in London. He was such a charmer that the ladies of Victorian London were totally enthralled as he flew over their heads, performing without a net. He was almost without clothes as well, for there is a photograph showing an extremely muscular man dressed in nothing more than a diaper-style loincloth.[1] Ironically, in our more liberated times, the leotard is the modest one-piece black garment that little girls and aspiring young ballerinas wear to dance class.

In America the song was featured by the singing clowns of the old-time circus, and a copyright claim was filed for it on March 31, 1868.[2] In the original song, the girl who eloped for love was turned into an aerialist herself, forced to support her master.[3] "Since women were never aerialists, the thought that one might be, added to the glamour for rural audiences."[4]

"The Man on the Flying Trapeze" was widely parodied, with many versions in the 1880s and 1890s. Wherever Jennie Devlin was when she heard it, she already knew about the "scandalous" Mormon practice of multiple marriages, a subject for many sensational stories and, in this song, a fate on a par with other perilous situations a woman might endure. But note that the worst punishment for this wicked young woman was to run a boardinghouse — as Jennie herself did for many years.

1. Waites and Hunter, *Illustrated Victorian Songbook*, 124. For current text, see Blood-Patterson, ed., *Rise Up Singing*, 80.
2. Spaeth, *Weep Some More*, n.p.
3. Randolph *Ozark Folksongs*, 4:231–32.
4. Ibid., 3:266.

Ta-ra-ra Boom-de-Ay

1.
"Oh, mama dear and what is that
Hanging from that lady's hat?"
"Hush your noise, you sassy brat.
They are streamers to her hat."

2.
Jingle, jingle, up and down.
Sleighs are flying through the town.
Jingle, jingle, don't you hear?
Merry sleigh bells far and near.

Get a sleigh that's large and wide.
Let the children have a ride.
Mary-Ellen, Tom, and Ann,
George and Jane and little Fan.

Yes, there's plenty of room for all.
Get another blanket shawl.
Tuck them in. Away they go,
Jingle, jingle, through the snow.

Jingle, jingle, now we meet,
Faces gay and horses fleet,
While we shout and laugh and sing,
And the merry sleigh bells ring.

Grandma Deb: "These are just some extry words. You know, a parody."

"Ta-ra-ra Boom-de-Ay" was a very great music-hall success.[1] Many versions and many parodies are to be found in the *Check-List* and other collections. The tune was so popular that, once again, Grandma Deb did not bother to give us the words that we already knew. She offered, instead, these two little songs. Usually new words that are grafted to the tune of a humorous song are also comic. "Oh, mama dear and what is that?" is an excellent example of this. The rousing "Ta-ra-ra Boom-de-Ay" would fit as a jolly chorus after the child's song about the lady's hat.

"Sleigh Song," despite Grandma Deb's describing it also as a parody of "Ta-ra-ra," actually is, this time, just what she said about many of her songs, "a nice piece to sing to the kiddies." Here a well-known tune was used as a vehicle for a song totally different in words and mood. It really is a separate song, not a parody.

1. Waites and Hunter, *Illustrated Victorian Songbook,* 104–6.

The Little Valley

Can Jen - nie re - mem - ber or has she for - got, the man - y hap - py hour spent in

glee? Does she sigh when she thinks of the one that she loved, when a

lit - tle girl she played up - on my knee? From this val - ley they say you are

go - ing.__ We shall miss your bright face and sweet smile. You have

tak - en from us all the sun - shine,__ that bright - ened our path for a

while. Then come sit here a - while e'er you leave us.__ Do not

hast - en to bid us a - dieu, But re - mem - ber the bright lit - tle

val - ley__ and the hearts that have loved you so true.

Can Jennie remember
Or has she forgot,
The many happy hours spent in glee?
Does she sigh when she thinks
Of the one that she loved,
When a little girl she played upon my knee?

CHORUS:
From this valley they say you are going.
We shall miss your bright face and sweet smile.
You have taken from us all the sunshine,
That brightened our path for a while.

Then come sit here a while e'er you leave us.
Do not hasten to bid us adieu,
But remember the bright little valley
And the hearts that have loved you so true.

Grandma Deb: "Funny, she has my name. But I didn't have nobody to mind whether I ever went or not."

The *Check-List* has only the Jennie Devlin song with this title, but there are several in the book marked "Red River Valley," and, most likely, they are all related. Although the popular song "In the Bright Mohawk Valley," by James Kerrigan, appeared in 1896,[1] there were earlier versions in folksong tradition in Canada, several decades earlier.[2] It is possible that, as the song traveled, it might have been heard by young Jennie Hess; she never knew in which part of Canada she had lived with the Stevensons. On the other hand, there seems to be no way to date when she did learn it.

By either title, "Red River Valley" or "In the Bright Mohawk Valley," the intriguing question is, Who is leaving whom? In the Canadian songs, the girl is of mixed blood, pleading to the British soldier who is leaving because the troops have been recalled after putting down a revolt in the Northwest Territories. Carl Sandburg said the song was "a cowboy love song."[3] The Lomaxes found the singer was a desperate cowboy; it is the girl who is leaving.[4] But in some versions in the Ozarks, the abandoned lover is "a dark maiden."[5]

Looking at all these disparate interpretations, nowhere do we find anybody even remotely resembling Grandma Deb's speaker. Hers is not a love song; nobody is going to die by suicide or from heartbreak. This is a normal child who grows up and leaves home. The singer has a grandparental quality in his or her references to "Jennie's" childhood, apparently speaking for a community of people who will miss her.

Was there a personal element in Grandma Deb's recollection of this song? Why does the girl who is leaving her loved ones have the same name as the singer herself? Of all the questions that we have about these songs—Where did she learn them? What changes did she herself make, as she mulled over them, searching for meanings? How many tricks had her memory played on her repertoire? — no question is more intriguing than this one, concerning the identity of "Jennie."

1. Blood-Patterson, ed., *Rise up Singing*, 56.
2. Fowke, "'The Red River Valley' Re-Examined," 163–71.
3. Sandburg, *American Songbag*, 130.
4. *Folk Song, USA*, 221.
5. Randolph, *Ozark Folksongs*, 4:204.

Busker's Song

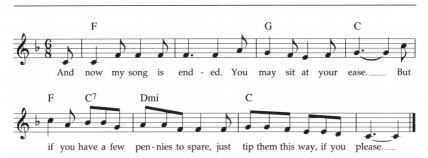

And now my song is ended,
You may sit at your ease,
But if you have a few pennies to spare
Just tip them this way, if you please.

SELECTED BIBLIOGRAPHY

Abrahams, Roger D., ed. *A Singer and Her Songs: Almeda Riddle's Book of Ballads.* Baton Rouge: Louisiana State University Press, 1970.

The Arkansas Woodchopper's World's Greatest Collection of Cowboy Songs with Yodel Arrangements. Chicago: M. M. Cole, 1931.

Belden, H. M., ed. *Ballads and Songs Collected by the Missouri Folklore Society.* 2d ed. Columbia: University of Missouri Press, 1955. Rpt., 1973.

Bilhan, P. P. *Soul-Winning Songs.* Kansas City, Mo.: Lillenas Publishing Company, 1895.

Blood-Patterson, Peter, ed. *Rise Up Singing.* Bethlehem, Pa.: Sing Out Corp., 1988.

Brewster, Paul G. *Ballads and Songs of Indiana.* Folklore Series, No. 1. Bloomington: Indiana University Publications, 1940.

Bronson, Bertrand Harris. *The Ballad as Song.* Berkeley and Los Angeles: University of California Press, 1969.

Brown, Frank C. *The Frank C. Brown Collection of North Carolina Folklore.* Vol. 2, *Folk Ballads.* Vol. 3, *Folk Songs.* Edited by Henry M. Belden and Arthur Palmer Hudson. Durham, N.C.: Duke University Press, 1952.

Campbell, Olive, Dame, and Cecil J. Sharp. *English Folk Songs from the Southern Appalachians.* New York and London: G. P. Putnam's Sons, 1917.

Carmer, Carl. *Songs of the Rivers of America.* New York: Farrar and Rinehart, 1942.

Cazden, Norman. *Folk Songs of the Catskills.* 2 vols. Albany: State University of New York Press, 1982.

Chambers, Robert. *Book of Days.* 2 vols. Edinburgh: W. and R. Chambers, 1862–64.

Chappell, William. *Old English Popular Music.* New edition by H. Ellis Woodbridge. New York: Jack Brussel, 1961. Based on Chappell's original collection of 1859. This volume also contains material by Frank Kidson. See Kidson, *Traditional Tunes.*

Charms of Melody, or Siren Medley. Sets of English broadsides and large songsters. Dublin. No. 33, *The Scold.*

Check-List of Recorded Songs in the English Language in the Archive of American Folk Song to July, 1940. Washington, D.C.: Library of Congress, Music Division, 1942.

Child, Francis J. *The English and Scottish Popular Ballads.* 5 vols. Boston: Houghton, Mifflin, 1882–98.

————. Manuscripts. 30 vols. Edited by G. L. Kittredge. In Harvard College Library.

Coffin, Tristram. *The British Traditional Ballad in North America.* Philadelphia: American Folklore Society, 1950. Reprinted with supplement by Roger DeV. Renwick. Austin: University of Texas Press, 1977.

Cox, John Harrington. *Folk Songs of the South.* Cambridge, Mass.: Harvard University Press, 1925.

Cray, Edward. *The Erotic Muse.* 2d ed. Urbana: University of Illinois Press, 1992.

Damon, S. Foster, ed. *Checklist: Fifty Old American Songs (1759–1858) in the Harris Collection of American Poetry and Plays.* Providence, R.I.: Brown University Library, n.d.

D'Urfey, Thomas, ed. *Wit and Mirth: or, Pills to Purge Melancholy.* 1719–20. Rpt., 2 vols. New York: Folklore Library Publishers, 1959.

Eddy, Mary O. *Ballads and Songs from Ohio.* 1939. Rpt., with foreword by D. K. Wilgus. Hatboro, Pa.: Folklore Associates, 1964.

Egle, William H. *History of Pennsylvania.* Harrisburg, Pa.: Dewitt Goodrich, 1877.

Ford, Ira W. *Traditional Music of America.* New York: E. P. Dutton, 1940.

Fowke, Edith. "'The Red River Valley' Re-examined." *Western Folklore* 23 (no. 3): 163–71.

Fuson, Harvey H. *Ballads of the Kentucky Highlands.* London: Mitre Press, 1935.

Geller, James J. *Grandfather's Follies.* New York: Macauley, 1934.

Harker, David. "The Price You Pay: An Introduction to the Life and Songs of Laurence Price." In *Lost in Music,* edited by Avron Levin White. Sociological Review Monograph No. 34. London: RKP, 1987.

Harvard College Broadsides Printed in England in the Nineteenth Century. 4 vols.

Henry, Mellinger Edward. *Folk-Songs from the Southern Highlands.* New York: J. J. Augustin, 1938.

"The Hutchinson Singers." *Palimpsest* 18: 145ff.

Illustrated History of Allegany County, New York, 1806–1879. Beers and Company, 1879.

Johnson, Helen K. *Our Familiar Songs and Those Who Made Them.* New York: H. Holt, 1889.

Jones, L. C. "Folksongs of Mary Wyatt and Henry Green." *Bulletin of the Folk-Song Society of the Northeast* 12 (1937): 14–18.

Jordan, Philip D., and Lillian Kessler. *Songs of Yesterday: A Song Anthology of American Life.* New York: Doubleday, Doran, 1941.

Kidson, Frank. *Traditional Tunes.* London: Oxford University Press, 1891.

Korson, George. *Pennsylvania Songs and Legends.* Philadelphia: University of Pennsylvania Press, 1949.

Laws, G. Malcolm, Jr. *American Balladry from British Broadsides: A Guide for Students and Collectors of Traditional Song.* Philadelphia: American Folklore Society, 1957.

————. *Native American Balladry: A Descriptive Study and Bibliographical Syllabus.* Rev. ed. Austin: University of Texas Press, 1964.

Leach, MacEdward. *The Ballad Book.* New York: Harper and Brothers, 1955.

Leach, MacEdward, and Henry Glassie. *A Guide for Collectors of Oral Traditions and Folk Cultural Material in Pennsylvania.* Harrisburg: Pennsylvania Historical and Museum Commission, 1973.

Lomax, Alan. *The Folk Songs of North America in the English Language.* New York: Dolphin Books, Doubleday and Company, 1975.

_____. *Penguin Book of American Folk Songs.* Baltimore: Penguin Press, 1964.

Lomax, John, and Alan Lomax. *American Ballads and Folk Songs.* Foreword by George Lyman Kittredge. New York: Macmillan, 1934.

_____. *Folksong: USA.* New York: Duell, Sloan, and Pearce, 1947.

MacKay, Gordon. "Devlin Still Picks Winners after 64 Years as Handicapper." *Courier-Post* (Camden, N.J.), December 1, 1937.

Mahan, Bruce, and Pauline Grahame. "Play-Party Games." *Palimpsest* 10.

Marks, Edward P. *They All Sang—from Tony Pastor to Rudy Vallee.* As Told to Abbott J. Liebling. New York: Viking Press, 1934.

Miner, Charles. *History of Wyoming.* Philadelphia: Crissey, 1845.

Nettl, Bruno. *Folk Music in the United States.* 3d ed., rev. by Helen Myers. Detroit: Wayne State University Press, 1976.

Opie, Peter, and Iona Opie, comps. *The Oxford Dictionary of Nursery Rhymes.* London: Oxford University Press, 1951.

"Orphan Trains." *Smithsonian,* August 1986, 95–103.

Randolph, Vance. *Ozark Folksongs.* Rev. ed. 4 vols. Columbia: University of Missouri Press, 1980.

_____. *Pissing in the Snow and Other Ozark Folktales.* Urbana: University of Illinois Press, 1976.

Rembault-Smith, E. F. *A Little Book of Songs & Ballads, gathered from Ancient Musick Books, MS and Printed by E. F. Rembault-Smith.* London, 1851.

Rice, Sara Sigourney. *Warner's Series: Forty-four Readings and Recitations.* Vol. 9. 1890.

Sandburg, Carl. *The American Songbag.* New York: Harcourt, Brace, 1927.

Sankey, Ira P., et al. *Gospel Hymns.* Boston: Bigelow and Main, 1892.

Sankey, Ira P., and Dwight L. Moody. *Sacred Songs: Hymns for Young People.* Boston: Bigelow and Main, 1894.

Scarborough, Dorothy. *On the Trail of Negro Folk-Songs.* Cambridge, Mass.: Harvard University Press, 1925.

_____. *A Song Catcher in the Southern Mountains.* New York: Columbia University Press, 1937.

Sharp, Cecil James. *American English Folk-Songs Collected in the Southern Appalachians.* New York: Putnam, 1918.

_____. *English Folk Songs from the Southern Appalachians.* 2d ed. Edited by Maud Karpeles. 2 vols. London: Oxford University Press, 1932.

_____. *Folk-Songs of England.* 5 vols. London: Novello, 1908.

Shoemaker, Henry W. *Mountain Minstrelsy of Pennsylvania.* Philadelphia: Newman F. McGirr, 1931. Originally published Altoona, Pa., *Times-Tribune Press,* 1931.

Skinner, Charles, ed. *The Arbor Day Manual.* Syracuse, N.Y., 1896.

Smith, Reed. *South Carolina Ballads.* Cambridge, Mass.: Harvard University Press, 1928.

Spaeth, Sigmund. *Read 'Em and Weep.* New York: Doubleday, Page, 1927.

_____. *Weep Some More, My Lady.* Garden City, N.Y.: Doubleday, Page, 1927.

Thomas, Jean. *Devil's Ditties.* Chicago: W. W. Hatfield, 1931.

_____. *The Singin' Fiddler of Lost Hope Hollow.* New York: E. P. Dutton, 1938.

Thompson, Harold. *Body, Boots, and Britches.* Philadelphia: J. B. Lippincott, 1940.

Vaughan Williams, Ralph. *Folk-Songs from the Eastern Counties.* London: Novello, 1923.

Vaughan Williams, Ralph, and A. L. Lloyd. *The Penguin Book of English Folk Songs, from the Journal of the Folk Song Society and the Journal of the English Folk Dance and Song Society.* Harmondsworth, Middlesex: Pelican Books, 1959.

Waites, Aline, and Robin Hunter, comps. *The Illustrated Victorian Songbook.* London: Michael Joseph, 1984.

Warner, Anne. *Traditional American Folk Songs.* Syracuse, N.Y.: Syracuse University Press, 1984.

Werner, Edgar, ed. *Readings and Recitations Series.* New York: 1890, 1892.

Wilgus, D. K. "The *Aisling* and the Cowboy: Some Unnoticed Influences of Irish Vision Poetry on Anglo-American Balladry." *Western Folklore* 44 (October 1985): 255–300.

————. "The *Aisling* and the Cowboy, II: 'Rocking the Cradle.'" Typescript. Paper presented to the California Folklore Society, April 20, 1985.

————. *Anglo-American Folksong Scholarship since 1898.* New Brunswick, N.J.: Rutgers University Press, 1959.

Williams, Alfred. *Folk Songs of the Upper Thames.* London: Duckworth, 1923.

INDEX

A Note on the Author

KATHARINE D. NEWMAN founded MELUS, the Society for the Study of the Multi-Ethnic Literature of the United States, in 1974 and is editor emeritus of its journal. She is the author of a number of books and articles on multi-ethnic literature and culture. Now retired and an independent scholar, she was a professor of English at West Chester State University. In 1993 she began studying a little-known field, literature about old people, and taught a course on that topic, Literature for the Reflective Years, in her hometown of Encinitas, California. Her favorite old characters are Oedipus, King Lear, and Jennie Devlin.

Books in the Series Music in American Life

Sing a Sad Song: The Life of Hank Williams
Roger M. Williams

Long Steel Rail: The Railroad in American Folksong
Norm Cohen

Resources of American Music History: A Directory of Source Materials
from Colonial Times to World War II
D. W. Krummel, Jean Geil, Doris J. Dyen, and Deane L. Root

Tenement Songs: The Popular Music of the Jewish Immigrants
Mark Slobin

Ozark Folksongs
Vance Randolph; edited and abridged by Norm Cohen

Oscar Sonneck and American Music
Edited by William Lichtenwanger

Bluegrass Breakdown: The Making of the Old Southern Sound
Robert Cantwell

Bluegrass: A History
Neil V. Rosenberg

Music at the White House: A History of the American Spirit
Elise K. Kirk

Red River Blues: The Blues Tradition in the Southeast
Bruce Bastin

Good Friends and Bad Enemies: Robert Winslow Gordon and
the Study of American Folksong
Debora Kodish

Fiddlin' Georgia Crazy: Fiddlin' John Carson, His Real World,
and the World of His Songs
Gene Wiggins

America's Music: From the Pilgrims to the Present
Revised Third Edition
Gilbert Chase

Secular Music in Colonial Annapolis: The Tuesday Club, 1745-56
John Barry Talley

Bibliographical Handbook of American Music
D. W. Krummel

Goin' to Kansas City
Nathan W. Pearson, Jr.